AC 112

The Challenge of Child Abuse

Anglo-American conferences:

1971: **Medical Care**

SBN 9501555 1 9

1973: **Drug Abuse**

ISBN 0 9501555 5 1

1974: **Continuing Medical Education**

ISBN 0 9501555 7 8

Reports of these conferences may be obtained
from The Publications Department, Royal Society
of Medicine, Chandos House, 2 Queen Anne Street, London,
W1M 0BR, or through any bookseller

1976: **Sexually Transmitted Diseases**

ISBN 0 12 164150 3

1977: **Care of the Elderly**

ISBN 0 12 244950

Published by Academic Press Inc (London) Ltd

The Challenge of Child Abuse

Proceedings of a Conference
sponsored by the
Royal Society of Medicine
2–4 June 1976

Edited by
ALFRED WHITE FRANKLIN

1977

ACADEMIC PRESS   London
GRUNE & STRATTON   New York

ACADEMIC PRESS INC. (LONDON) LTD
24/28 Oval Road
London NW1

U.S. Edition published by
GRUNE & STRATTON INC.
111 Fifth Avenue
New York
New York 10003

Library of Congress Catalog Card Number: 77 71798
ISBN (Academic Press): 0 12 265550 8
ISBN (Grune & Stratton): 0 8089 1056 6

Printed in Great Britain at
The Spottiswoode Ballantyne Press by
William Clowes & Sons Limited
London, Colchester and Beccles

Participants

Dr Leonard Arthur, MB, MRCP   *Consultant Paediatrician, Derbyshire Hospital for Sick Children*

Mrs Gill Gorell Barnes, MA, MSc   *Central Council for Education and Training in Social Work*

Detective Superintendent Peter S. Bayliss   *Derbyshire Constabulary*

Dr Arnon Bentovim, MB, FRCPsych, DPM   *Consultant Psychiatrist, Hospital for Sick Children, Great Ormond Street and the Tavistock Clinic*

Miss Margaret Booth, QC, LLM   *Barrister-at-law*

Professor Sydney Brandon, MD, FRCPsych, DCH   *Professor of Psychiatry, University of Leicester*

Ms Anne Campbell, BA   *Department of Experimental Psychology, Oxford*

Miss Jan Carter, BA, DipSocStuds, MSc   *Principal Researcher, Day Care Project, National Institute for Social Work, London*

Mrs W. E. Cavenagh, JP, PhD, BScEcon   *Barrister-at-Law; Lately Professor of Social Administration and Criminology, Birmingham University*

Mr J. B. Chapman   *Court Welfare Officer, Royal Courts of Justice, London*

Dr Christine Cooper, OBE, MA, FRCP, DCH   *Consultant Paediatrician, Department of Child Health, University of Newcastle-upon-Tyne*

Miss Joan Court, AAPSW, MSW(Smith)   *Social Work Service, DHSS*

Mrs C. M. Desborough, MA   *Research Officer, Social Work Project, Department of Social and Administrative Studies, University of Oxford*

Professor G. R. Dunstan, MA, HonDD, FSA   *Professor of Moral and Social Theology, King's College, University of London; Canon Theologian of Leicester Cathedral*

Dr Alfred White Franklin, MA, MB, BCh, FRCP   *Consulting Paediatrician, Saint Bartholomew's Hospital, London*

Mrs Joyce Heath, BA, AMIMSW   *Senior Hospital Social Worker, Derbyshire Hospital of Sick Children*

Professor Ronald W. Hepburn, MA, PhD   *Professor of Moral Philosophy, University of Edinburgh*

Ms Carolyn Okell Jones, BSc Hons   *Part-time Project Leader, National Children's Bureau; Part-time Tutor in Applied Social Studies, Bedford College, University of London*

Dr Dermod MacCarthy, MD, FRCP, DCH   *Consultant Paediatrician, Institute of Child Psychology*

Mr Andrew Mann   *Children's Rights Workshop*

Dr Walter Milburn, MBE, TD, DL, MB, ChB, MRCGP   *Police Surgeon, Derby; Adviser in Forensic Medicine, Derbyshire Hospital for Sick Children*

Miss Sue Mountain, BA   *First-year student, post-graduate Diploma in Social Work, University College, University of Cardiff*

Dr J. E. Oliver, MB BS, MRCPsych   *Consultant Child Psychiatrist and Consultant in Mental Sub-normality, Pewsey and Burderop Hospitals, Swindon*

Mr John Pickett, AAPSW   *Regional Social Work Manager, NSPCC, Manchester*

Dr Martin P. M. Richards, MA, PhD   *University Lecturer in Social Psychology, Cambridge*

Miss Jane Rowe, OBE, MA   *Director, Association of Adoption and Fostering Agencies*

Professor Michael Rutter, MD, FRCP, FRCPsych, DPM   *Professor of Child Psychiatry, Department of Child Health and Adolescent Psychiatry, Institute of Psychiatry, London*

Dr P. D. Scott, CBE, MD, FRCP, FRCPsych   *Consultant Psychiatrist, Bethlem Royal and Maudsley Hospital and Home Office*

Dr Joanna Shapland, MA, DPhil, DipCrim   *Research Fellow in Criminology, King's College, University of London*

Dr R. E. Smith, MB, ChB   *General Practitioner, Derby*

Lord Taylor, MD, FRCP, FRCGP   *Visiting Professor of Medicine, Memorial University of Newfoundland*

Miss Jill Tibbits, BA   *Chief Probation Officer, Surrey*

Dom Benedict Webb, MA, MRCS, LRCP   *Monk of Ampleforth*

Chief Superintendent Mary Wedlake, MBE   *Metropolitan Police*

Dr. Arthur Hyatt Williams, MD, FRCPsych, DPM   *Consultant Psychiatrist, Tavistock Clinic*

The taller child, whose height is on the 50th percentile, is aged 5 years 1 month, and is only nine months older than the dwarfed child. By courtesy of Dr Dermod MacCarthy (see p. 97)

Foreword

I am glad of this opportunity to send a message to those attending the symposium on child abuse organized by the Royal Society of Medicine.

The problems of child abuse which can be defined as prevention, recognition, treatment and management, touch on the responsibilities of many professions. It is, therefore, particularly appropriate that those taking part represent a wide range of professions and disciplines.

As you know, my Department has always emphasized the importance of sharing information and expertise. We advocate the coming together of all who have knowledge of particular cases in mutual confidence and undeterred by professional demarcations, something that is easier to advocate than to achieve. We understand how there may be inter-professional disagreements about what is in the best interests of the child or his family; mutual misunderstandings of the intentions and motives of others; concern about how information gained in confidence from a patient or client may be used by others. Only by overcoming these difficulties can we hope to achieve our common goal, namely to find and apply in each case the solution which will be in the best interests of the child and his family. I welcome the opportunity provided by symposia such as yours, which bring together representatives of such differing professions to discuss how best to improve our ability to deal well with these tragic cases.

I have noted with special interest your intention to consider child abuse within a wider spectrum. The increased awareness of the subject in our changing society is significant, and all this can benefit from the lessons to be learnt in this wider context from the studies of the stresses and strains, social, financial, psychological, physical, which contribute to child abuse.

In the kind of crises which arise there is always the danger of concentrating too much on first aid. We need to stand back to study underlying factors in this as in other fields. We in the Department and all those concerned with the welfare of families and children in the country as a whole look forward with interest to reading the reports of your discussion.

DAVID OWEN

Department of Health and Social Security
June 1976

Contents

1. Introduction

Alfred White Franklin

Reflections on child abuse, this barely believable aberration of family life, this seeming reversal of natural instincts, challenge many accepted and comforting feelings about human behaviour. Assumptions hitherto regarded as axiomatic fall like ninepins in a gale of emotion, while distrust and recrimination all too often bedevil relationships between helper and client, between one kind of helper and another, and between society as a whole and client and helper alike. This book comprises a set of articles on the subject of child abuse by a number of authors and includes accounts on the philosophical and friendly discussions that these articles engendered; a genuine symposium fulfilling in every way the dictionary definition.

It began when Donna Bradshaw, originator of F.L.A.C. (Family Life Achievement Centre) and later of the National Committee for Prevention of Child Abuse, asked from Chicago whether the Royal Society of Medicine would sponsor an international meeting in London on child abuse. The Society agreed, but somehow the American enthusiasm waned. The international meeting withered away; the plant took root and blossomed. The then President, Sir John Stallworthy, gathered a committee consisting of Professor Winifred Cavenagh, Miss Joan Court, Professor Michael Rutter, Miss Olive Stevenson and Mr Reginald Wright, and invited me to join them and to submit a programme as a basis for the symposium.

The original theme was to be "child abuse — sickness or crime?" The intention was not to discuss once more the practical details of diagnosis and management, of registers, of police and social worker action, of legal sanctions and of court orders, but rather to move the discussion of child abuse into the more general context of deprivation within the family, of family psychopathology, and of perversion or failure of family functioning.

In 1946, James Spence* professed a simple outlook on the purposes

* The Purpose of the Family. Convocation Lecture, 1946, National Children's Home, p. 33.

of the family. "It exists," he wrote, "first, to ensure growth and physical health; secondly, to give the right scope for emotional experience; thirdly, to preserve the art of motherhood; and fourthly, to teach behaviour." Much has been learned in the thirty years since Spence wrote these words that would have caused him to modify his statement, although nothing that could have altered his views. "Motherhood" would certainly have given place to "parenthood" despite the increased importance attached to the mother–infant interaction; father has his place. Spence's four general purposes remain valid and one thing about child abuse is strikingly clear — the abusing family fails on all four counts.

Many factors threaten both the integrity of family life and its competence to perform its functions: among these are immaturity of parents, sexual promiscuity, pregnancy and especially repeated pregnancy among teenagers, illegitimacy, a succession of consorts and cohabiters, low intelligence, poor self-discipline, a degraded self-image, and alcohol or drug dependence, misuse and overdose. Factors of another kind are chronic disease and disability, mental or physical or both in parents or in child, with a proportion of aggressive psychopaths, sadists and schizophrenics. Poor quality housing, frequent moves of home and changes of employment, low income and even a criminal record are common concomitants. The appearance of child abuse in several generations raises as well the possibilities of a genetic influence or of a cultural matrix that casts each new member in this deforming mould.

Common experience ought to be met with scepticism but not with unbelief. It deserves scientific study which requires the collection of carefully controlled observations. Everyone knows that all of the adverse factors and concomitants described above have a prevalence throughout Western society, variable in size and distribution but not inevitably leading to child abuse. An ambitious programme of study was therefore outlined.

We need [it was claimed] a study of family psychopathology and family breakdown to show the nature and the extent of the crimes with which they are associated, and not only of non-accidental injury. We need, also to study the effects on family life of some of the more easily identified adverse contributing factors and concomitants of child abuse, for example,

the effects of drug dependence including alcoholism,
the success rate of families after adolescent "marriage",
the relationship of inadequate housing to unsuccessful family life,
the relationship between unemployment and bad housing,
the relationship between chronic handicapping disease and family breakdown,
the relationship between child minding and deprivation.
An even more difficult study, but one of great importance, is the follow-up

of abusing families in relation to the treatment meted out — rehabilitation of the family at home, separation, management and supervision by the social services or the probation service, police action and prison sentences.

The fact that this information is needed in order that the problems of child abuse may be put into proper perspective is true; but if the symposium was ever to materialize, we would not be able to await the collation and analysis of such observations. The theme of sickness or crime was abandoned, but the question "is child abuse a crime?" is discussed by Jan Carter in Chapter 16. The final programme was then outlined. This was to begin with paediatric and psychiatric descriptions of abusing families followed by accounts of their work from social workers, probation officers and psychiatrists, including the preparation of reports and their value in court. On the second day we would discuss the family, its importance in society and what happens to a child when his family fails in its functions from the initial bonding between baby and mother, through childhood deprivation to failed parenthood in the next generation.

We wanted to raise the question of the nature of aggression and why it found expression in non-accidental injury to children, to be met by the reaction of society in punishment and retribution under the law. We wanted also to examine what followed from treating the abusing parents as criminals and to ask the question whether attempts to rehabilitate the family might more often succeed if such parents were seen differently, for example, as disturbed people suffering from psycho-social stress. The family was failing its children, was society in some way failing the family?

At Miss Court's suggestion and with the co-operation of the Derby team, a diagnostic case conference was to be held during the meeting. This was expected to raise for discussion some, at least, of the difficulties of inter-professional co-operation and the sharing of confidential information. The final question was this. Accepting that child abuse is a family affair, nevertheless the abuse is a personal activity just as all forms of management are in the final analysis and in practice transactions between people. Is there any way in which to help a person, stressed as he may have been by a combination of adverse factors with perhaps some crisis as the last straw? Can the arm raised to strike be halted in mid-air? Religious belief, ethical propositions, psychiatric insight, have any of these the power to influence the abusing parent? Can any of them help to gain for the child the security and the loving care on which his health, physical, emotional, intellectual and social, absolutely depends?

As the papers came in, a certain pessimism became obvious, particularly over rehabilitation of the family if the child was to be protected from the harmful effects of emotional deprivation or physical abuse. He might be saved from actual physical injury only to live in a rejecting and emotionally depriving family atmosphere. In this way, some study of the effectiveness of alternative family care was added to the programme (see Chapter 11).

In the event the programme moved into directions of its own. The papers were circulated for study before the meeting and each author allotted a quarter of an hour to summarize his main points. Plenty of time remained for discussion, the discussions at each session being recorded by two different reporters. The editor, who took his own notes, had the task of rendering down these lively exchanges of opinions and ideas and of rearranging their content to provide the accounts with which the book is punctuated. Most participants are actively engaged in the practical tasks of diagnosis or management, but perspectives differ. As we tried to accommodate our own ideas to those of others and as we listened to others examining our ideas from their different angles, basic assumptions seemed to be being challenged. We were compelled in facing these challenges to ask a number of questions which had not been foreseen and which had certainly not been included in the programme. Some of these challenges and questions together with some of our shared anxieties are discussed in Chapter 23.

Some textual alterations have been made by authors as well as by the editor, who has also changed the order of the papers into what he conceived as a more logical sequence. The details of the case conference, in the preparation of which the participants assuredly took great pains, are banished to the Appendix, but the discussion to which this led and which provided one of the high points of the meeting is incorporated in the final chapter.

Acknowledgements

Lord Taylor of Harlow opened the meeting in his usual genial and charming manner. We are grateful to him and to Lady Taylor for making the long journey from Wales.

Thanks are due to the Right Honorable David Owen, Minister of Health at the time, for his encouraging message now printed as a foreword.

This seems the appropriate place to pay tribute to the Staff of the Royal Society of Medicine for the trouble that they took over the preparation and management of the meeting, and for the Society's generous hospitality to the participants. Especial thank are due to Miss Muriel Mitchell who acted as conference secretary. Thanks too are due to Mr John Davies and the Society's Publications Department for their help in preparing this book for publication.

2. Three Abusing Families

Christine Cooper

The presentation of these three case reports with summaries of the discussions that followed introduces the subjects of child abuse, deprivation, neglect and battering, in a practical manner. In these reports are to be found the bases for many of the problems of diagnosis and management which still perplex and often defeat those charged with the responsibility of aiding families in trouble and of protecting babies from danger. The difficulties into which life's experiences plunge members of so-called multi-problem families are also well illustrated.

Case 1: Mary, Born 24 Sept., 1973

Mary was first brought to hospital when she was 8 months old, on account of a black eye and badly bruised cheeks. Her weight was on the 25th centile line.

The mother was aged 16 years at the time of Mary's birth. She was the fifth of nine children with various fathers in a Roman Catholic multi-problem family. The records from several hospitals and social service departments have not all been collated. Openly rejected by her own mother, she attended an E.S.N. school. A vague history of a head injury and seizures could represent non-accidental injury. At 14 years, she was received into care at her mother's request as being "beyond control", having often run away. She continued to run away from whatever home she was in, drank to excess, became sexually promiscuous and six court orders were made for burglary, theft, drunkenness and assault. Recommended to an approved school by a child psychiatrist, who found her "very disturbed", she took several overdoses and stabbed herself in the abdomen with a broken bottle.

When she became pregnant with Mary, she went home to her mother, but following "ructions" she was admitted to a mother and baby home to which she returned after a normal delivery. Her wish for Mary's adoption was overruled by her mother and there followed another overdose one month after delivery. Mary was placed by the social services at 6 weeks with a foster mother where frequent visits by her mother caused great nuisance in the foster home, and at 6 months she was taken back by her mother who moved many times but was based mainly at her own sister's house, the dwelling of another problem family with neglected children.

At this time Mary's mother was attending a V.D. clinic where she was already well known. She was again taken to Court for soliciting, for being drunk and disorderly and for assaulting a policeman. The baby was not registered with a doctor, nor had the social services notified the health visitor of her return home. The mother told the clinic health visitor not to visit and threatened that any visitor would cause her to "disappear" with the baby. Shortly afterwards the probation officer, during a home visit, found the baby bruised and arranged for her admission to hospital.

In hospital, Mary was alert and thrived. A care order was obtained in the juvenile court and plans were made for fostering. Unfortunately, the baby became infected by her mother with dysentery so that she was moved to isolation where, as a carrier of bacilli, she remained for 8 weeks. The series of nurses who played with her did not furnish a real mother substitute. She was discharged from hospital at 10 months to a foster family with three teenage daughters and experience of thirty-four foster babies. They planned to adopt Mary, who settled in well and was disturbed only when her mother visited.

Mary was 14 months old when the marriage of her foster-parents suddenly broke down. She was moved abruptly to a new foster family where the parents have three boys (14, 12 and 9 years old) and a foster daughter of 18 years and where she will remain. The foster-parents say that they cannot afford to adopt her.

At the time of Mary's admission to hospital, aged 8 months, her mother was unfriendly and difficult in the ward, quarrelling with the staff and other visitors. After an original denial, she acknowledged hitting Mary "but not nearly as hard as my mother used to hit me." She showed no affection for her daughter but occasionally played with her as with a doll. She took more overdoses, but refused to see the psychiatrist.

Successfully prosecuted for ill-treating her baby, she was sent to borstal, becoming pregnant again on discharge. She delivered prematurely at about 34 weeks a girl who died with an intraventricular haemorrhage at 48 hours. The mother, now aged 19 years, was deeply distressed during this baby's illness and loud in protestations of grief at the baby's death. Plans had, in fact, been made for requesting a care order for this baby with a view to long-term fostering and adoption.

Discussion

Dr Cooper posed the following four questions.

1. Could it be predicted with absolute certainty that such a disturbed girl would fail to provide adequate mothering for her second baby?

2. To what extent should doctors and social workers "persuade" severely disturbed mothers to relinquish new-born babies for adoption?

3. Should a care order have been requested for Mary at the time of birth or at 6 months when the mother took her home?

4. What should be done about the inevitable next pregnancy, assuming that the mother mismanages contraception, and refuses psychotherapy and all offers of friendship and help?

In the discussion there was general agreement that failure of mothering could be predicted. This family provides another example of the families which Miller has labelled with "the four Ds", dull, disturbed, deprived and dilapidated. The mother's problems can be blamed, in part at least, on rejection, abuse and possibly battering by her own mother. Is she redeemable? Can we legislate to protect her from herself and her own self-destroying impulses, which are associated with refusal of all help? She could under present law have been "dealt with" in two legal categories, as someone under the age of 21 years who is mentally subnormal and as someone in urgent need of psychiatric treatment. Plenty of kindness towards her is available in the social service as well as from doctors. However, her need is not only for kindness but for authority and we seem now to lack the courage and we clearly lack the will to use authority. It would be possible to make a treatment plan which could allow the mother to maintain charge of her baby, but success or failure should be assessed at the end of a definite period and failure should lead to removal of parental rights. Fostering from birth under a care order might have protected Mary but would not have prevented the nuisance and disturbance in the foster home and the emotional disturbance for Mary. Family planning advice appears inappropriate. Contraception requires both foresight and care, and only compulsory sterilization could be relied on to prevent further pregnancies and compulsory termination to prevent the birth of more babies. The serious interference with civil liberties that would be needed probably prevents the adopting of both these practices. The ambivalence of society is here displayed. No one should stop the mother from having more children; the social services are in deep trouble when she does have more.

Case 2: Peter, Born 22 Oct., 1973

First contact with Peter was at 12 weeks of age when he was admitted to hospital with (?) osteitis of the left tibia. Although fever and a raised sedimentation rate supported the diagnosis of infection, X-rays showed a tiny chip fracture and a skeletal survey 12 days later showed gross periosteal reaction in the left tibia with similar but milder changes in the right tibia. There was no history of injury, although the X-rays were typical of wrenching injuries of infants' limbs.

The mother, unmarried and aged 18 years, was living with a 17 year old consort at her father's home, the family consisting of grandfather, who was a labourer, and six younger siblings. The two older sibs were married and away from home. The grandparents had divorced following violence between them. The mother was small, thin, neat, very reserved but polite and attentive in manner. She gave up work 2 weeks before birth with a normal delivery of a boy at 38 weeks. He weighed 4 lb 15 oz (2.240 Kg) and was separated from the mother to be nursed in a special nursery for 2 weeks, the mother going home after 1 week. Peter's father had been under a supervision order for school non-attendance, had appeared in court on a charge of "taking and driving away" and was given a conditional discharge. He appeared pleasant, sensible and more forthcoming than the mother and both visited Peter in hospital for several hours daily, seeming fond and concerned. A few days after the admission, the mother "remembered" that her 3 year old nephew had fallen on Peter's leg but she could not account for the other injurities. Such an accident could not have produced the injuries present. Only 2 years later did they reveal what was previously denied, that Peter had cried a lot when a baby.

Twenty-four hours after Peter's admission, the parents were interviewed by the police, although who brought the police in has never been revealed. The mother's family were used to police involvement in minor delinquency and in family rows and regarded silence as the only sensible policy. This intervention, with its reinforcement of silence, is considered to have had a damaging effect on later work by doctors and social workers. Denial of injuries continued and the police took no further action.

When Peter was 3 months old, the social service department obtained an interim care order in the juvenile court with a full care order 4 weeks later. The parents still denied inflicting injury. An orthopaedic surgeon at first advised contesting the case, but reversed his advice later and Peter was sent to a residential nursery to await fostering and a plan was made for intensive case-work help for the parents; these plans failed because of the reorganization of the social services. In the event, the baby remained in this nursery until he was

2 years and 2 months old, appearing to develop normally. The parents visited once or twice each month and for one week the mother was admitted to the nursery where she was noted to manage Peter technically well but not to make any real relationship with him. The parents saw the child psychiatrist once but failed to keep further appointments.

When Peter was about 15 months old, the parents married and were housed next door with one of the mother's sisters and her family. The father remained unemployed. At this time the mother became pregnant again and a new social worker began to work with the family. He shared the parents' view that they had now a cosy home, were getting on well with each other and could manage Peter at home perfectly well. They continued to deny that they had caused him any injury and because of this denial together with uncertainty about how they would cope with the pregnancy and the new baby, the paediatrician and the child psychiatrist strongly opposed revocation of the care order, and Peter remained in the nursery.

When Peter was 23 months old, his baby sister was born at 35 weeks gestation, her birth weight being 4 lb (1.814 Kg). Once again mother and baby were separated while the baby remained for 3 weeks in the special nursery. The mother visited daily to give bottles and wash, but seemed remote and failed to interact with the baby. After discharge home, the baby was easy to manage and thrived. The parents then threatened to go to Court to seek revocation of the care order.

The paediatrician and the child psychiatrist maintained their view that Peter would not be safe from injury if returned to his parents' care, a view not shared by the Area Director of Social Services and a lawyer acting for the local authority. The decision was made to return Peter to his parents' care after a 4 week period of preparation and, when the sister was 3 months old, he went home. Two weeks later he was urgently readmitted to hospital with marks on his cheek and bruises on his neck and chin. Bruised buttocks and scattered bruises on the trunk were also seen when he was fully examined in hospital.

The father admitted chastising his son for hitting the baby and for throwing the cat on the fire. Peter was aged 2 years and 3 months! His father maintained that the boy understood what he was doing and that he needed firm discipline. Peter was readmitted to the original nursery and awaits long-term fostering. The baby, after a week away during the crisis, remains at home. The parents have seen the child psychiatrist once and missed five further appointments. It is now apparent that the father is the dominant partner in the marriage and has an authoritarian, rigid, disciplinary approach to family life, and this is being discussed in relation to the future of the family.

The social service department produced further information about the mother during Peter's second admission. They have known her family for years, the mother and several of the siblings having been in care for short periods. The mother was a very poor scholar, truanted and at 16 had become depressed. She had taken several overdoses, twice before and twice after Peter's birth.

Discussion

Dr Cooper drew attention to a number of points for discussion including the difficulty of the original diagnosis of the leg lesion, the early police involvement, delays and difficulties in carrying out the first plan of management, the change of policy when the new social worker took over and the return of the child home when a team of inexperienced social workers successfully opposed the experienced medical and psychiatric recommendation.

In the discussion, anxiety was expressed that there were still many professionals who were difficult to convince that parents did physically damage their children. After one battering incident the chances of another were greatly increased. This kinship again demonstrated that non-accidental injury and abuse were no more than parts of the complex problems existing in some families. The grandparents' marital history was important in setting the scene and the whole family was involved. The question was raised of when, during the development of a human being, does his comprehension of childhood arise and what is the origin of his understanding and acceptance of the quality of childhood behaviour. Presumably, in the old fashioned large families, the older children learned from and practised on the baby, and the baby in due time on nephews and nieces. Play provided important experience. In some women's liberation circles, girls were discouraged from playing with dolls, a policy in this context judged to be harmful. No-one suggested that, on the grounds of equality of the sexes, boys should be encouraged to play with dolls. The effect of too early police intervention was regretted. It was suggested that social workers who lacked practical experience, might be too much swayed by strongly held political ideologies. Closer co-operation and mutual understanding was still lacking in some areas between the various professional groups.

Case 3: Carolyn B., Born 23 July, 1960

Carolyn was brought to hospital from school in a state of intense uncontrollable fear and refusing to go home. Her story introduces some of the problems of abuse as it affects older children.

On admission, she claimed that her mother had tried to strangle her and that she would kill herself if sent home. She had some minor scratches and little red fingernail indentations on her neck. She calmed down on learning that she could stay in the hospital, but when, an hour later, her mother arrived, she began to quake visibly and cried silently until her mother left. She said that while helping her mother to wallpaper the lavatory she had cut a strip too short. Her mother in a rage seized Carolyn round the neck, shook her violently and pushed her downstairs. The presence of the marks on her neck and a few bruises on trunk and legs lent support to the story.

During her stay in hospital, this half-caste Asian pre-pubertal girl of 13 appeared intelligent, attractive and friendly, and she was good with the babies and toddlers in the ward. She repeatedly asked not to be sent home and the trembling recurred at each of her mother's visits.

Carolyn remained in the hospital for 9 weeks and gradually unfolded her history, calling an aunt to witness. This aunt, a stable, sensible woman, with four children of her own, had been doing her best for some years to help and befriend her nephews and nieces in their very deficient, troubled and sometimes dramatic home life. The social services had been concerned also about the family, but now for the first time, the attempt was made to collate all the information through an extensive psychosocial investigation.

In April 1974, at the time of Carolyn's admission, the family consisted of:

Mrs B., mother, 36 years
Mr B., step-father, 44 years
Jack, 5 October 1958
Carolyn, 23 July 1960
Margaret, 27 September 1961
Leonard, 15 March 1963
Alfred, 25 May 1964

The mother, Mrs B., who appeared an attractive, intelligent woman, was the third of four siblings and claimed to have enjoyed a happy childhood. She was in fact illiterate, although intelligent, and her brother, the kind aunt's husband, revealed that she had been severely ill-treated by her father throughout her childhood. He was an extra-marital child and had also suffered at the hands of the father. At 17 years, Mrs B. became pregnant and later married the father but left him, placed the baby, Jack, with her own mother, moved to London and had two more babies, Carolyn and Margaret, in quick succession by two different Asian men. Margaret at 3 months was placed voluntarily in care as the family was living in a caravan, and at 6 months, because her mother had not visited her at all, was moved to Yorkshire to a foster home. Here she remained until, at the age of $4\frac{1}{4}$ years, she was suddenly returned home at her mother's request.

In the meantime the mother had married a second husband, a

Caucasian, and had two sons, Leonard and Alfred. Soon the parents separated and then divorced. The two husbands have had no further contact with the children. Later the mother married Mr B., but they had had no children. He appeared a spruce, intelligent man interested in and knowledgeable about his step-children.

Carolyn was the first known victim of violence, sustaining a fracture of the right forearm at the age of 3 years 2 months, followed 1 month later by a fractured right elbow which mysteriously refractured 3 months later. The joint remains severely deformed with only 40° of movement. At 3 years and 7 months, a mid-shaft fracture of the left tibia was followed 2 weeks later by a similar fracture on the right. The orthopaedic registrar raised the question of non-accidental trauma and the radiologist of direct physical violence, but the orthopaedic consultant did not agree and contented himself with a negative investigation for fragile bones. Facial injuries and bruises were noted at this time. Six months later Leonard, aged 18 months, appeared in hospital with a fractured right humerus.

During the next year, the police recorded a complaint by Mrs B. that Carolyn, aged 5 years 9 months, had been sexually assaulted. What had happened was that Carolyn had enraged her mother by not returning home from school one evening. Mrs B. stuck pliers into Carolyn's vagina to make her bleed and then called the police. The police surgeon examined the child, but no action was taken.

At this time, Mrs B. had had Leonard and Alfred, and at the end of 1965 took Margaret home. It is hardly surprising that, joining her estranged mother and her unknown family and four children, this 4 year old child presented considerable behaviour problems, so that by the age of 7 years she was admitted to the child psychiatry unit for wandering from home and pilfering at school. When she had been home for 6 months, she had a fracture of the humerus followed by a dislocation of the right elbow joint. The hospital had been consulted on account of vomiting during meals and a number of nervous symptoms. At the age of 6 years her height was on the 10th and her weight below the 3rd centile.

The summer of 1966 seems to have been an especially stressful time. Carolyn was admitted to one hospital for acute abdominal pain and vomiting, now considered to have been due to fear; Margaret had her first fracture, treated at another hospital; Leonard came under review for failure to thrive, at a third hospital, and Alfred, after a lacerated index finger, was assessed at yet another unit, also failing to thrive, "social causes" being blamed. In retrospect, it looks as if some rather half-hearted discussions about the family took place, resulting in alerting the general practitioner and recommending him to contact the children's officer should any more injuries occur. Further traumas were certainly inflicted. Carolyn had a number of slashes with a razor during 1967 and 1968, but serious consideration of the family was delayed until 1969. Alfred, who had had a greenstick fracture of the left forearm, was admitted in the November for investigation of migraine, and Leonard, who had had a severe subluxation of his left thumb, which has left permanent damage, was noted in September to be very thin with a weight below the 3rd centile. A case conference was held and family violence diagnosed. The mother's consort was then in jail for assaulting a neighbour and they had separated, so that home was now considered to be safe for the children with supervision from the health visitor. The consort was blamed for the children's injuries.

In 1971, the mother married Mr B. and, at the time of Carolyn's admission in 1974, the family was living on an adequate income in a self-contained house. The parents on interview seemed reasonable and in charge of a united, respectable, artisan family. However, later investigation showed the falseness of this façade. Mr B., like Mrs B.'s two other husbands and her various consorts, is a violent man. During the 3 years of marriage, the police have been called more than once to marital rows in the night. It was Carolyn who usually summoned help from her aunt. During one incident, Carolyn, aged 12, arrived in her nightie, crying and frightened, saying, "Come quick, me dad's going to murder me mum!" Mrs B. was found lying in Margaret's bed surrounded by broken furniture and bleeding from cuts in her arm. A problem about housekeeping money was blamed. The police has been called, order restored, the wounds stitched and husband and wife were reconciled in the casualty department. According to the children, Mrs B. had slashed her own arms as she had previously slashed with a razor both Carolyn and Alfred. The children have all their lives witnessed recurring scenes of violence between their mother and a number of men and there can be no doubt that the mother has repeatedly physically assaulted each of her children. Apart from the known incidents of physical trauma, the amount of punishment and emotional trauma can only be guessed. Mrs B., who admits to having a bad temper and to "getting a bit high at times", believes that any ill-treatment she may have had from her own father was punishment well-deserved. It is hardly surprising that Carolyn refused to go home.

In the management of the family, first the idea that the stories were part of a plot by the children to discredit their mother had to be discarded. The kind aunt, too, could have been a trouble-maker and she was certainly not always on good terms with her sister-in-law. However, she was an entirely credible witness, no testimony being volunteered and saying only as much as was needed to answer questions asked. The children at this time were unanimous in wanting to get away from home and all were prepared to describe past events in their mother's presence once they had moved out of her care.

The mother saw a psychiatrist who found no evidence of depression nor of mental illness and diagnosed a severe personality disorder with an hysterical overlay. He considered her to be unamenable to psychiatric treatment.

The decision made was to remove all the children from the parents' care and this was done after school one Friday evening. The mother was warned on the day that this would happen and also what would be said by her children at a meeting to be held with them, the doctor and the social worker on the following Monday. The psychiatrist expected that this "confrontation" might be very disturbing to the mother, but had no fear that she would attempt suicide. The mother naturally denied the truth of all that her children described but was entirely unmoved. At the end of the Monday meeting, she produced a bag of sweets and a comic for each of the children.

At the meeting she was told that she would not be prosecuted but that she should get a solicitor to help her in the juvenile court where all the evidence of the children would be taken. On the other hand, if she preferred, the children could be removed under Section II of the Children Act 1948 and she could have a fresh social worker to help her. On Tuesday morning she visited the social service department and signed all the Section II papers apparently unmoved. At the same time she asked for a smaller house.

Since then Mr and Mrs B. are divorced and Mrs B. relies heavily on her own mother, now a widow. This lady had had a stormy and violent time with her first husband whom she had divorced. Later she had married a quiet and docile man who had died of cancer a year before. Mrs B. is having remedial reading help and seems much calmer. Jack remains in the boys' hostel and will be out of care soon when he reaches 18. Carolyn and Margaret rediscovered Margaret's Yorkshire foster-parents and planned to move there. Unfortunately while arrangements were being made, the foster-mother suffered a fatal stroke and the foster-father became ill. Carolyn has therefore gone to live with the kind aunt very disturbed and under psychiatric treatment, but Margaret remains in the children's home and is awaiting fostering.

Leonard and Alfred remained in the family group home for 6 months during which time Mrs B. paid regular visits. They were unhappy there and at the new school which they had to attend. After much thought, at their vehement request and following some trial weekends with mother at home, Leonard and Alfred returned home, and so far no problems are known to have arisen.

Discussion

Dr Cooper, who confessed to not knowing where to begin or end, so many were the questions raised, selected the following seven.

1. Would the significance of these recurrent injuries be missed today by hospitals, schools or social service departments?
2. Would it be sensible to leave any children with the mother in the light of what is known?
3. Both the younger boys begged to go back to her and promised to report any further incidents, but would they "cover up"?
4. In the elucidation of the family problems, the children were invited to tell the true stories of the various incidents to the workers in the presence of the mother. Could this confrontation be criticized as too traumatic an experience for them?
5. The children were removed under Section II to spare the need for them to give evidence in court. Would it have been wiser or safer to go to court for care orders?
6. How should a colleague be dealt with who is unable or unwilling to recognize obvious child abuse?
7. Who should have the responsible task of collating all the information from different hopsitals and social service departments and who has the immense amount of time that it takes?

In the discussion, the belief was expressed that the significance of this kind of story is widely recognized and that fewer colleagues needed now to be convinced. Much has happened in the 13 years since Carolyn's first fracture to enlighten society. The mother was generally regarded as unsafe to have the care of children. Her actions, if explained by her need to act out the violence that she felt inside herself, were bound to be repeated, she had a problem of grossly distorted relationships and was considered by the psychiatrist who saw her as unamenable to psychiatric treatment. Children did have a strong sense of loyalty to their parents, but the feeling was that, as in this family, they could be gently persuaded to reveal the truth and that this was an acceptable procedure. The collection of family information presented a formidable task, especially when there were many moves of house and many changes of name. Dr Oliver raised the question later and it was agreed that, in view of the importance of collating all this material and of the time that it required, some special arrangements had to be made.

Although some supported supervision orders, the majority considered that as they were at present laid down they gave insufficient strength to the supervisor and therefore a false sense of security. The argument that they could readily be changed to care orders paid too little heed to the crisis nature of events in abusing families.

3. Some Studies of Families in which Children Suffer Maltreatment

Jack Oliver

Parents and guardians who are responsible for cruelty to young children are not a homogeneous group of people. They cannot be neatly categorized as mad or bad, or of limited intellect. On the other hand, it is equally naive to take the line that "anyone can batter their child" or "there but for the grace of God go I". Only one series of studies so far has systematically compared the child rearing practices of large numbers of parents of battered children and controls in a disciplined way (Smith and Hanson, 1974b).

The significant behaviour patterns of battering parents included:

(a) much smacking of very young children,
(b) undemonstrativeness with very young children,
(c) carelessness over the whereabouts or well-being of young children with lax supervision,
(d) obedience demanded from very young children.

The contrast between unkind pestering (a and d) and neglectful rearing (b and c) indicates a destructively inconsistent child-rearing pattern. The parents either "did not enjoy the child" or the child "meant everything" to them. Either way, the rearing was deficient, because babies and toddlers need cuddling, kindly control, nurturing and practical loving kindness, rather than frustrated passion. Too often there has been a failure to grasp the difference between loving (giving practical love and kindness) and loving (frustrated, disappointed or perverted passion, in which the parents' emotional needs swamp all else). There is as much difference between loving-kindness in rearing and destructive exploitation of the child to satisfy insatiable emotional urges in a parent, as there is between happiness in sexual love and destructive lust.

Parents of battered children may well differ in their rearing practices from control parents of comparable social background, even more than was shown by Smith and Hanson (Oliver, 1976a).

There have been repeated warnings against failing to diagnose cruel rearing practices or child-battering by parents who appear to be monied and respectable, and even among the influential members of their community. By contrast researchers concede that child neglect occurs mainly in lower social-class families. The ensuing paragraphs emphasize the predominance of child abuse (battering and active cruelty cases) in multi-problem families, most in the lowest social class, who contributed a disproportionate number of cases. Although under-represented in north-east Wiltshire, some battered and cruelly treated children came from superficially "respectable" homes, whose parents were plausible people.

The Birmingham team showed that battering occurs alongside a constellation of other social inadequacies or failures of adaptation, rather than in isolation. Pre-marital pregnancy, illegitimacy, absence of the child's father, marital disharmony and rejecting attitudes towards the child are precursors of battering. The children are likely to be reared in broken homes and are at risk of social maldevelopment and death. Battering parents nevertheless compared reasonably with other low social-class groups in their standards of income and in food expenditure (Smith *et al.*, 1974). As a group they differed appreciably from parents of a comparable social class in the same locality in other ways, as indicated in the following extracts:

Several interesting psychiatric features emerged. Abnormal personality was a significant finding among parents of battered children. ... Mothers were generally emotionally immature and dependent. Nearly half were of subnormal intelligence. Battering may at best be regarded as an ineffectual method of controlling a child's behaviour. ... One third of the fathers had a gross personality defect and nearly half the mothers were neurotic. ... Nearly a third of the fathers had a criminal record. Although the follow-up period was brief, nevertheless six fathers committed further crimes after the child abuse incident, thus emphasizing the criminal element ... 16 of the brothers and sisters had been battered. ... We have found that where parents have a personality disorder and a record of one or more crimes, and deny that the child has been battered, an optimistic outcome is rather unlikely. We feel it is essential to obtain a care order if further battering incidents are to be prevented. Although efforts must be made to rehabilitate battering parents, this should not be at the expense of the safety of the child (Smith *et al.*, 1973).

Hession, reporting to the Select Parliamentary Committee on Violence in the Family, estimated "that about 40% of 'discovered' cases of serious injuries come from families with at least one parent with an I.Q. lower than 75" (Hession, 1976). Thus studies in London, Birmingham and north-east Wiltshire all emphasize that the parents of battered children are very frequently people with borderline subnormal, subnormal or severely subnormal intelligence.

Subtle, semi-concealed, but profound disorders of personality in parents have been the factors most strongly associated with child abuse within the family. These lead to severe emotional problems, and child-like or distorted methods of coping with life (Steel and Pollock, 1968). Kempe in the U.S.A. and many of his colleagues and followers have been remarkably optimistic about treating such parents. Techniques of treatment are suggested which aim to carry distressed and inadequate parents, thus protecting their children (Kempe, 1974). These have been summarized as "transfusion of mothering (from therapist to parent)". Kempe now feels that this demanding task need not fall only on professional people; help from lay groups (e.g. Parents Anonymous) should be vigorously martialled (Kempe, 1974; Kempe and Helfer, 1972).

Selwyn Smith and the Birmingham team are much more sceptical. They emphasize training in rearing for young parents and others liable to respond. However, prompt care-order proceedings and efficient methods of protection for young children at risk are essential for the rather high proportion of abusive parents who show a constellation of social inadequacies and who are liable either to continue to be unable to rear properly, or to persist in cruel practices. Cogent arguments are also presented by the Institute of Family Psychiatry, directed against archaic ideas on the care of children which had been prevalent in the U.K. and the U.S.A. Children require love and freedom from pain and fear. To achieve this, a proportion need to be reared by people other than their biological parents (Howells, 1974).

Bonding Failure

In the City of Oxford, Ounsted and his colleagues place emphasis on the failure of bonding between parent and child, and direct treatment accordingly (Ounsted *et al.*, 1974; Lynch, 1975). A similar analogy would be to treat a faulty marriage, rather than either or both marital partners separately. Ounsted's group recognizes untreatable parents, but find these a minority. Direction of treatment for the remaining families is firm. There is maximum surveillance of the children at risk, with legal proceedings if necessary to restrain the parents. These need not harm the treatment and the parents are both emotionally supported *and* controlled in a polite humane way. Drugs which impair self-control can increase the risk of bonding failure and release violence to young children, so that certain tranquillizers can be as dangerous as alcohol (Lynch *et al.*, 1975).

Studies in North East Wiltshire

Table 1 shows certain characteristics of 67 parents, most of them young, of severely abused young children in north-east Wiltshire (Oliver et al., 1974; Baldwin and Oliver, 1975). These parents had presented a façade of normality, including some previously designated "subnormal" or "E.S.N." by other professionals. The characteristic plausibility of the parental behaviour had been determined by their own defective rearing, a generation earlier. They learned the superficial social routines, and were adept at modifying their accounts of rearing practices or abusive incidents to attune to the attitudes of the listeners. They watched and listened for the slightest cues which betrayed the attitudes of the people with whom they were concerned, and reacted by anger, evasion, projection of blame, withdrawal, denial or most characteristically *attenuation of their stories*. Having themselves been victims in childhood, they had lifelong experience of these ways of behaving.

Most abusive or neglectful parents had no yardstick with which to measure normality within the life of the family. They often therefore misrepresented themselves and this was not necessarily through conscious lies, deceit or the omission of information. They frequently presented an ideal or façade bearing little relation to reality. Sentimentality could conceal irresponsibility in essentials. Sentimental or idealized versions of the parents' own upbringing often had led professional people to record misleading accounts of neutral or innocuous family histories. Parents commonly made global statements which indicated a belief in the normality of their own upbringing. These general accounts contradicted and contrasted dramatically with unpleasant specific accounts given in detail. Such parents usually appeared unaware of these discrepancies, and became bewildered when their previous statements were compared. Comparison of different agency records sometimes proved more revealing and more reliable than direct interviews in assessing capacity to rear, the effectiveness of case-work treatment and the safety of vulnerable young children within the household.

Those parents who had been given "subnormal" or "borderline subnormal" labels often had suffered impairment of intellect as a consequence of severe psychological deprivation in their own past rearing (Oliver and Cox, 1973). The deleterious effects on children of poor rearing by mentally retarded parents, and the interaction between adverse genetic and socially disadvantageous influences are discussed by Blackie et al. (1975). Our experience is that dull, deprived parents with multi-agency involvement continue to be incompetent rearers, whatever supportive treatment is offered. Furthermore, their families

Table 1
Frequency of certain characteristics in 67 parent figures of the severely abused children

Characteristic	Present No.	Present %	Absent No.	Absent %	Not applicable No.	Not applicable %	Not known No.	Not known %	Total No.	Total %
In childhood										
1. Severe or moderate physical abuse	28*	41.8	17	25.4	—	—	22	32.8	67	100
2. Severe or moderate neglect	28	41.8	16	23.9	—	—	23	34.3	67	100
3. Severe or prolonged mental abuse	39	58.2	4	6.0	1	1.5	23	34.3	67	100
4. Illegitimate or pre-marital conception	10	14.9	47	70.2	—	—	10	14.9	67	100
5. Abandoned, institutionalized or fostered	18	26.9	33	49.3	—	—	16	23.8	67	100
6. Prolonged (over 1 month) separation from one or both parents	28	41.8	21	31.3	—	—	18	26.9	67	100
7. History of E.S.N. or special schooling	11	16.4	37	55.2	6	9.0	13	19.4	67	100
8. Conduct, learning or emotional disorder	33	49.2	11	16.4	6	9.0	17	25.4	67	100
9. Extensive agency support (Oliver and Cox, 1973)	26	38.8	14	20.9	6	9.0	21	31.3	67	100
In early adulthood										
10. History of stealing, violence, sex offences or other criminal behaviour	31	46.3	34	50.7	—	—	2	3.0	67	100
11. Extensive agency support (Oliver and Cox, 1973)	45	67.2	21	31.3	—	—	1	1.5	67	100
12. Chronic physical ill-health or disability	17	25.4	50	74.6	—	—	—	—	67	100
13. Episodes of unconsciousness	19	28.4	48	71.6	—	—	—	—	67	100
14. History of uncontrolled drug or alcohol use	8	11.9	54	80.6	—	—	5	7.5	67	100
15. Borderline or moderate mental subnormality	20	29.8	45	67.2	—	—	2	3.0	67	100
16. Personality or neurotic disorder	51	76.1	10	14.9	—	—	6	9.0	67	100
17. History of suicidal attempts or gestures	20	29.8	43	64.2	—	—	4	6.0	67	100
18. History of psychiatric treatment	39	58.2	24	35.8	—	—	4	6.0	67	100
19. History of psychiatric inpatient treatment	23	34.3	38	56.7	—	—	6	9.0	67	100

* Includes 10 cases in whom severe or moderate physical abuse was probable but evidence was not complete

also tend to be complex, with different cohabitees, and different half and step sibs of the originally attacked child, in different places in different permutations at different times. The capacity of such parents to form *useful protective bonds* with their children, rather than shallow sentimental attachments, or emotionally exploiting relationships, is strictly limited. These latter situations lead to neglect, abandonment or further active ill-treatment of the originally presenting children, or of their sibs (Oliver *et al.*, 1974; Baldwin and Oliver, 1975; Stevenson, 1920; Bruce-Chwatt, 1976; Oliver 1976b, c).

Historically, whole cultures have accepted cruel practices to children (Oliver, 1976a; Radbill, 1968; Solomon, 1971; Bloch, 1973). In the U.S.A., Milgram (1974) has described how people who are not sadistic or cruel by nature can permit, or take part in, cruel practices. There has been a sustained campaign in the U.S.A. and U.K. to treat the parents of maltreated children, rather than to condemn them. Nevertheless untreatable parents exist and they must be recognized. There are therefore dangers in proselytizing campaigns calling for a humane attitude towards cruel parents, unless these are accompanied by firm statements that their children will not be subjected to further suffering and will receive good rearing. Care orders are frequently necessary to protect the children, not to punish their parents. In any locality, not only must pre-battering tense or distressed parents feel free to come for help, but the "at risk" parental population must also know that firm responsible action will be taken by people in authority to ensure the protection of young children.Where this dual policy operates, parents on the fringes of cruel rearing practices respond: "I know of a little baby down our street, who was taken away because her mother was cruel — I'm not as bad as her Mum was, but I don't want to get that way."

Characteristics of Abusing Families

Rates and Repetitions

Prevalence cannot be measured without some form of agreed definitions. The following provides working definitions.

I. *Assault Cases* These range from blatant and/or prolonged battering to irate or unjustified damaging blows to a baby, toddler or young child, which caused professional involvement.

II. *Neglect/Ill-Usage Cases* The neglect cases ranged from starved, or repeatedly dehydrated or abandoned young children to young children irresponsibly left on their own for varying periods. Examples of blatant irresponsibility in failing to provide minimum essentials of parental care for younger children came from a variety of agencies. The criterion for inclusion in the maltreatment (neglect/ill usage) numbers was a situation caused by the

Table 2

Results, maltreated children under 12 years in N.E. Wilts. Population of 44 846 children under 12 in the areas considered (1971 census). The ratios of assault to neglect/ill-usage children were as follows: 65–71 = 1 : 4.24; 72–73 = 1 : 2.36; 65–73 = 1 : 3.52.

Time interval—(years inclusive)	Type of care (all children under 12)	Numbers of affected children over the time interval. (Repeat cases not counted)	Numbers (of affected children under 12) per 1000 (children under 12) for the relevant time interval	Rate per 1000 children under 12 per year
1965–1972, with first half of 1973 (8½ yrs)	Maltreatment (all types)	1921	(42.8)	(5.0)
	Assaults	425	(9.5)	(1.1)
	Neglect/ill-usage	1496	(33.4)	(3.9)
1965–1971 (7 years)	Maltreatment (all types)	1374	(30.5)	(4.4)
	Assaults	262	(5.8)	(0.8)
	Neglect/ill-usage	1112	(24.7)	(3.5)
1972 with first half of 1973	Maltreatment (all types)	547	(12.2)	(8.1)
	Assaults	163	(3.6)	(2.4)
	Neglect/ill-usage	384	(8.5)	(5.7)

parents which necessitated professional involvement on behalf of the children.

Abandonments and receptions into care with repeated capricious removals were often considered forms of parental neglect.

Table 2 shows the maltreatment rates for children of under 12 years identified in north-east Wiltshire. The numbers are not likely to represent the full totals for the following reasons.

1. The definitions of abuse/neglect/ill-usage depended on professional intervention on behalf of each child, so that the better the services and the more conscientious the workers, the worse the situation appears. The converse also applied. Reporting and intervening on behalf of maltreated children in north-east Wiltshire was as patchy as it is elsewhere.

2. Further cases from the period under consideration are still coming to light.

3. Ideally, for adequate ascertainment, each agency dealing with children should have had a team personally collecting and collating information, rather than just one child psychiatrist and one sociologist collating for all the agencies.

Maltreatment cases as defined by the working definitions topped eight new cases per 1000 children under 12 years in 1972/73 (Oliver, 1976b, c). The figures therefore are comparable with the projections by Light of Harvard (1973) that 1% of children under 18 are victims each year and, more remarkably, with Chesser's figures (1951) from N.S.P.C.C. sources in England and Wales, that 1% of children under 15 are victims each year. Table 1 is not really adequate to give a rate for children under 12 years old of abuse/maltreatment at some time in their childhood, but this rate cannot be less than 4% (Oliver, 1976c). Chesser's comparable figure is 6 or 7%. These numbers do not imply disagreement with estimates made by Clegg and Megson (1968) and the Plowden Committee that orders of one in ten children are victims in their own homes, or that children from one home in ten are brutally beaten (Hession, 1976). The figures here merely give the minimum rates highlighted by professional agencies in north-east Wiltshire of maltreatment of such magnitude as to require or precipitate professional intervention on behalf of the child.

About 16 or 20 medical/nursing health and welfare agencies can be involved with child welfare and protection in Britain. There are five or more social welfare organizations which can be similarly involved. There are also the penal/legal organizations (e.g. the police) and the professionals associated with education (teachers, education welfare officers, educational psychologists). For severely ill-treated young children under the age of 5 years in north-east Wiltshire, the medical/nursing agencies were much more involved than all the others put together. The paediatrician was most often the key professional person, but a large variety of other professionals were principally or solely involved in more than three-quarters of the total cases (Oliver *et al.*, 1974; Baldwin and Oliver, 1975).

Chesser (1951) rightly made a strong point of studying "re-opened" or "hard core" cases.

Approximately 50% of all the 99 622 children reported to the N.S.P.C.C. in 1949/50 had previously been under the Society's notice, arising out of an entirely different incident which had been dealt with and the case closed at least 6 months before the event occurred, which once again necessitated recourse to the N.S.P.C.C. There is thus a very substantial hard core of cases in which children suffer repeated neglect and cruelty, and which not even the persistent efforts of the N.S.P.C.C. can eradicate permanently.

In north-east Wiltshire the same applies. For the 38 severe abuse cases, there was a mean of 5.9 incidents per child (at different times). In less than 10% of cases, the battering took place over a period of hours, and less than 25% of the children were battered over 1 day to 2 week periods. Nearly half suffered abuse over a period of 1–10 months, and nearly a third suffered over a period of 1–8 years. 63–72% of the 65 sibs at risk also suffered abuse. Of the 100+ children at risk in these families, only 14% appeared to have been well-cared for (Oliver *et al.*, 1974). Furthermore, nearly 40% of the mostly young parents were already receiving multi-agency support; in this, the findings were comparable with various New York studies, which have emphasized child abuse/neglect in multi-problem families (Simons *et al.*, 1966). Comparable analyses of "reopened cases" have not been possible for the larger numbers considered in Table 2. Our impression is that the same considerations apply, though the proportion of hard-core abuse/neglect families may be less than 50%. The principal difference between our findings in 1965–73 and those of Chesser in 1949–50 was as follows. Many of our problems involving distress to children "repeated" through *different* agencies. Only a minority of families repeated (following a closed or lapsed case) with the *same* agency.

Repetitions are carefully considered in a recent comprehensive report from the Manchester and Leeds special units of the N.S.P.C.C. (Rose *et al.*, 1976). Re-injury rates in Manchester (following up battering cases in 1973 and 1974) of 20 and 18% were felt to be high especially in view of the short follow-up period of one year. Pre-notification rates of re-injury for the 2 years were 60% and 34%. Injuries to sibs are not mentioned. The authors make the following points: (a) younger children are most at risk of battering and re-injury; (b) the most vulnerable rebattering period is usually within the three months immediately following the initial injury; (c) professional intervention and management may reduce rates of re-injury substantially (Rose *et al.*, 1976). Seventy per cent of cases were managed on a voluntary basis; yet 12 months after initial notification, 50% of the Manchester notified children ". . . had some experience of removal from home and/or statutory control. For about half the cases, management procedures had resulted in more than two changes of residence for the child during this period." Again the fate of sibs is not mentioned. Skilled, organized and professional support was available to the parents, yet half the index children were seen to require initial or additional protection from their parents by the Society within one year of the notification. Ascertained and actual re-injury rates before and after treatment are a fundamental consideration, but not the only crucial one for the children.

Family Patterns

Families in which there is severe child abuse were characterized in a retrospective study by their large size, youthfulness, instability, criminality, and by gross excesses of psychiatric and physical illness and disability. Similar features were found in a prospective study of comparable families (Baldwin and Oliver, 1975). So marked were these features that, even in the absence of controls, it is likely that they identify a group of inadequate and unhealthy families to whom severe physical abuse is largely confined. These results are in accord with those of Smith and his colleagues in the Birmingham area (Smith *et al.*, 1973, 1974; Smith, 1975). Large size was also a very marked feature of the battering families studied in Leeds and Manchester by the N.S.P.C.C. (Rose *et al.*, 1976). Oliver and Cox (1973) described a problem of family kindred with battering and neglect of young children over three generations, pointing out the massive and largely ineffective support given. Seven spouses of members of this family came from other socially-chaotic kindreds where mental and/or personality disorders were present. This pattern had been seen in many Swindon and north-east Wiltshire families, implying assortative matings. Abusive, neglectful and problem families were remarkably often linked with each other by transient association and cohabitation, brief marriages or unsuspected kinships (Oliver and Cox, 1973; Oliver 1976c).

This point is also highlighted by the pilot study on the Intergenerational Cycle of Deprivation, from Edinburgh (Paterson and Inglis, 1976). In a preliminary series of conclusions, the authors state the following:

We believe that the cycle is intensive, that multiple difficulties in addition to the generational patterns occur in a relatively small number of cases, households or family pedigrees within any one social-work department caseload. We are of the opinion that because of the intensity, *because of the interconnection with other families exhibiting similar difficulties* and because of the spatial distribution of the type illustrated in this sample, these "problem families" appear to constitute a major part of the departmental caseload.

Another large problem family, which also has multi-agency involvement, consists of a borderline subnormal mother and nine children. Some of the children are dull or subnormal, and most have been neglected, maltreated or abandoned. This local family unit is linked by cohabitation or kinship with five or probably six other local battering families! This sort of information can only be ascertained by energetic, sceptical and lengthy personal searches for and collation of information. Much professional co-operation, knowledge of alternative names, previous surnames and forenames, localities and local record systems, is also required in order to find the true extent of the social pathology and the effectiveness (or ineffectiveness) of case work or other interventions.

The pattern for at least 40% of battering parents is as follows: Rapidly enlarging young families of vulnerable children; multiple social problems; multi-agency involvement, with children often going for varying spells into various types of care; complex families, with transient cohabitations, and numbers of half and step sibs. As this 40% consists mainly of young parents, it will rise as time goes on. Each affected family will increasingly resemble a classical "problem family" with neglected, intermittently attacked, abandoned or incompetently reared children who create the nucleus for social epidemics in years to come. Many "problem families" with older children have semi-concealed indications that the same children, when they were young, were battered, maltreated or neglected. Families with pseudo-respectable, tense parents of higher social standing do sometimes produce severely battered babies, but the bulk of child maltreatment cases in a locality are drawn from multi-problem families.

Publications are split, approximately, in the ratios 3 : 2 : 1 into those finding that sibs of presenting child victims are usually also victims, those which concede that sibs are sometimes victims and papers which make a great play of individual children being singled out for cruel treatment. Our findings generally are in line with the first group and, although it is conceded that all variations of abuse occur, *most* parents who maltreat one child will maltreat his sibs, his step sibs and/or his half sibs. The abuse of one child may well be much worse and more specifically discriminatory than the abuse or maltreatment of the others. It may be different for each sib in type, severity, frequency and the length of time over which the abuse occurs. Florid abuse and/or neglect occurs when there is a potentially abusive/neglectful parent and bonding failure between the mother and the particular child victim (Ounsted *et al.*, 1974).

The demarcation line between the sorts of parents who assault their children and those who neglect them is not clearly defined (Young, 1964). Most attacked children had also been neglected. The neglected children from notorious problem families had also been frequently and unnecessarily and unjustifiably assaulted. The cruel parent in the higher social class was not materially neglectful and tended to specialize in confidential pacts with doctors. The parent in the lower social class was more often involved with a number of different social agencies.

Collating Problems

There was a dichotomy between small isolated family units of two (mother and child only) to four individuals, and huge problem families, the ill-treated children forming part of a network of socially incompetent people. Often the latter families extended their social (and medical) pathology over several generations with multiple files on sibs and uncles and aunts, step and half-sibs and cohabitees (Oliver and Dewhurst, 1969; Oliver and Taylor, 1971; Oliver and Cox, 1973; Oliver *et al.*, 1974; Oliver, 1976b). Multi-agency involvement often resulted in "paper depots" of uncollated and unstandardized files in which items of "hard data" on abuse and neglect of children were buried in sheaves of socio-psychological observations on adults and bureaucratic administrative correspondence about the individuals within the families who had created a problem for society. Where the family and personal histories of the isolated family units who were not part of a large *local* problem family complex could be pursued, one or both parents were usually found to have escaped from their unhealthy or problem family backgrounds in other parts of the country. Such parents were usually young, were failing to cope with their own children and were continuing the child abuse from one generation to another (Oliver and Dewhurst, 1969; Oliver and Taylor, 1971; Oliver and Cox, 1973; Oliver *et al.*, 1974). The pregnancy or the marriage had been the means of escape from their unhappy homes.

In many abusive and neglected families, there were alternative forenames and alternative surnames, and different dates of birth were frequently given for any one child. The parents could be adept at concealing episodes of treatment or at underplaying the different agencies involved with themselves or their children at different times. The importance of this is that treatability of abusive parents is more likely to relate to the number of different maltreatment incidents and the length of time over which children within the family have been poorly reared, than to the severity of a single assault, however terrible the consequences. The frequency of pathologies in these families is suggestive of clustering of disorders and is reminiscent of Newcombe's

(1966) finding of greatly increased relative risk in siblings of handicapped and stillborn children for a wide range of conditions, including
accidents, poisonings and violence. This is clearly a subject for detailed
study for which a system of linked medical records depicting the
primary and inter-generational family relationships would be
necessary. If disease clustering in such families were confirmed and its
nature and extent specified, there could be important implications for
both medical knowledge and the organization of health and social
care. Child abuse appears to be but a manifestation of widespread,
heterogeneous, but often severe medical and social pathology affecting
virtually the whole family. In some families the social disturbances
were obvious, albeit underplayed, but in other, superficially more
respectable, families, they were mostly concealed. Multiple pathology
and the consequent disability may become so overwhelming that the
means of coping with the difficulties of living are no longer available to
the adult members. For many abusive and neglectful families, violent
impulsive aggression, shifting dependence on acquaintances and
relatives and deep ambivalence towards health, social welfare and
social control agencies on which extraordinary demands are made,
become a characteristic way of life.

The Children

A high proportion of severely abused children suffered brain damage
and impairment of intellect (Oliver *et al.*, 1974; Oliver, 1975; MacKeith,
1974, 1975; Bax, 1975; Smith and Hanson, 1974a). Seven per cent of
children on the roll of three special (E.S.N.) schools in Wiltshire had
already been recorded as having been subjected to ill-treatment before
the maltreatment lists were half completed (Myers, 1975).

Much recent research concerns malnutrition, under stimulation and
subsequent brain and intellectual development (Lewin, 1974; Dobbing, 1974a, b; Stewart, 1975; Watts, 1976). Reference has already been
made to the susceptibility of children's I.Q. to adverse rearing,
particularly by mothers of low I.Q. (Blackie *et al.*, 1975). Furthermore,
more than one half of a follow-up (8 months to 9 years) group of
children with "failure to thrive" as a consequence of neglect by their
parents showed evidence of continued growth failure, emotional
disorder, mental retardation or combinations of these handicaps
(Bullard *et al.*, 1968). There is, therefore, much to indicate that poorly
reared and maltreated children can suffer impairment of intelligence
as a direct result of assaults, or more commonly, as a consequence of
the combination of neglect, underfeeding, understimulation and/or
unkindness within the home setting.

At least 2.8% of children admitted to subnormality hospitals in Wiltshire have severe brain damage as a consequence of assaults involving ferocious shaking or battering. These children had previously been biologically normal. Larger numbers of children, at least 16% of those who end up in subnormality hospitals, appear to have been victims of sustained abuse. Many, but probably not all of these additional ones, were biologically abnormal before the assaults. These numbers do not take into account the neglected children who end up in subnormality hospitals, or those whose mental subnormality results from malnutrition and/or psycho-social deprivation.

Adults from two recently seen families subtly but firmly extruded damaged children from their households into our care, whilst talking of having new children by new partners. Such extruded damaged children in subnormality hospitals are forgotten and rarely or never visited. The relatives of damaged children can project blame on hospital staff either wildly, or as a displacement of unhappy conscience. Relatives of loved children in subnormality hospitals rarely make unjustified complaints, in contrast to the relatives of unloved children who have been harmed at home. There is an unrealized concentration of child victims of severe abuse or maltreatment involving the brain in subnormality hospitals. These hospitals, as well as serving their functions towards mentally handicapped children from kindly families of origin, also function as the last refuge of children secretly damaged and subsequently rejected and extruded from their families.

Specific and Non-specific Evidence

It is of utmost importance to realize that features which are highly specific to abusive families may be less important in practice than much commoner but less specific features. Excessive crying or hyperactivity in the child may have many causes. The parent may fail to attend the clinic for many reasons. Nevertheless, excessive crying or hyperactivity in children and non-co-operation in appointments and attendances by adults are also features strongly associated with families in which there is severe child abuse. These relatively common features may be found in 15 or 20 abusive families for every one family in which there is a child showing "frozen watchfulness".

The following is a list of the most important injuries and conditions which occur in children and their siblings compiled from the study of 60 severe abuse families. The items are listed in the order of frequency of importance. The first 13 items are in roughly the same order as for the larger numbers of families considered in Table 2. Intermittently maltreated children can look convincingly normal even to skilled observers. Some children alternated between features such as irritability/crying and withdrawal/apathy.

1. Non co-operation by parents or substitute parents over appointments and attendances; reluctance or refusal to allow professional people, such as health visitors or social workers, to see children when the homes were visited, features shown by at least three-quarters of severely abusive families.

2. Persistent crying reported by neighbours and/or irritability, so that the abusive or neglectful parent often refers to the child in pejorative terms such as "nasty ... vile-tempered ... evil-tempered ... bad-natured ... foul-tempered ...", a feature reported in nearly half the presenting children and one third of their sibs. (N.B. most, but not all, "impossible" or irritable children became quiescent, calm, tractable and lovable after a period of loving care.)

3. Withdrawal, listlessness, apathy, unresponsiveness, the abusive parent referring to the child as "useless ... lazy ... worthless ... backward ... well behind his brothers ... etc., a feature reported in nearly half the presenting children and one-fifth of their sibs.

4. Marked fear of parents or other adults, with abnormal displays of fear in certain circumstances or situations, e.g. fear of certain uniforms or of bathing, a feature reported in nearly half the presenting children and one-fifth of their sibs. (A proportion of our abusive parents used suffocatory techniques as a punishment measure, including holding children under water and placing polythene bags over the head.)

5. Hyperactivity or repetitive motor/muscular activity, reported in over a quarter of the presenting children and one-fifth of their sibs. It is now generally accepted that hyperactivity and hyperkinesis can often be more closely related to faulty or defective rearing in early life than to organic factors (Editorial, 1975).

6. Pallor and/or anaemia, reported in a third of the presenting children.

7. Bruising of the head (check under the hair).

8. Bruising of the body and limbs.

9. Bruising of the face (including inside, on and around the mouth) and ears.

10. Severe napkin rash, often with infections on old unhealed areas.

11. Fits and losses of consciousness.

12. Speech defects.

13. Defects in walking, e.g. the child does not learn to walk or is "always falling over" or "unsteady". Bruising is interpreted as a result of this falling tendency. The reality may be that the child is "punch drunk" or weak, and the bruising occurred *as a result of abuse* which also contributed to the unsteadiness and failure in standing upright. Some children felt safer down, rather than risk the danger of standing up.

Others (mostly toddlers) were injured whilst escaping from blows, running up or down stairs.

14. Episodes of bronchitis and pneumonia.
15. Fractured ribs.
16. Fractured skull.
17. Intracranial bleeding without skull fracture.
18. Burns and scalds.

The duration of abuse for a particular child varied from 1–4 hours to 1–8 years. Some mothers maltreated several different children in the family over decades, and could not be considered "safe" until they had reached the end of childbearing and rearing.

For our series, there was an average of six unpleasant recorded incidents per child, mostly injuries, but sometimes other features, such as episodes of partial suffocation. Relatives, neighbours and occasionally the parents themselves sometimes emphasized that the worst intervals of abuse occurred during periods when the "case" had been closed, or had lapsed, and records were not being made. It is important to note that some unequivocally (but usually intermittently) ill-treated young children were *not* noticed to be abnormal in their appearance or behaviour by playschool teachers, infant teachers, doctors, social workers or other professional people. Some maltreated young children appear to adapt happily to controlled, happy social groups and *appear* to relate well to (and lie on behalf of) abusive parents.

"False Love"

It is not well enough known that many ill-treated children cling to abusive parents, rather than showing expressions of fear and distress. Such emotional expressions may have been suppressed by secret, harsh deconditioning within the family setting; more often the infant appears to be imprinted with attachment for the abuser. This sequence often confounds the observer, and even experienced social workers and health visitors must be on their guard. This phenomenon, of "false love", has been described in the children of cruel nannies (Gathorne-Hardy, 1972), but not so far for biological parent-child interactions. It is important for the following reasons: (a) professional people are deceived, and fail to persevere in initial firm action to protect the child; (b) this phenomenon causes professional people to "close cases", many of which are subsequently reopened by another department, to relax supervision or to make unjustified claims for successful case-work treatment of abusive or neglected families; (c) abnormal and unhealthy patterns of emotional life are set up in the child, as the basis of later neurosis or personality disorder; (d) most abusive and neglectful parents were reared with cruelty, unkindness or incompetence. They frequently present a façade of normality, including normal personal and family histories, yet they have immature personalities or cruel attitudes behind this façade. The "false love" phenomenon in one generation may give rise to episodes of otherwise inexplicable child battering in the next or subsequent generations.

Professional people have been warned to be on their guard when they observe the *apparent* need a maltreated child has for its biological parent (or parent *in situ*). "The unwary often negate the diagnosis of child abuse when they observe such children's [apparent] need for their parents" (Irwin, 1975). "The attachment of children to parents who by all ordinary standards are very bad is a never ceasing source of wonder to those who seek to help them" (Bowlby, 1951). The tendency has nevertheless been to assume that, although vigilance should not be reduced as a result of this phenomenon, there must be some sort of innate bond representing a fundamental emotional requirement for the child. The reality is that children of all ages show this biological adaptation which usually tends to protect them. This adaptation does not always work in abusive families. Indeed, even children who are being slowly poisoned by their parents also tend to cling to and protect the parent. Such children collude in the poisoning and suffer sadness and intense anger when separated from their parents (Rogers *et al.*, 1976).

Conclusions

Studies in all countries agree about the wide extent of child abuse within the family (Oliver, 1976c). They disagree about the relative importance of different causes and, markedly, about the treatability of the majority of abusive parents. The reasons for the differences are analysed in the following two sections.

Optimistic Commentators

1. Certain treatment centres (e.g. Denver, U.S.A., or The Park, Oxford) appear to have developed energetic and skilled regimes which treat bonding failures between battered young children and their parents. The majority of referred families are accepted for treatment (80–90%). Severe rebattering seldom occurs.
2. Much sociological research indicates that social changes at different times and in different countries have improved conditions for the family. The suggestion that these may in turn have improved the quality of rearing on a wide scale provides room for scepticism (Oliver, 1976c).

Pessimistic Commentators

1. Florid rebattering episodes may only occur in a minority of skilfully treated abusive families (10–20%). Nevertheless indifferent rearing usually continues, with episodic abuse/neglect incidents involving either the originally attacked child or his brothers and sisters.

2. Radiologists were needed to prove the extent of severe battering to most paediatricians, psychoanalysts, psychiatrists and social workers. Highly specialized research methods are necessary to assess the effects of other forms of unkind or incompetent rearing, and the effects of case-work or other treatments on abusive parents and their families. We do not know how ineffective the armies of social workers, doctors, health visitors, teachers, probation officers and others are in improving rearing practices.

3. A large reservoir of poor rearers are not touched by existing treatment facilities. The multi-problem families who have maltreated their poorly reared youngsters and caused damage to their emotional and intellectual life are often not identified. The adults waste the resources of the community in time and energy expended by medical/social/penal agencies without benefit to their children or to themselves. These represent larger numbers than the relatively few parents of battered children who reach treatment centres.

Rehabilitation of the Family not an Ultimate Aim

Research in north-east Wiltshire and elsewhere has cast considerable doubt on the possibility of rehabilitating severely abusive or neglectful families. Making rehabilitation of the family an aim at all, let alone an ultimate aim, permits many children to remain in unhappy surroundings. It encourages an attitude which delays action (such as care order proceedings) to ensure the future of young children, permitting "problem family" situations to arise and the ill-used young child to become the disturbed, delinquent or unmanageable older child. Furthermore, rehabilitation of the family is often not a practical aim and may represent an over-optimistic or even arrogant attitude by the doctor or social worker. Many trends and many other people in society can also influence either the family group or individuals within the family.

Rehabilitation of the family only succeeds when it helps the child towards the fullest happiness and potential. It may, or may not, be one of the correct methods of treatment, and there is a danger in presenting rehabilitation of the family as an ultimate aim since the correct treatment for an ill-treated child may be to ensure loving foster care and ultimate adoption. Children have a right of loving care and they may only be able to receive it from competent foster or adoptive parents (Howells, 1974; National Childrens Bureau, 1974).

I see some danger in statements from authoritative sources like the quotation from a report from the British Paediatric Association and British Association of Paediatric Surgeons below. Most of the recommendations in the report are practical, and it is only fair to state that some exceptions to the "Rehabilitation of the Family" theme are recognized. Nevertheless this theme recurs as a basic aim.

In practice the management and treatment of "non-accidental injury" present in the first instance clinical problems for which the doctor must assume clinical responsiblity. His primary aim is to treat the injury and to protect the child from any repetition; his ultimate aim is to rehabilitate the family. But these aims cannot be achieved by the doctor alone, and unfortunately in present circumstances and in some cases neither complete protection nor lasting rehabilitation is attainable.

Some parents are treatable. These even include parents who may have committed severe acts of violence which have caused lasting brain damage to one child.

A tense conscientious, albeit unstable, young woman who has lost control and shaken her young baby, even to the point of brain damage or death, *might* benefit from "rehabilitative" treatment. Existing (and future) children might reap the rewards, for the family could become a healthier unit, rather than the nucleus for the spread of further social pathology for two or more generations.

This is a different treatment proposition from the borderline subnormal, emotionally deprived or intermittently mentally-ill girl who has escaped from a chaotic family background to marry a psychopathic youth. He in turn is often from another problem family, with a diversity of social/pyschiatric disorders. There may have been multiagency involvement on both sides of each family in the preceding generation, little of which appears in any one set of notes!

My experience leads me to conclude that in a high proportion of cases from this latter background, particularly those where there has been repetition, or violence has occurred over a long period of time, complete protection of the well-being of children in that family cannot be attained. As long as rehabilitation of a family such as this is regarded as an ultimate aim, children remain in both immediate and long term danger of both physical and lasting emotional damage.

References

Baldwin, J. A. and Oliver, J. E. (1975). Epidemiology and family characteristics of severely abused children. *Brit. J. Prev. Soc. Med.* **29**, 205–221.

Bax, M. (1975). The effect of child abuse on the neurologic and personality development of children. Developmental medicine and child neurology. (Paper given by H. P. Martin during Annual Meeting of the American Academy for Cerebral Palsy) 1974, p 389.

Blackie, J., Forrest, A. and Witcher, G. (1975). Subcultural mental handicap. *Brit. J. Psychiat.*, **127**, 535–539.

Bloch, H. (1973). Dilemma of "battered child" and "battered children". *N.Y. St. J. Med.*73, 799–802.

Bowlby, J. (1951). Maternal Care and Mental health. *Bull. W.H.O.* 3, 355–533.

Bruce-Chwatt, L. (1976). Female "circumcision" and politics. *Wld Med.* **11**, 44–47.

Bullard, M. D., Glaser, H. H., Heagarty, M. C. and Pivchik, E. C. (1968). Part XI: The abused child. Failure to thrive in the "neglected" child. *In* "Annual Progress in Child Psychiatry and Child Development". Ed. S. Chess and A. Thomas. New York; Chapter 32.

Chesser, E. (1951). "Cruelty to Children". Victor Gollancz, London.

Clegg, A. and Megson, B. (1968). "Children in Distress". Penguin, Harmondsworth.

Dobbing, J. (1974a). The later development of the brain and its vulnerability. "Scientific Foundations of Paediatrics". William Heinemann Medical Books, London; Chapter 32, pp 565–577.

Dobbing, J. (1974b). Intelligence after malnutrition. *Lancet* 1, 802–805.

Editorial (1975). Hyperactivity in children. *Brit. Med. J.* **4**, 123–124.

Gathorne-Hardy, J. (1972). "The Rise and Fall of the British Nanny". Arrow Books, London (i.e., see pp 213 and 246).

Hession, M. (1976). Violence in the family. Memorandum submitted to the Select Parliamentary Committee in May 1976 by the Institute of Child Psychology.

Howells, J. G. (1974). "Remember Maria". Butterworth Press, Brisbane, Toronto, Wellington, Durban, London.

Irwin, C. (1975). The establishment of a child abuse unit in a children's hospital. *S. Afr. Med. J.* **89**, 1142–1146.

Kempe, C. H. (1974). Duty to report child abuse. *Western J. Med.* **121**, 229.

Kempe, C. H. and Helfer, R. E. (1972). "Helping the Battered Child and his Family". Lippincott, Philadelphia and Toronto.

Lewin, R. (1974). Malnutrition and the human brain. *Wld Med.* **10**, 19–21.

Light, R. J. (1973). Abused and neglected children in America: a study of alternative policies. *Harv. Educ. Rev.* **43**, 556.

Lynch, M. A. (1975). Ill-health and child abuse. *Lancet* 2, 317–319.

Lynch, M. A., Lindsay, J. and Ounsted, C. (1975). Tranquillizers causing aggression. *Brit. Med. J.* **1**, 266.

MacKeith, R. (1974). Speculations on non-accidental injury as a cause of chronic brain disorder. *Develop. Med. Child Neurol.* **16**, 216–218.

MacKeith, R. (1975). Speculations on some possible long-term effects. *In* "Concerning Child Abuse". Ed. A. W. Franklin. Churchill Livingstone; pp 63–68.

Milgram, S. (1974). "Obedience to Authority". Tavistock, London.

Myers, P. A. (1975). Can education help break the pattern in familiies where there is cruel, neglectful or incompetent rearing? Thesis for the University of Oxford Department of Education Studies; see p 45.

National Children's Bureau, (1974). 11th Annual Review.

Newcombe, H. B. (1966). Familial tendencies in diseases of children. *Brit. J. Prev. Soc. Med.* **20**, 49–57.

Non-Accidental Injury in Children (1973). Introductory comment from B.P.A. and B.A.P.S. *Brit. Med. J.* **4**, 656–660.

Oliver, J. E. (1975). Microcephaly following baby battering and shaking. *Brit. Med. J.* **2**, 262–264.

Oliver, J. E. (1976a). Letter to *Brit. J. Psychiat.* **128**, 509. Parents of battered children.

Oliver, J. E. (1976b). Child abuse. From Social Crises in Service Communities, Amport House Symposium. Survey Dept. Neuro-Psychiatric Centre, Princess Alexandra's R.A.F. Hospital, Wroughton, Wilts.

Oliver, J. E. (1976c). The extent of child abuse. *In* "The Battered Baby Syndrome", Ed. Selwyn Smith. M.T.P., Lancaster; Chapter 1, Sections 1–4 (in press).

Oliver, J. E. and Cox, J. (1973). A family kindred with ill-used children: the burden on the community. *Brit. J. Psychiat.* **123**, 81–90.

Oliver, J. E., Cox, J., Taylor, A. and Baldwin, J. A. (1974). Severely ill-treated young children in north-east Wiltshire. Unit of Clinical Epidemiology, Oxford Record Linkage Study, Oxford Regional Health Authority.

Oliver, J. E. and Dewhurst, K. E. (1969). Six generations of ill-used children in a Huntington's pedigree. *Postgrad. Med. J.* **45**, 757–760.

Oliver, J. E. and Taylor, A. (1971). Five generations of ill-treated children in one family pedigree. *Brit. J. Psychiat.*, **119**, 473–480.

Ounsted, C., Oppenheimer, R. and Lindsay, J. (1974). Aspects of bonding failure: the psychopathology and psychotherapeutic treatment of families of battered children. *Develop. Med. Child Neurol.* **16**, 447–456.

Paterson, A. and Inglis, J. (1976). Intergenerational cycle of deprivation. (D.H.S.S. and University of Edinburgh Joint Study.)

Radbill, S. X. (1968). A History of Child Abuse and Infanticide. *In* "The Battered Child". R. E. Helfer and C. H. Kempe. University of Chicago Press, Chicago and London, Chapter 1, pp 3–17.

Rogers, D., Tripp, J., Bentovim, A., Berry, D. and Goulding, R. (1976). Non-accidental poisoning. *Brit. Med. J.* **1**, 793–796.

Rose, N., Owtram, P., Pickett, J., Marran, B. and Maton, A. (1976). Registers of suspected non-accidental injury. A report on registers maintained in Leeds and Manchester by N.S.P.C.C. Special Units. N.S.P.C.C.

Sarsfield, J. K. (1974). The neurological sequelae of non-accidental injury. *Develop. Med. Child Neurol.* **16**, 826–827.

Simons, B., Downs, E. F., Hurster, M. M. and Archer, M. (1966). Child abuse. Epidemiologic study of medically reported cases. *N. Y. St. J. Med.* **66**, 2783–2788.

Smith, S. M. (1975). The battered child syndrome — some research findings. *Nursing Mirror* June 12th, 48–52.

Smith, S. M. and Hanson, R. (1974a). 134 battered children: a medical and psychological study. *Brit. Med. J.* **3**, 666–670.

Smith, S. M. and Hanson, R. (1974b). Interpersonal relationships and child-rearing practices in 214 parents of battered children. *Brit. J. Psychiat.* **127**, 513–525.

Smith, S. M., Hanson, R. and Noble, S. (1973). Parents of battered babies: a controlled study. *Brit. Med. J.* **4**, 388–391.

Smith, S. M., Hanson, R. and Noble, S. (1974). Social aspects of the battered baby syndrome. *Brit. J. Psychiat.* **125**, 568–582.

Smith, S. M. and Noble, S. (1973). Battered children and their parents. *New Society* **26**, 393–395.

Solomon, T. (1971). Symposium on child abuse. Held at New York University Medical Centre, New York City, June 15th, 1971. *Pediatrics* **51**, **ii**, 773–776.

Steele, B. F. and Pollock, C. B. (1968). A psychiatric study of parents who abuse infants and small children. *In* "The Battered Child". Ed. R. E. Helfer and C. H. Kempe. University of Chicago Press, Chicago.

Stewart, R. J. C. (1975). How malnutrition handicaps children. *New Society* 13th Feb., 378–380.

Stevenson J. (1920). "Two Centuries of Life in Down". The Linehall Press, Belfast, Dublin; pp 215–216 and 462.

Watts, G. (1976). Malnutrition in context. *Wld Med.* Feb., 25, 57–60.
Young, L. (1964). "Wednesday's Children". McGraw-Hill, New York, Toronto, London.

Discussion

Professor Brandon began the discussion with a warning against the assumption that we possess therapeutic omnipotence. We could construct what we believed to be the optimal plan, that seemed best under all the circumstances. We must be prepared for failure and then for the permanent removal of the child. Oliver stressed his point that too much emphasis had been placed on rehabilitating the family. His experience in a mental colony of children whose brains had been permanently damaged by non-accidental injury and his studies of complex kinships made up of people whose life history showed that safe parenthood would be beyond their reach had made him pessimistic. Making family rehabilitation one of the main therapeutic aims simply prolonged the danger period for the child.

However, if more children were to be removed permanently or for periods of years from their parents, who would provide the family life that was essential for their growth and development? Adoption, which had its own problems, could provide security, good bonding and the two-way relationship between parents and child. Adoption was not always available and was never a rapid process. The idea that fostering care was better than leaving the child in a battering family while the family was being treated had some support. This raised the further question of whether the rehabilitation of parents was possible in the absence of their child. An attempt ought to be made to achieve bonding within the family first.

The kind of families that Oliver had studied were exceptional and not the ones usually encountered. For these, rehabilitation as parents was beyond anyone's ability to achieve. What was certainly more important than the rehabilitation of the family was to ensure that the child was provided with those essential contributions which could only come from a secure and loving relationship within a family.

4. Battering in Relation to Other Deviant Behaviour

Peter Scott

Syndromes and specific deviant behaviours resemble living organisms in evolving through states of youthful vigour and certainty, cross-fertilization from other fields with the production of new variants and finally dissolution. There may be some usefulness in considering our youthful "battered-child syndrome" together with some of the older forms of deviant behaviour, especially "delinquency" and other forms of crime. It is possible that by so doing some stages of enquiry may be abbreviated and blind alleys avoided.

Definition is always difficult in deviant behaviour because there is usually no more than a description of behaviour to depend upon, so that tautology is common. Lawyers can only state that crime is behaviour punishable by legal process, and the best we can do with the battered-child syndrome is "non-accidental injury to a child under x years of age" — a sort of definition by exclusion. As with crime and delinquency, the definition serves practical, legal and administrative purposes quite effectively, but means nothing clinically, there being so many quite different paths by which this behaviour might have been reached.

The incidence of crime and battering have resemblances: once there is awareness of the problem, the incidence burgeons and we have no idea whether it is real or apparent, whether it is due to better ascertainment, whether with increased tolerance those afflicted have less need to hide the tendency and greater willingness to seek help, or whether there is greater police or different court or coroner activity, or some mysterious deterioration amongst parents. Certainly the public responds to both with similar waves of alarm, each precipitated by some dramatic case or report; anxious committees of enquiry into social deviants of various sorts have been reporting for at least 400 years, and their recommendations for one type of deviance are often perfectly applicable to the others.

The distribution of most "deviances", and certainly delinquency and battering, includes those of any race, colour, creed or political system. Whether it is confined to man is not certain. Some animals, notably the Harlows' monkeys, exhibit fairly typical battering under experimental conditions, and it is worth noting here that those conditions are deprivations rather than exposure to violence during their own infancies. Many animals will desert, kill or eat their offspring under conditions of stress, and such behaviour (we have to face) may have species survival value. Henry Maudsley, founder of the hospital in which I work, indicated that crime may be due to the misapplication of valuable human qualities.

Studies in Causation

The history of the study of causation in crime and delinquency reveals stages which, to some extent, can be seen to be recapitulated in the battering syndrome. The stage in which a single factor is held to be central in the causation is common to both. The single factor, like the sorcerer's touchstone, has been eagerly sought, frequently found, but never validated. Most attractive has always been the single medical, especially organic, factor, because this would make the whole anxiety-provoking condition understandable, predictable and treatable without the necessity for tiresome changes in society or long term caring and dependency of which all services seem to be so afraid. In delinquency we have had a succession of such single factors — brain damage at birth, under nourishment, endocrine disorders, type of bodybuild and (amongst social and psychological causes) mental deficiency, broken homes and the like. In battering, early emphasis was placed on psychosis, dullness of intelligence (still a firm runner), E.E.G. abnormalities, physical exhaustion, experience of battering during the childhood of the perpetrator (still widely accepted as *the* cause), social isolation and so on. Many of these monistic theories are really the result of the inevitable selection of cases for particular workers. Doctors have been particularly at risk here, and have elevated to the status of diseases many widespread social phenomena, simply because only a few exceptional examples are referred to them. Only the interdisciplinary, epidemiological studies can correct these errors, and such studies are very urgently needed in the battering area. They would settle the question of whether the battering parent is qualitatively different, or simply part of a continuum, ranging from non-punitiveness, through harshness, to battering. If the analogy with other "deviances" hold good, then the answer almost certainly will be "both", for experience now shows that deviances usually have a small so called hard core compounded of the extreme end of the distribution curve together with a few qualitatively different "ill" persons, while the remainder of the large penumbra shades imperceptibly into the general population. At least studies should be planned with this double distribution in mind thus avoiding some possibly inconclusive results.

Another lesson to be learnt from delinquency research is that a given measurable factor may correlate with the syndrome at both ends of its scale. For example both very high and very low intelligence has a negative correlation with recidivism, possibly because the person with a really low I.Q. is always supervised and anyway bungles his attempt, and, on the other hand, the intelligent man is more likely to have money, lawyers and perhaps the ability to find alternative satisfaction or to see consequences. The extremes of social types have been claimed to correlate with delinquency at both ends of their scales. Crime may be caused by poverty and, it is claimed, by the pampering of some children of wealthy parents. It is likely that similar double correlations may obtain in battering.

Some of the best studies of delinquency and crime have shown that these deviances occur amongst a constellation of other social insufficiences. Robins' (1966) beautiful 30 year follow-up study of delinquents demonstrates this very clearly.

Oliver's (Oliver *et al.*, 1974) excellent battering studies from north-east Wiltshire show a similar clustering of social and psychiatric pathology, and Newcombe (1966) finds that the siblings of battered children have a greatly increased incidence of a variety of accidents, poisonings, violence and other disasters. It seems that it is not only old age which "commeth not alone". Just as undetected and *formes frustes* of crime contribute to a large "dark figure", so it is certain that much serious child abuse never comes to light. The Newsons' in their study (1965) of child rearing practices in a northern township found that 62% of children at 1 year and 97% at 4 years are subject to physical modes of correction, 8% of them daily. While this is not battering it shows a rather alarming tradition of punitiveness which may lower the threshold for the relatively few predisposed parents.

In every discussion on baby battering, we hear that all mothers sometimes feel like battering their babies and when daughters make such statements to their parents, it carries much conviction and suggests a close similarity with crime, in that nearly everyone has been aware of the impulse of crime. In battering and other felonies, we have to accept that the wish is normal (in the statistical sense). But at the same time, there are some deviants and some batterers whose impulses towards their babies are exceptional, rare and, even in phantasy, pathological. In both conditions it is a combination of abnormal phantasy, deficient control and provocative circumstances which has to be guarded against. Oliver and Taylor (1971) describe five generations of ill-treated children from the same extended family. This is reminiscent of the many genealogical studies of crime and degeneracy made around the turn of the last century. Most famous is Richard Dugdale's "The Jukes" (1877) which concerns a Dutch settler (born about 1730) who settled in New York State. 709 of his progeny were traced; more than a quarter had been in pauper care, 140 of them criminals, 60 thieves, 50 prostitutes and 7 murderers. The other is Henry Goddard's "The Kallikaks" (1912) in which, of 480 descendants of the union of a soldier and a bar-maid, 143 were feeble minded, while the soldier's legitimate progeny showed no such tendency.

All deviant behaviours turn out to involve widely different types of person, so that classification and typologies become essential, and these are almost always readily interchangeable amongst the deviations; the same broad categories crop up again and again. As Don Gibbons and others have found with crime, there is no single characteristic personality profile of the battering parent and it follows that there can be no single treatment approach.

Crime and Psychiatry

The relationship of crime to medical and psychiatric illness is very slight, and the presence of such illness does not necessarily imply causation. Even such an excellent candidate as epilepsy, when properly studied, does not seem to correlate with crime to any significant extent. So it seems to be with battering. Some psychotic patients do commit crimes; according to Böker and Häfner (1973) mental patients and defectives considered together show no higher incidence of acts of violence than do mentally sound persons. Schizophrenics are by far the most likely amongst psychiatric patients to commit acts of violence, but even so the rate is extremely low (5 in 10 000). The corresponding figure for the affective psychoses and subnormals, together, is 6 in 100 000. Marital partners, lovers and children, they say, are most at risk particularly from patients who have had affective psychoses and delusions.

However, the manner in which schizophrenic or endogenously depressed parents attack their children is quite different from that of non-psychotic parents. Depressed parents usually plan the attack carefully and may try to make it as painless as possible, though their experience is so lacking that the assaults are often dreadfully bungled. The schizophrenic parent does not usually carry out repeated attacks, but is more likely suddenly to strangle the child, dash him to the ground, or throw him out of the window or over the balcony; paranoid delusions of persecution do not often centre upon small children. The relationship between depression and violence is uncertain, but direct observation shows that depression and violence are quite independent of one another; the one may precede or follow the other or they may occur together; this suggests a linkage in parallel rather than a causative or releasing relationship as is so often claimed. Both are closely related to frustration and loss, and probably arise in common from this source.

In summary the relation between child killing, or attempts to kill, and psychiatric illness is probably higher than in Böker and Häfner's figures because of the well-known linkage between the family and violence, but it is very doubtful if the repeated and escalating pattern of the battering syndrome is any more common in psychotic than non-psychotic parents.

A further important similarity between crime (particularly other forms of violent crime) and battering is the difficulty in predicting repetition. We know from the Baxstrom studies of Cocozza and Steadman (1974) that prediction of violence is over-inclusive. "If we attempt to distinguish the potentially dangerous patient" they write, "we double our error by identifying as dangerous all of a group of patients when only a third of them will live up to their expectation".

The early ignorance about the dangers of repetition of battering had one advantageous consequence, in setting up a natural experiment which would be quite unrepeatable with our present knowledge. Some cases of 10 years ago were treated with such lenience by the courts that a young mother who had battered a child to death was allowed home, with only nominal supervision, to look after her remaining children, yet came to no harm and successfully reared two further babies. This is not to say that our present caution is wrong or needless, but it does suggest that, as with crime, our prediction is over-inclusive and that further attempts either to improve prediction or to substitute newer forms of support and supervision should be sought. Since prediction in other deviancy has on the whole consistently been found wanting and is likely to be so with battering, the alternative solution should capture priorities.

Treatment and its Results

In treatment, we see that elsewhere the medical model has not been a success. As stated, the link with medical and psychiatric disability is slight so that the involvement of the medical profession is only really essential for diagnosis. However, as in crime, the role of the doctor will probably continue to be large owing to the long tradition of helping, the wider basis of his training and the greater trust which the profession still attracts.

On the basis of the similarities already discussed, it is predictable that group methods of treatment, including mutual help between patients, in an open, community-based setting, with varying degrees of professional supervision, are likely to be the direction for development. The day nursery at which groups of parents would also be accepted seems essential, at some stage for the majority of cases, with a small proportion of highly supervised family accommodation for the more difficult cases.

Experience with a variety of deviants and criminals shows that a very high proportion can be safely contained within the community provided the support is sufficiently intensive and appropriate, but that it has to be continued for very long periods, and shows a marked tendency to relapse when the help is withdrawn. It is very probable that battering parents will often react similarly. It is already apparent that battering parents are indistinctly divided into those who are afraid that they may batter and those who actually might. Those who fear it and are registered as batterers or potential batterers may swell the numbers considerably and absorb the more intensive care which should be reserved for the more serious cases. A third group is beginning to appear of those who (like some who threaten suicide) are using this very powerful, almost irresistible, weapon to manipulate the social services. In the present climate of scape-goating the social services for society's own defects, a mother with a small baby if she has the know-how and a degree of importunity, can get more or less what she wants. Fairburn's (Fairburn *et al.*, 1975) division into severe and low risk groups recognizes these problems.

Research on the effectiveness of treatment in crime and delinquency has not been very successful. Unless the subjects, the methods and the treating agents are classified and separately assessed, then whatever the treatment or lack of treatment the same basic results emerge. The process of classifying these three aspects is so difficult as to defeat most projects. It is likely that the same difficulties will be experienced with battering parents, although there are differences in this area, notably that the treatment is essentially crisis intervention and that the child's chances of physical rebattering fall off sharply after the age of five.

Finally, the similarity between crime and battering is woefully apparent in another area — the almost total neglect of prevention. Such efforts that exist are really early treatment of established or ascertained cases. The methods used to stop battering should be identical for all the deviant behaviours. Anything that helps in one case will almost certainly work in others. Basically such prevention, as far as present knowledge indicates, is a matter of the cultural, economic and political aspects of child rearing practices.

This could perhaps be the subject of the next conference to which, in addition, there should be invited experts in education, architecture, town planning and economics, and of course the politicians.

References

Böker, W. and Häfner, H. (1973). Mentally disordered violent offenders. *Soc. Psychiat.*, 8/4, 220–229.

Cocozza, J. J. and Steadman, H. J. (1974). Some refinements in the measurement and prediction of dangerous behavior. *Amer. J. Psychiat.* 131, 1012–1014.

Dugdale, R. (1877). "The Jukes". Putnam's, London.

Fairburn, A. C., Jones S. and Moore, C. (1975). Child abuse: A scheme of interdisciplinary linkage and co-ordination. Submitted for publication.

Goddard, H. H. (1912). "The Kallikaks". Macmillan, London.

Newcombe, H. B. (1966). Familial tendencies in diseases of children. *Brit. J. Prev. Soc. Med.* 20, 49–57.

Newson, J. and Newson, E. (1965). "Patterns of Infant Care in an Urban Community". Penguin, Harmondsworth.

Oliver, J. E. and Taylor, A. (1971). Five generations of ill-treated children in one family pedigree. *Brit. J. Psychiat.* 119, 473–480.

Oliver, J. E., Cox, J., Taylor, A. and Baldwin, J. A. (1974). Severely ill-treated young children in north-east Wiltshire. Unit of Clinical Epidemiology, Oxford Record Linkage Study. Oxford Regional Health Authority, Research Report No. 4.

Robins, L. (1966). "Deviant Children Grown Up". Williams and Wilkins, Baltimore.

Discussion

The essence of the problem was to be found in child rearing. Recent years have seen traditional practices reviewed in the light of scientifically controlled observations on both animals and man. The stage had now been reached for politicians to understand the newer knowledge; it was politicians, and politicians alone, who could enable this knowledge to be put into practice. It was also necessary for children and adolescents to realize that rearing a family was good but that it was also difficult and at times uncomfortable. School experience trained children to live democratically together and began the process of socialization. It could also teach them about infant and child behaviour. Difficult secondary-modern schoolgirls could be sent to care for younger children in infants schools, although not every child could learn how to be a good parent.

It was true that what could be done by improving living conditions was limited, but bad conditions must contribute to deprivation and abuse. Moral support and sensible advice from a visiting health visitor could help. In the end the mother is alone with her baby, no one is due to come in for a long time, the baby is crying and nothing makes him stop. What is she to do? Re-introducing the cradle and rocking chair might be of some help. The earlier physical maturation of girls was by no means matched by emotional or intellectual maturity. Parenthood without emotional maturity led to great stresses and some escape route was essential such as a crisis nursery. Mothers do assault their babies in the presence of witnesses, but they are less likely to do so when they lose their feeling of helplessness and isolation. More refuges for violent families are badly needed.

5. The Psychiatric Report in Cases of Non-Accidental Injury

Sydney Brandon

Psychiatrists show as great a diversity of personality experience and interest as members of any other specialized professional group. All share the basic training and experience in psychiatry, on which their professional skill depends, but a "psychiatric" assessment and report may call for much more than this. Those asking for such reports should consider why it is required and how it may be used, and should ensure that the psychiatrist consulted has the appropriate knowledge and skills.

The General Psychiatrist

The general psychiatrist is skilled in obtaining a psychiatric history from and performing a physical and psychiatric examination upon an individual, interpreting information obtained from the subject and other sources and on the basis of this data offering a psychiatric diagnosis, prognosis and treatment plan. His knowledge of treatment resources enables him to recommend the most appropriate form of and place for such treatment and his knowledge of the natural history of psychiatric illness permits him to make some prediction of the risk of violence to others or of self injury. Such predictions are, however, heavily dependent upon factors outside the individual and are at best statements of probability.

The psychiatrist will frequently find, particularly in individuals referred because a court or social agency requests an opinion rather than because the individual is ill or distressed, that no formal psychiatric diagnosis is justified. The pressures against the categorical statement "no psychiatric abnormality found" are however considerable. Psychiatric assessment involves not only medical skills but judgement about personality, motivation and interpersonal relationships, together with an exploration of psychopathology and the eliciting of "neurotic" symptomatology such as somatic anxiety or depression reactive to circumstances.

Many apparently inexplicable or foolhardy acts become comprehensible in terms of an individual's life experience and current circumstances; many neurotic defences or deviant personality traits may be adaptive in some situations and maladaptive in others. Thus the "understandability" of some events, the difficulty in defining the ranges of normality and pressure from the individual, his advisors or the court, may lead the psychiatrist to attach a diagnostic label to the behaviour of a "normal" individual under stress.

The psychiatrist may be invited in a number of ways to play a part in a battering situation and to give evidence in court. Because he had been consulted by one or other parent on account of personal distress before the events, he may be asked to see his patient after an attack likely to lead to prosecution, by the patient himself, distressed by his violent outburst or its consequences or seeking medical protection or justification. The request for consultation may come from a medical colleague involved in the incident, from a social-work agency, from the probation service, from the defence solicitor or from the court. Whilst this by no means exhausts the list of referring agencies or their motivation in seeking a psychiatric opinion, it does illustrate a range of expectations. A psychiatrist, consulted because he has already been involved with the patient, may have no particular forensic experience or knowledge of child abuse. The defence solicitor may consult a psychiatrist because he is known to be an impressive witness in court and always willing to "do his best" for his "patient", the solicitor's client. Sometimes the solicitor will seek more than one medical or psychiatric opinion and use the report most favourable to his client.

The probation service or the court may seek a psychiatric opinion through the prison service or on the basis of almost random factors such as which consultant in the area is willing to make a report before the accused is again due in court. Where the psychiatrist has no on-going commitment to the individual referred or to the referring agency, the recommendation to the court is less likely to be rooted in reality. There is a world of difference between "I am willing to take on this individual for treatment in such and such circumstances" and "this patient should receive certain treatment [from someone else in an unspecified place]".

The Forensic Psychiatrist

The psychiatrist with particular forensic experience may be called upon to identify or exclude formal psychiatric disorder. When this is present or where the patient was affected by other "medical" factors, including drug treatment, he would be expected to indicate the influence of the disorder upon:

(a) the capacity to form intent;
(b) motivation;
(c) impulse control.

Such a report in the case of an indictable offence may assist the court in arriving at the legal judgement of guilt or innocence and, where the verdict is one of guilty, to bring forward factors which may be considered in mitigation of the offence. Reports may justify a verdict of unfit to plead, of not guilty by reason of insanity or may be considered only in determining sentence.

In considering capacity to form intent, the mental state at the time of committing the alleged act must be deduced and may well bear little or no relationship to current functioning. Briscoe (1975) has recently advocated a much broader concept of impairment, arguing that in the past we have been too preoccupied with the presence or absence of "madness" but should be concerned with the intensity of emotional feeling and whether this is outside the generality of normal experience, or of the accused's control. Recently, there has also been an attempt to modify the legal attitude to impairment of intent through drunkenness and other drug intoxications with attention paid to the effects of certain drugs which in therapeutic dosage may either inhibit normal control mechanisms in aggression or actually induce uncharacteristic "rage reactions" (Brandon, 1975).

The Community Psychiatrist

The psychiatrist with particular experience of or interest in community psychiatry may be called upon in agency consultation with the social service or probation departments, N.S.P.C.C. units or other groups concerned with the management of child abuse or may be involved as a member of the team providing service to the individual family. His report or assessment is then for the group or team and only incidentally for the court. Normally he will have a clear on-going commitment to the agency, the family or the treatment team. Since the team is multi-disciplinary and may involve individuals from social and probation services, voluntary agencies, the police, the primary medical-care team, the community health and hospital services, it is not always appropriate that the psychiatrist should be the team member who reports to the court. Clearly, in detailing injuries to the child, the paediatrician or general practitioner are the appropriate experts. However, in assessing the prognosis in terms of development and maturation, family cohesion, risk of further injury or in recommending optimal placement of the child, the expertise which is shared may be vested largely in any member of the team. Not every team member is however acceptable to the courts as an expert witness. The qualifications and experience of social workers vary very widely, the particular knowledge and expertise of an individual health visitor may not be apparent to the court and the techniques of the witness box and skill in coping with cross examination have to be acquired. At present, it appears that the courts are more willing to accept, as authoritative expert witnesses, medical practitioners whose qualifications and experience can to some degree be recognized from their objective qualifications and posts held, and whose bearing in the witness box gives them a reasonable prospect of actually presenting to the court the material which they regard as relevant. Thus for the present, in both prosecutions and care order cases, the team is likely to call upon a medical member to appear in court. The psychiatrist is often best equipped as witness and may be more concerned with the broader issues being considered than the other doctors involved.

The Psychiatrist's Report

I do not wish to enter the "psychiatry unlimited" controversy, but it is clear that psychiatrists are often invited to intervene in or report upon situations which are virtually devoid of psychiatric content. Formulating a psychiatric history and making a psychiatric examination involves the collection of a wide range of personal, social or psychological data, and diagnosis involves judgements regarding personality function and development and a variety of interpersonal processes. The nature of psychiatric care is such that the psychiatrist is inevitably involved in aspects of community and family life which lead to knowledge and experience outside the normal range of medical education and this may encourage him to offer opinions or make judgements about other matters than mental illness. In 1971, Kahn made the following observation:

In deviation from the normal, particularly where behaviour is concerned, there may not necessarily be a medical contribution at all, the treatment may be purely legal or social action. The aim is to bring the behaviour into conformity . . . the psychiatrist comes into the study of some human problems only by invitation and this invitation may not be wholehearted. It is as if the psychiatrist is expected to claim authority in many problems of living only to have that claim challenged even while his help is being sought.

The sheer folly or the apparently bizarre nature of the behaviour of individuals, regarded by psychiatrists as showing no psychiatric abnormality, leads some workers to press for formal diagnosis and such diagnoses may lead in turn to unrealistic expectations of treatment success.

The question then arises about what should be presented to the court. Both court and witness should be aware that selection of information inevitably occurs. In practice the court may question the witness to elicit information not revealed in the report in order that bias may be detected or the covert motivaton of the witness revealed for the enlightenment of the court. The objectives of court reports or the strategies employed to influence the decisions of courts have been little studied. The social inquiry reports of probation officers apear to have at least three distinct functions. First is "tariff" in reverse (Davies, 1971). Through the medium of the social enquiry report, the sentencer determines where on the continuum of social need the offender stands and sentences him accordingly. Second are "strategic" interventions (Hardiker, 1975) in which the report attempts fuller social diagnosis and prognosis and incorporates an actual recommendation in accord with this professional social-work judgement. Third are strategic interventions of a more complex variety incorporating bias and recommendations which offer positive discrimination in favour of vulnerable groups or accord with an anti-custody or other ethos.

Where the psychiatrist is approached by a parent accused of child abuse or is asked by the court or its officer to prepare a "forensic" report, the issue may appear straightforward but it is unlikely to be less complex than the state of affairs relating to social inquiry reports. The doctor is primarily consulted in order to report upon the offender, he assesses intent, motivation and impulse control in terms comprehensible to the court and with knowledge of the current state of the law on such matters as diminished responsibility. His factual diagnosis may already have been influenced in borderline areas by the pressures previously alluded to but he is now able to influence the court by selectively reporting historical or other data and by biased or judgemental interpretation of such information. This may have a tariff effect and be used by the court in determining the nature or severity of punishment or may be strategic in intent. Many complaints about psychiatric evidence to the courts relate to strategic presentations which reflect "permissive" "liberal" or "soft-option" attitudes rather than judicial opinion, whilst professional views based on diagnostic and prognostic knowledge occupy an intermediate position.

The strategic recommendations also reflect knowledge of and direct personal involvement with various facilities. Prison-service psychiatrists are more likely to recommend institutional sentences; health-service consultants are more likely to recommend out-patient treatment and do so more frequently if their report is based on examination during remand on bail than in custody (Gibbens *et al.*, 1975). The psychiatrist is more likely to recommend therapy if he sees the accused in a clinic setting within his own catchment area than when he is acting purely as a medico-legal consultant.

The Psychiatrist's Functions

Listed below are some or all of the multiple functions that a psychiatrist, in child-abuse cases, would be required to perform.

1. The identification of psychiatric disorder in any family member which requires physical or specialized psychological treatment.
2. The recognition of psychopathic disorder and the provision of advice and support to those involved in the management of affected individuals.
3. The diagnosis of neurosis or personality disorder appropriately managed exclusively by or jointly with social workers.
4. Psycho-social diagnosis; a review of the total situation with an attempt to assess the interaction of constitution, illness, environment and psychopathology, and to contribute a "psychiatrist's view" to the case conference.
5. Reviewing the child's environment, development, nature of parent-child relationship and other factors with a view to ensuring that reasonable conditions are provided for growth and maturation. Examining and predicting the consequences of alternative life situations for the child.
6. Acting as research worker or resource.
7. Functioning as a member of the care team or as an external consultant/advisor.
8. As a medical resource person participating in professional education; facilitating interprofessional collaboration and acting as an advisor at the area liaison committee level.
9. Staff support — professional and personal.
10. Maintaining realistic expectations of the effects of psychiatric intervention.

As indicated, however, a psychiatrist may become involved coincidentally in a case of abuse when his "psychiatric" opinion is requested on some related matter or when, like any other professional "care giver", he becomes aware of an actual abuse or an "at risk" situation. He may then wish to be directly concerned with the care team but it would be quite appropriate for him to pass the problem to a colleague operating specifically as a community psychiatrist or as consultant to the appropriate agency.

There must now be a general acceptance that the management of non-accidental injury demands interprofessional collaboration of a high order with shared communication and a willingness to blur professional boundaries and to share professional tasks. Any professional who becomes aware of an "at risk child" has a clear responsibility to establish that adequate supervision or surveillance is provided. The case conference probably offers the most effective means of co-ordinating interprofessional involvement providing an opportunity for the sharing of information, arriving at a consensus plan for management and above all clearly defining the task of each member with one individual designated as the key worker through whom all information must be channelled, though another member may have responsibility for reconvening the case conference if required and for maintaining communication with all members.

The psychiatrist will usually be in a peripheral position rather than carrying day to day responsibility for care. As consultant he participates in assessment and diagnosis, he may be consulted when decisions regarding the future of the child are being made and is likely to be called upon to give evidence in court if the parents are to be prosecuted or the child taken into care.

Three aspects of the consultant's relationship to the field workers deserve special mention. First the peripheral nature of the psychiatrist's involvement and the fact that he is a member of a different profession can facilitate his function as consultant and counsellor to the worker carrying the main burden of direct work with the family. No worker in the field of non-accidental injury, regardless of seniority or experience, should engage in direct work with such a family without regular supervision or frank discussion of the case with an experienced worker. The collusion which exists between parents can insidiously incorporate the most experienced worker. When an injury occurs after real progress in some aspect of work with the family, the worker is almost inevitably drawn into collusive denial of the nature of the injury. Even during supervision or peer group sessions among workers and supervisors with a day to day commitment to the work, these collusions and evasions may escape detection. For an "outsider" hearing an account of progress, it is often enough simply to ask "will you say that again?" — the painful insight into the incident of "falling downstairs" might well be more difficult to accept if provoked by an everyday colleague.

The stress of intensive work with these families places a considerable burden on the field worker. Counselling and support must be provided and this will be mainly professional rather than personal. It is necessary to provide regular discussion and ventilation of the problems of management as well as reassurance of the adequacy and effectiveness of the worker's contribution. This is particularly important in those cases where one or other parent shows evidence of a severe personality disorder, for here the psychiatrist can help in setting realistic treatment goals and in helping the worker to acknowledge treatment failure without experiencing a sense of personal failure.

Adequate professional support and consultation is a most important prophylactic against emotional disturbance in the field workers, but at times some personal help may be required. A psychiatrist working with the field staff may offer informal counselling without either party specifically acknowledging the nature of the intervention. When more formal help is required, rapid and informal referral will help to sustain the field worker until the pressure can be relieved.

A dilemma exists in organizing work with violent families between developing expertise and maintaining long term care on the one hand and the personal demands on the worker on the other. I believe that no worker should spend more than a limited period exclusively in intensive case work with such families. The work needs to be leavened with teaching, administrative, supervisory or social-work tasks of a different kind which are satisfying to the worker and do not produce conflicts of time allocation.

The second function of the psychiatrist in the care team to be considered is his part of the deliberations about the long term care of abused children. Paediatricians and psychiatrists share a particular concern about the effects of a hostile or inconsistent environment on physical, emotional and cognitive development. Abused children vividly illustrate the cycle of deprivation in reproducing disordered behaviour patterns in later life. Intensive and skilled intervention in these families offers some prospect of breaking the cycle but is demanding in terms of time and resources. Screening programmes leading to early identification of families at risk will never attract sufficient resources for effective intervention with the use of current techniques. Even with established cases, we must make parsimonious use of resources and invest where there is some prospect of a return. It is important that treatment interventions should have defined objectives and progress be assessed at intervals. In those families where there is a member with a severe personality disorder or where other factors raise serious doubts about the outcome, a "trial of therapy" should be undertaken. Intervention and management methods aiming to maintain the integrity of the family are no longer justified if intensive help has been provided and no progress made within a defined period.

The struggle to maintain a family group, which would fragment or explode into violence without it, places too great a burden, not only on resources, but upon the family itself and particularly on the children. In those families that are able to use the help offered, the children have some prospect of normal maturation. Those families where the child's life is punctuated by separations, neglect or violence are nurturing major problems for the next generation. The longer a child is exposed to this hostile environment, the less effective later intervention is likely to be. A child eventually taken into long term care at 8 or 9 years of age following a life-time of abuse may well fail to respond even to massive intervention at that time, whereas adoption or long term fostering in the first year of life might have produced a normal child and adolescent.

Earlier total deprivation of parental care should be considered in a few families, in the interest both of the children at risk and of society at large, despite the very real risks of injustice and the need for bureaucracy. Such deprivation raises serious questions regarding future pregnancies, child minding and unemployment for that small but dangerous group of parents who are particularly unresponsive to treatment. Possibly earlier, permanent removal will require both changes in the law and specific guidance on the constitution and procedure of the group which will make the recommendation for removal. Action as drastic as this can only be justified if resources are available to provide high-quality continuing care for the removed children and compassionate, concerned support for the deprived parents.

However, whether within the framework of existing legislation and practice or in a changing situation, an informed psychiatrist has skills of relevance to aspects of the family assessment and can make a significant contribution to the debate regarding the fate of the individual family. He also has an important part to play in providing or securing specialist help for the individual family members who are separated as a result of these deliberations. I am convinced that there are many situations in which the health and social adjustment of both parents and children can be improved by facilitating dissolution of the family group and others in which the interests of the child have to take precedence over the emotional needs of the disordered parents.

Finally, the psychiatrist will frequently find it necessary to deny unrealistic expectations of psychiatric intervention. He may also have to assert that, though there is a considerable overlap between the areas of interest of psychiatrists, social workers and related professionals, the psychiatrist is a medical specialist with specialist skills and knowledge and his professional task is quite distinct.

This paper has strayed from the narrow confines of the psychiatric report and I make no apology for this because a psychiatrist interested in the field of non-accidental injury has a much broader contribution to make. The courts or social agencies may request specialist single-interview psychiatric reports from experts of their choice but to do so is to narrow their range of options. Such a report will deal effectively with the presence or absence of psychiatric illness and such medico-legal questions as the capacity to form intent, but may well fail to contribute to the management of the particular situation. Wherever possible, a psychiatrist should play a full part in the interprofessional network providing care and protection for abused children.

References

Brandon, S. (1975). "The Non-Barbiturate Hypnotics: use and abuse in sleep disturbance and hypnotic drug dependence". Ed. A. D. Cliff. Excerpta Med., Amsterdam.

Briscoe, O. V. (1975). Assessment of intent — an approach to the preparation of Court Reports. *Brit. J. Psychiat.* 127, 461–465.

Davies, M. (1971). Social enquiry for the courts: an examination of the current position in England and Wales. Paper presented to the Anglo-Scandinavian Research Seminar in Criminology, Norway.

Gibbens, T. C. N., Soothill, K. L. and Pope, P. (1975). Remands for medical reports. Paper presented to the National Criminology Conference, University of Cambridge.

Hardiker, P. (1975). Recommendations in Social Inquiry Reports (in press).

Kahn, J. (1971). Uses and abuses of child psychiatry. *Brit. J. Psychol.* 44, 229–238.

For Discussion see p 78.

6. Protective Casework and Child Abuse: Practice and Problems

John Pickett
Andy Maton

> "Make this the last — children bring you
> nothing but trouble" (A mother's message to her
> daughter on the birth of her first child)

> "As is the mother, so is the daughter"
> (Ezekiel XVI 44)

This paper is a subjective and descriptive account of our work as social workers with families where non-accidental injury has occurred. We have not attempted to set our families in the context of different diagnostic models, or to compare our work with other therapeutic programmes, or to make of it a validated piece of research. We look on it rather as a useful basis from which such attempts can be made.

The paper amounts to a reflective conceptualization of the usual process that our work with families tends to follow. It therefore expresses what we have come to find ourselves to be doing, rather than any *a priori* set of assumptions about the way our casework should proceed. The material derives from and is illustrated by our experiences with 57 families with whom we have worked intensively since 1973.

The Special Unit

The Manchester Special Unit became operational in January, 1973 (Owtram, 1975). It had been set up by the N.S.P.C.C. in conjunction with the Manchester Social Services Department and the city's Child Abuse Policy Committee.*

The Unit is staffed by a team leader and five team members, who are

---

* Estimated populations in 1972: total 535 490; 0–14 years 125 800.

all experienced, qualified social workers, a full-time health visitor, seconded by the area health authority and a unit co-ordinator with responsibility for managing the register and monitoring procedures, and for arranging case conferences. A unit secretary and typists complete the establishment. Staff are supported by consultants in paediatrics and psychiatry. We also have seven voluntary workers providing a variety of services to families in the role of "family friends".

From the beginning, we have been concerned with two primary functions and others deriving in part from them. Our primary aim has been to offer therapeutic casework and case management to families where non-accidental injury has definitely or very probably occurred. Our second principal function is concerned with the overall management procedures in Manchester (Pickett, 1976). From 1973 we have operated a register of suspected non-accidental injury and the associated monitoring procedure. More recently, the Manchester Child Abuse Policy Committee added to our consultation work the specific responsibility to convene, chair and minute case conferences. We have always seen it as an important part of our task to be available as consultants to case conferences or individual professional workers involved in this type of case. In the three years 1973–75, we have been represented at 580 case conferences and consultations in the Greater Manchester Metropolitan County. There have been 699 notifications to the register covering the same area.

In addition, we have a particular contribution to make in disseminating knowledge and increasing general awareness of this form of child abuse. We are also concerned with increasing that stock of knowledge and developing further therapeutic techniques and skills. We have contributed to an epidemiological study based on register data (Rose *et al.*, 1976) and are increasingly wanting to make an evaluation of our therapeutic intervention.

So far we have accepted 57 referred families. In nearly all of these cases we accepted repsonsibility as primary social worker in response to a recommendation by a case conference. It was understood that we would be able to offer an intensive level of social work. We therefore tended to take families where the diagnosis and prognosis seemed set at the more serious end of the spectrum.

The features of the case that suggest a poor prognosis for the child would include psychiatrically diagnosed psychopathy, or a chronic pattern of anti-social behaviour, bizarre or instrumental injuries which seem to suggest an element of premeditation in the attack on the child, severe malnutrition, neglect or rejection, consecutive battering of siblings, chronic, self-perpetuating stresses and persistent hostility towards potential sources of help.

The Children and Their Parents

The following description of our cases is based on an analysis of 20 of them accepted during the 1974–75 period (Hyman, 1976). Although describing the families with whom we are working, this description is not necessarily a fair representation of the whole range involved in non-accidental injury (Skinner and Castle, 1969; Castle and Kerr, 1972; Smith and Hanson, 1974; Oliver *et al.*, 1974; Gil, 1970).

Most of the injured children were first and only children (85%), and their age averaged 14 months. Very often their birth or the preceding pregnancy was associated with something negative (Lynch, 1975; Richards and Bernal, 1972; Richards, 1974; Klaus *et al.*, 1972). In 75% there had been an abnormal pregnancy (in 45% an abnormal delivery); 30% were separated from their mothers for some period of the early months of their life; and 20% of them suffered neonatal illness. Thirty per cent of the children suffered serious injuries and in 55% of the cases protective action was taken in the juvenile court.

The parents were typically young: 75% of the mothers were under 20 years and 80% of the fathers were aged 18–22 years. Pre-marital pregnancy and unstable sexual relationships characterized the parents' relationships. Half of the mothers were not living with the child's natural father at referral and around 50% of the fathers were not living with the mothers during pregnancy. In 45% of the cases, there was a history of husbands abusing their wives and in 25% of the sample, there was reciprocal abuse of the husband by the wife. Thirty percent of the fathers had a problem with alcohol, and 35% of them had a criminal record. Twenty-five percent of the mothers had made a suicide attempt. Inadequate accommodation was common. Forty-five percent of the families shared accommodation and 40% of the families occupied one or two rooms. Thirty percent of the fathers had frequent changes of job and in 35% of the cases there were financial problems.

Although many of our parents share common characteristics, there are important differences in their psychopathology and these differences have implications for treatment. For example, one very disturbed mother, with an I.Q. of 56, seriously injured her young baby. Much of our work has been focused on helping her to separate from a child she cannot nurture and getting her established in an adult training centre and on to a reliable family planning regime. In another case, young parents in seriously overcrowded conditions produced twins, and the mother had a puerperal depression. The fractious, difficult twin was injured and received into care with the parents' consent and a programme of rehabilitation quickly established, which had good prospects of a successful outcome. While most of our parents share some characteristics to a greater or lesser extent, individual families may diverge significantly from the generalizations that follow.

We are presented, with monotonous regularity, with chronologically young parents, manifesting severe degrees of immaturity and personality disorder (Baher *et al.*, 1976; Court, 1974; Reiner *et al.*, 1959). Retrospective analysis of early-life experience usually elicits memories of harsh parental attitudes, often accompanied by discontinuity in parenting. One young mother had 19 changes of caretaker in between the ages of 8 months and 17 years. Little wonder that her capacity for making lasting relationships in adulthood was seriously impaired. Low self esteem and a poorly integrated sense of the self are common and are usually marked by massive defences of projection and denial, aimed at deflecting from consciousness the reality of their inner weakness. This accounts for their hostile, aggressive, or weak, compliant responses and persistent shift of responsibility from the self to others, or a variety of external forces.

Many of these parents were damaged early in life at the pre-verbal stage of development so that verbal techniques based on a psycho-analytic model are initially of little effect (Polansky *et al.*, 1971). Caring has to be expressed in concrete, demonstrative ways. You have to *show* you care, not *say* you care (Winnicott, 1965). Both historically and currently the parents are alienated from their own parents and families. They yearn for love and attention and will act out to a dangerous degree in order to get it but at the same time will negate efforts to help because of their fear of rejection. They are not likeable people and a poorly motivated social worker will be easily put off by them.

Like other practitioners, we have found that many of our parents tend to perceive their child egocentrically and to fail to perceive and respond to the child's needs. Gratification of their own needs is a primary motivation for their interaction with the child (Davoren, 1974; Steele and Pollock, 1974; Morris and Gould, 1963). Major reliance on projection leads to serious distortion in their perception of the child. This inability to empathize is not confined to their child but pervades all relationships. When her social worker went sick, one mother complained in anger "he's no right to be sick, I'm bloody sick and he should be here". She was quite unaware of her lack of empathy or concern. Her own needs overwhelmed all else.

It is usual to find both parents sharing similar characteristics. It is as if the marriage allows mutual frustration to continue. There seems to be a reciprocal willingness to support the status quo accompanied by compliance with the act of abuse by the "non-abusing" partner, as if mutual hostility is worked out. As previously noted, marital violence is common. Physical interaction seems to be a mode for the discharge of tensions and the expression of conflict, and it can be seen as an extension and intensification of verbal abuse which is also common (Goode, 1971). In these families, aggression is a constant element in family interactions and there is a "taboo on tenderness" (Suttie, 1935) and love with emotional distance and wariness characterizing relationships. As many of our parents are also socially disadvantaged, impinging social pressures add to the burden of intra-psychic tensions and conflicts. Alternative modes of relieving discomfort and tension are not available and the parents are turned in onto themselves and their children in a cataclysmic process of self destruction.

The Social Work Process

Initial Contact

Child abuse is symptomatic of serious problems in parenting, but it is rare for abusing parents explicitly to present themselves for help. They usually present their children to doctors, health visitors and social workers as problems, without admitting to having inflicted abuse. Often, their fear of retribution and stigmatization is compounded by the presence of professional denial as well. The observer does not want to believe what he sees, and so the perpetrator, the victim and the potential source of help join together in collusive silence (Underhill, 1974). Therefore, the problem has to be re-enacted; problems that are unresolved are repeated and in child abuse repeated injury is very common (Skinner and Castle, 1969). In most of our cases, there is a history of repeated injury at the time of referral. This is important because it tells us something about the parents' expectations of us. Their expectation is that we will deny the existence of a problem, like other sources of help that they have met. Our capacity to stay rooted in reality will have a critical influence on the outcome of the crisis. Our presence may be seen to extend and perpetuate their crisis, because we not only keep the crisis in their consciousness but confront them with the reality of their actions and the possible long term consequences for themselves and their child.

The crisis for the parents can be said to be fourfold. First, there are the precipitating stress factors that swept away their controls and reduced them to violent reaction; second, there is the actual abusing incident; third, there is the aftermath of consternation, fear of repetition and maybe guilt; and fourth, there are the social consequences of their actions symbolized by our presence. These elements present both a threat and an opportunity to parent and helper. Crisis, as we know, is potentially a productive time and offers us an opportunity to lay the foundations for subsequent management and therapy.

In this initial phase, we are presented, with a serious dilemma. We know from experience that it is important that we focus on the parents, appealing to their narcissism by paying great attention to their needs and feelings. However, our child-protective responsibilities also mean that we have to assess, with great care, the circumstances in which their child has been injured. We have to combine empathy with confrontation (Day, 1965; Garner, 1959, 1961; David, 1974). "You've been listening to my problems all this time and you haven't spoken about Julie yet", to which the worker replies, "Well, shall we do that now?"

Although initial contact has its own specific and immediate objectives (Goldberg, 1975), it is the origin point of an ongoing flow of work and therefore has to be placed within the wide context of the initial phase of therapy (Pollock and Steel, 1972). In this fairly prolonged phase, we attempt to establish a model of good parenting within the context of control. In other words, we have to achieve the presentation of an integrated self, pursuing two goals.

1. We encourage a large element of dependency on the worker, who offers understanding, empathy, help, support, reliability and dependability.

Dependency is the first step towards establishing some measure of basic trust (Erikson, 1950). Once established within an individual relationship, attempts are then made to encourage a more generalized sense of trust within a wider context of relationships.

2. We impose some degree of control on a family situation which has clearly broken down in a massive and fundamental way.

Statements of understanding and acceptance are very important. That is not to say that one leaves the impression that one condones what has happened; this has to be made explicit because the control element in the relationship is an important source of strength to parents with poor ego controls (Wasserman, 1967). Care is taken in the initial contact to explain our function as child-protective social workers, explaining the work of the Special Unit and the ways in which we would like to help. It is important at subsequent interviews to reiterate much of what is said at initial contact, which is often lost because of anxiety. Care is taken to explain who we are, writing down our name and the names of colleagues, giving information about our availability and "round-the-clock" service.

We explain what we know of their child's injuries and our belief that the injuries are non-accidental. Usually, where the child is in hospital (which accounts for the majority of the Unit's cases at referral), the paediatrician will already have seen the parents, to hear their explanation of the injuries and to explain his diagnosis and its consequences to them. In this way, initial contact will have been prepared for and planned and will probably occur at the hospital.

We encourage parents to ventilate feelings caused by the confrontation with them. We do not seek to interrogate, nor to demolish their much needed psychological defence mechanisms. We demonstrate concern without collusion. We introduce the parents to the fact that, at least potentially, the injuries and breakdown of parenting have important implications for the future. The usual form this would take, where the child is in hospital, is to explain that for the time being at least the child should remain there. Our powers to obtain a place of safety order are explained and the legal implications of the injuries are made explicit. We explain the processes of decision making that have to occur once a diagnosis of non-accidental injury has been made and keep parents informed of developing decisions and encourage their participation in the decision making process, as far as is possible. Their sense of powerlessness should not be unnecessarily reinforced.

The reaction of parents to the content of the initial contact is widely variable ranging from strong denial and flight to frank admission accompanied by immense relief (Pollock and Steele, 1972). "It's a terrible feeling when you have to go on and on hitting and hitting and not being able to stop. It's like a bad dream and you feel awful about it. When you can tell somebody it becomes real and you can stop it" — on admission of abuse.

It helps, if we understand that we are dealing with parents who are difficult to reach and communicate with. They will strongly deny any need for help and this denial may persist long after they have come to accept our help. There is a danger of being drawn into the parents' collusion and dealing superficially with the problem. We have to understand that the parents are presenting themselves for help as well as their children. They expect to be judged, accused and punished. Throughout their lives they have received a lot of negative reinforcement from authority figures. They are hurt children. We need to tone down their expectations of attack. Typically, they will react with aggression and hostility or will appear to be co-operative and submissive, adopting a passive identification with authority (Pollock and Steele, 1972). Both responses will mask fear and desperation and should not be taken at face value but recognized as important clues as to what is going on in the mind of the parent. Paradoxically, our understanding and sympathetic approach sometimes produces strong feelings of suspicion. Often it is a perplexing experience for them. This is summed up by the mother who said "You have been here for nearly an hour and I am still waiting for you to lay the law down, like all the other social workers, but you haven't done so, *and I can't understand why*". The variations in response constitute important diagnostic clues for us as we enter the critical phase of diagnosis and management planning.

Establishing the Initial Management Plan

Immediately following the initial contact, a programme of regular home visiting is established, aimed at completing a number of tasks which are part of the initial phase of therapy.

We discuss with the parents events leading up to the child's injury and obtain as full an understanding as possible of the precipitating circumstances. A detailed study of the total family is needed in order to formulate a psychosocial diagnosis and prognosis (Pollock and Steele, 1972). We find it difficult to understand the resistance that some social workers have to taking formal social histories. Most of our clients seem to accept the need for this kind of history taking, especially if one carefully explains to them that, in order to understand and help effectively, it is important that we know those we are trying to help. They need to ventilate and want to talk about their situation and experiences. This process is important in trying to help parents towards a recognition of the need for help and acceptance of dependency. Often the history given in the initial phase of treatment differs significantly from the information given later and this difference can be a useful measure of developing trust. Like other workers, we have found a need to reach out and demonstrate our concern in concrete and practical ways (Baher *et al.*, 1976). Initial hostility and mistrust in one case began to recede when the worker turned up with a much-needed cot mattress.

Much of our work at this stage amounts to a process of evaluating therapeutic potential. Ideally, initial decisions should be taken while the child is safe in hospital. The important question to be asked is "Is the home safe for this child?" Far reaching decisions about the future of the child often have to be taken against a background of urgency and inadequate information. However, the lack of information should never be a reason for returning a child home to a situation which is not clearly understood.

The absence of reliable criteria to validate decision making is a serious handicap for worker, parent and child. There is a pressing need for research into the processes of decision making and the outcome. In the absence of reliable criteria we have to rely on what Stevenson (1975) has called "practice wisdom".

A combination of the following factors may indicate the need for at least temporary removal of the child.

1. One important consideration is the severity of injuries, including fractures, subdural haematoma, burns and extensive bruising, especially in children under 2 years of age; another is the bizarre nature of the injuries, such as sitting a child on an electric hot plate, multiple cigarette burns and instrumental injuries. The degree of

injury is no measure of the degree of risk, especially with early diagnosis. Quite minor injuries may be symptomatic of extreme pathological parenting and a history of repeated injury (even minor injury) is an ominous indicator.

2. Although young children are especially vulnerable to physical damage, we realize that a child of any age who suffers physical trauma also suffers emotional trauma.

3. The degree and extent of the psychopathology provides the most difficult assessment in the short time available before decisions have to be made. The extent and depth of denial, especially if accompanied by elusiveness and "hostile distance" from the social worker, collusion, lack of mutual support, a marriage under stress and alienation from extended family and a history of self-perpetuating stress and crisis are all important indicators that favour temporary removal of the child.

4. It is important to take into account the psychiatric diagnosis, if one is available. Where mental illness is diagnosed the extent and nature of the illness will be important factors in assessing the degree of risk to the child. For example, a schizophrenic illness which includes delusional, persecutory fantasies about the child is a very different matter than a puerperal psychosis managed by in-patient treatment in a mother and baby unit. Similarly, the degree and extent of so-called psychopathy and personality disorder varies widely as does understanding of the terms. A history of abnormally aggressive behaviour and a failure to learn from past experience, especially if accompanied by a sense of self-righteouness is indicative of substantial risk to the child.

5. It is important, although very difficult in the short-term, to assess the parents' perception of this particular child. Good parenting of siblings is not necessarily reassuring. Some children take on a special meaning and trigger the parents potential for abuse because of a complex, sometimes indecipherable process of negative identification (Goldberg, 1975). The classical role reversal frequently referred to in the literature is common (Morris and Gould, 1963). So too is "lack lustre" parenting, a joyless interaction between parent and child.

6. Another significant factor is the existence of acute or chronic stress arising from illness, or multiple social problems, especially where there is evidence that these problems are self-perpetuating and not easily mediated.

Where care proceedings are decided upon, we are faced with the task of resolving the essential paradox in the initial phase of management in its most concrete and explicit form. We encourage dependency to a basically benign parent figure at the same time as imposing control by an authoritarian parent-figure on a family situation that is out of control. We are in other words reflecting reality through a whole and integrated therapeutic person. But our clients' object relationships are so fragmented and disintegrated that some of them cannot hold together this paradox and all of them find it difficult. Their reaction may be a useful index of their degree of immaturity or disintegration (Guntrip, 1968). So far, only three parents have failed to hold together the therapeutic person to such an extent that they removed themselves from our treatment.

Out of a total sample of 57 cases, one mother took flight completely and removed herself from any source of help. This mother was psychopathic to a degree and had failed successively to mother four children. One had died, one was abandoned and we removed two from her, a seriously retarded two year old and a month old baby, permanently brain damaged following a subdural haematoma and skull fracture. In the three months that we held this mother in treatment, we instituted family planning but she is now probably out of reach of any known form of treatment.

A further two cases were transferred out of the Special Unit to the Social Service Department, because the negative transference proved too difficult for them and because we believed it was right to respect their wishes to be rid of us. In one of these cases, considerable therapeutic gains are being achieved by the Social Service Department; in the other case the outcome is more problematic. In many cases protective action became a focus for distrust and hostility endemic in the parents' personalities and may have impeded or retarded therapeutic progress but in the absence of a controlled study of daunting complexity our observations are purely speculative.

Our work does not support the view of some writers that it is not possible to hold together protective and therapeutic roles (Court, 1970; Jones and Jones, 1974; Jones, 1973). However, all child abuse workers are working in the context of minimal therapeutic gain. There is no room for dogmatism but a need for experimentation and controlled research.

Once we have decided to take protective action on behalf of the child, emphasis is given to keeping parents informed of events as they unfold. We arrange legal representation for them, review the evidence that we and others will be presenting, familiarize them with court proceedings and likely outcomes and their right of appeal. We emphasize that our protective action is as much in their interest as their child's. We try to help them understand the difference between care proceedings and criminal proceedings, a distinction they find hard to make. Our honest openness and concern for their rights reduces their feelings of powerlessness and makes explicit our respect for them.

At the same time we are usually active in intervening on their behalf to reduce external stresses, dealing with such problems as debts, bad housing and poor health. These are necessary procedures but they also provide a useful counterbalance to the controlling, protective elements in our work.

We do not try to impose acceptance of our management plan and we expect parents to disagree with us. But, as therapy advances and positive reactions begin to emerge, we see evidence of their attempts to bring together the paradox of our "goodness" and "badness" and the positives and negatives of our management plan. Typically, in this early phase parents either (a) respond with denial and hostility towards our intervention, but nevertheless at the same time display need and dependency, or (b) respond in a passive, compliant way, identifying with authority and seeking to placate. Once the management plan has been established (that is, once the order has been made when protective action is taken) both we and the parents are free to move into a phase of more extensive therapy.

Building a Relationship

Therapy, of whatever kind, whether psychiatric treatment, behaviour modification treatment, group work, etc. is based on a corrective relationship aimed at encouraging trust and dependency, with a major element of control.

The worker who enters their life offering warmth, understanding and concern is an enigmatic figure who is met with considerable ambivalence, being seen as a potential source both of help and of threat. The parent, although craving for nurture, deeply distrusts the worker offering it. Care has to be taken to avoid emotional proximity. The parent has to be allowed to preserve emotional distance and to move into a relationship at his or her own pace. Fear of authority and of rejection is an inhibiting factor. "It seems that in some ways I am asking for help from you and in others asking you not to get too close or involved in case I confuse you also" (Letter from a mother).

Despite frequent visits to the Unit, one mother continued to prefer the protection of a desk between herself and her worker, saying "I feel safer, I prefer it this way". This mother once asked the Unit Leader to become her worker. "He (her worker) is getting too close to me. You are stricter, sort of stern with me". She was asking for emotional distance and control.

Some parents seem to need a strong external super ego to protect them from their own lack of control and impulsiveness, while others have internalized harsh, punishing controls from which they need freeing. When they become less harsh on themselves, they become more benign towards their children.

We seek to enable our clients to develop basic trust both in themselves and in their worker and, at a later stage in therapy, as a generalized quality in an extended range of relationships. Initially, this is on the basis of a one-to-one relationship investing trust and dependency in the worker. From the outset we encourage parents to see their worker as one of a group of workers in the Unit, including other social workers, secretaries, office cleaners and voluntary workers. They are encouraged to visit the Unit and we provide fares and food, a kitchen and a room of their own, rarely entered without staff. Frequent use of these Unit facilities is often the prelude to entry into a parents' group, and into contact with our team of volunteers. At all times, attention is given to ameliorating external stresses, such as debts and housing problems, and to the health of both the parents and child, who are accompanied to ensure that appointments are kept. Support is given in using community resources and making contact with other agencies.

The whole process can be described as good parenting in the context of containment and control, but we are dealing with extremely capricious and wilful "children" who would try the patience of the best "parent". Constant acting and testing out occur. The worker's capacity for acceptance is tested out by failed appointments, disruption of carefully worked out plans, hostility and insatiable demands for time and attention. Any failure to meet these demands is interpreted as rejection. Establishing a basis for trust calls for the utmost dependability, reliability and concrete demonstrations of care and immediate response to the perceived crisis. This goes hand in hand with affirmations of the client's worth and value as a person.

At the same time, care has to be taken not to foster too much dependency and so reinforce their sense of low self-esteem and powerlessness. We are attempting at this stage to build on their limited capacity for reality-based object relationships, seeking to help them integrate both within themselves and others "goodness" and "badness". It is now that much work has to be done on their relationships with their own parents or caretakers (Jones and Jones, 1974). The worker has to be on guard against the negative transference this may arouse and against his own feelings of anger towards the withholding, punishing parent. Abusing parents need help to accept the reality of their own parents and to understand that they were not all bad. If they can, with help, release some love for them, an important therapeutic advance has been made.

Most parents go through a period of mourning, grieving for the loss of their own unfulfilled childhood. Social casework cannot fill this void. The most we can do is help them with the pain of reality, helping them work through some of their ambivalence about it. Beginning to be less punishing towards their own parents is another indicator of progress. During this work there is no attempt to promote insight for they do not have a sufficient ego strength to cope. We concentrate on their consciousness with such questions as, "was it hard to love your mother?" One mother responded with deep feelings of anger towards her mother who failed to protect her from a brutal, tyrannical father. She was immediately aware of her own failure to protect her daughters from repeated ill-treatment by her cohabitee. She was also able to see how her violent husband and later her violent cohabitee were perpetuating her childhood for her.

Growth is inevitably slow and almost imperceptible. Typically, there are regressions and recurrent crises followed by periods of quiescence and consolidation. Inevitably, the clients' own drive to grow or improve or succeed cannot overcome the massive existence of their own inadequacies. Sometimes the regressions involve repeated minor injury to the child. One mother describes how her own sense of deprivation, triggered by marital discord, resulted in repeated injury to her child.

He was always accusing me of things and he started to hit me. I began to hit Karen more. I began to take it out of Karen because I couldn't take it out of him. If I had just had a row with Bill, as soon as he left the house I would start hitting her. I tried to talk to the Welfare but she seemed to be on his side. I didn't tell her I had hit Karen. I couldn't tell anyone. I thought it was very cruel. I really regretted what I did to her but I couldn't control myself. I just kept on and on until I satisfied myself. I used to hit her with a belt and she was only a little tiny baby. I used to get a strap and hit her and hit her and hit her. I just couldn't stop and then when I did satisfy myself I got hold of her and really cuddled her. I could only cuddle her after I had hit her. It went on for a long time and Bill didn't know, he never bathed her or anything. She was a year old at the time. I don't really like to say it but I like her and I don't like her, its half and half. I want to love her but I don't really know how. I think to myself, why should I give her love when I haven't had any myself. I don't know what love is anyway".

This case illustrates the important interrelationships between child abuse and marital problems. Marital work and parent/child interaction form two major areas of concern in our work which should ideally involve both parents, but problems arise in the differing responses of the marital partners to our intervention. In some families we find that one of the partners, more usually the husband, so dominates the joint interaction that the other effectively withdraws from involvement, despite our efforts to prevent this happening. In one such family, for example, the quite serious personality problems of the wife became much more explicit only after she had left the home. In other families, where there is no such drive for dominance from one partner, we often find it is easy for one or other parent, usually the father, to opt out of involvement with us. We have to make a real effort to ensure that contact is maintained: in one such case regular visits at 8 a.m. had to be made to retain the involvement of the father.

Where the joint involvement of both parents is retained we sometimes find that they need us in the same sort of ways. They each may need us to have a very individual relationship with them and then find difficulty in sharing us equally. The other problems for the worker stem both from the client and from himself. The early dependency that most clients invest in him includes a readily understandable element of passive or active hostility. But there is also the client whose real hostility seems to be totally masked by an easy relationship and overt compliance with the worker. Here, the client's identification with the aggressor, that is to say the all-powerful parent-figure in the social worker, operates as a powerful psychological defence. Another client tries to make the social worker into a close personal friend, thereby reducing the authority figure to safe proportions. Such problems threaten the integrity of the workers as persons. For in the short term, our therapeutic effort may call for seeming collusion with at least some part of our clients' array of psychological defences, in an attempt to reduce the extent of our threat to them so that, in the long term, the major and fundamental therapeutic task can be achieved. In pursuing this task, we must not abrogate the need to keep other issues alive in the interaction; in particular the whole element of control and containment can never subside very far from the surface of our relationship. Also a whole range of important side issues will crop up and threaten to overwhelm the main therapeutic issue. There will be the occasional need to put in a lot of effort to modify external stresses not always of the client's causing.

Our parents may have serious misperceptions of themselves, each other, the social worker, or of their children, their parents or the whole world, but they have quick and often accurate perceptions of criticism, actual or implied, or signs of rejection. A change of mood, however slight, in the demeanour of the worker, as he maybe wearies in a lengthy contact, will not go unmarked by the parent. The worker's commitment to care is being tested out and if he adopts a bland, neutral "professional" image he will make little headway. Sustained therapy requires the worker to integrate his professionalism and agency responsibilities with himself as a real person.

A crucial part of the worker's task is to interpret the parents' needs and reactions to other sources of help, especially in contacts with alternative caretakers, whether the child is in full time or day care. Mismanagement can lead to disruption and breakdown of placements. Most parents are hostile and critical of alternative caretakers and they often elicit the sorts of responses that they anticipate in a self fulfilling way. When a mother, walking into a nursery playroom smoking a cigarette, was told that this was not allowed, her extremely aggressive response astounded the nursery nurse. Her behaviour becomes understandable only in the total context within which it occurred. Her three year old daughter was originally referred because of her failure to thrive and repeated inflicted burns. In this context, Betty's comment "they didn't have to remind me that I had burnt her" became explicit. Only sensitive interpretation to both mother and nursery staff preserved a day nursery placement for a child who is the subject of a supervision order.

Towards Independence

Once parents have come to trust their worker and have begun to generalize that trust through a network of relationships both in therapy and in the community, it is safe to assume that they have begun to make identifications and to imitate role models. This will often be reflected in the way that they handle problems, including inter-personal relationships. They will begin to bring partially, or completely resolved problems to us, seeking approval, whereas before they were seeking direction. They will begin to make their own choices and play a much larger part in finding their own way through life but still constantly seeking affirmation and approval (Pollock and Steele, 1972).

"I know I can phone the Unit if I have any problems, but I seem to have sorted them out for myself lately." This is the stage in treatment when parents are gaining more autonomy and beginning to make some real growth. Our objective is that the family should be able to stand on its own. We want the parents to develop their own powers of self control through a process of identification with others who have well developed internalized controls and values (Reiner *et al.*, 1959). In this phase we contrive to build on the foundation previously laid. The reduced need for psychological defences, at least between worker and parent, allows for rather more purely verbal interchange. The "thinking out" mode offers an alternative to the "acting out" mode through a process of modelling which oocurs within the therapeutic relationship. Parents learn that problems can be talked out, communications can be used to defuse points of interpersonal tension and there can be less resistance to learning. We think that this is the point in treatment which offers a major opportunity to introduce a programme of parent education aimed at modifying harmful child rearing practices.

In this phase in particular, we need to portray ourselves as real people with our own weaknesses as well as strength. One young mother was caught up in major feelings of ambivalence towards her husband and usually acted out her inter-personal tensions with provocative and violent behaviour. In one session she asked "do you have rows with your wife" Such a question does not call for a subtle reflecting back to the questioner but an honest answer to an honest interest in a real person in the worker. It betrays at least a potential desire to identify and incorporate a rather wider set of experiences and values. The mother is also asking "Am I normal?" as she seeks to explore the boundaries of her own feelings and behaviour.

In this phase we emphasize, rather more than we have done, the clients' responsibility in choosing and acting, and we leave them more exposed to the consequences of their action to test out their viability before we come to make decisions about reducing contact and disengaging from therapy. We give them short term goals and praise their success. Praise is important throughout therapy and every opportunity for ego enrichment should be taken but it can only have value if it is real and sincere. Care should be taken to set goals towards which they are motivated and which are within their potential to achieve. We expect them to do at least some of the things needed to resolve their problems. We feel encouraged when they begin to derive pleasure from their own achievements. "Last week I read to the children every bedtime and Mandy has started cuddling up on my knee. She feels as if she belongs now." In other words we are consciously limiting our parents dependency on us, whereas formerly we had gone out of our way to encourage it.

Disengagement from Therapy

In classical casework theory, the final phase is described as a complete and distinct entity to be completed at the end of therapy and called "termination" (Fox *et al.*, 1969). We prefer to think of the ultimate phase in our therapy as a gradual process of mutual disengagement, ebbing and flowing, but never coming to a complete end.

Many of our parents react badly to news of an impending reduction in contact. They often regress to previous dependent behaviour which they express by saying that the child is becoming difficult again, a statement guaranteed to increase our anxiety and prolong contact. Fear of abandonment is a constant factor, and any situation that may be interpreted as rejecting needs careful management. Notes are always left on failed visits, letters are sent if appointments have to be rearranged and, when workers are sick, co-workers are usually assigned. Cards are always sent by the primary worker when on holiday. All the parents receive birthday and Christmas cards and presents, and these links are maintained with parents who are only now seen infrequently. Each brief break in contact is carefully monitored so that we can observe the degree to which parents can tolerate separation and we take these opportunities to help them build up tolerance to separation. The actual process of disengagement usually occurs over several months as we progressively reduce contact and the parents dependency on us. The care of the children continues to be monitored by health visitors, day nursery staff and schools.

The Problem of Repeated Injury

Defining an injury as non-accidental is difficult, especially if the injury is minor and the child is active and getting into situations where bumps and bruises occur (Rose *et al.*, 1976). We know one doctor who insists that a black eye cannot be caused by a fall on to a flat surface and yet one of the authors saw a 14 month-old fall flat on his face onto a carpeted floor and sustain a black eye. We know of a child who suffered repeated minor bruising and then accidentally fractured her skull while in the care of the health visitor. Who would have believed the parents?

Repeated minor, undefined injury in children under our care is a major problem both for us and the parent. Any child already regarded as "battered" is under close surveillance which increases the likelihood of observed injury. Once a parent has been labelled as an abusing parent, there is a natural bias towards confirmation of the label. Isolated minor injuries in young, ambulant children are fairly common and often it is necessary to wait for a pattern of repeated minor injury, with all the possible consequences that that implies, before protective action can be taken. Each injury to a child has to be discussed and this constant confrontation can inhibit and destroy a therapeutic relationship. Even high levels of skill are no guarantee against failure.

This undermining and emotionally-exhausting work cannot be practised in isolation. However emotionally and professionally secure the worker may be, he will at times be drawn into the deep depressions and anxieties suffered by parents and will be crushed by the weight of the responsibility felt for the child. For him, good professional support and consultation are essential (Baher *et al.*, 1976; Spencer, 1970).

The Question of Rehabilitation

Throughout therapy careful observation is made of parent/child interaction and it is a recurrent major focus in therapy. Much reflective discussion is encouraged, in which we retrospectively examine the childhood experience of the parent. It is through this process that we come to understand what this child represents to them. Unless there is real modificaton of feeling and response to the child, nothing is really changing.

In most cases, where a child has been removed from the family on a care order, the question of rehabilitation looms large from the outset in the interaction between the parent and us. When we feel that the child has no foreseeable viable future within the family, we plan accordingly for the family to effect total separation from the child. Such a casework plan is an index of the severity of the parents' psycho-pathology and the poor prognosis for change. Some parents tacitly agree and make no effort to maintain contact with the child. Others take the opposite course.

In the majority of families, rehabilitation is a more viable possibility and, in a few of them, might be planned to occur relatively quickly. In all cases where a court order is made, the parents have a legal right to apply for a revocation of the order and such applications can succeed despite our definite opposition. This possibility is a proper constraint on our professional freedom, but the question of rehabilitation may hamper our therapeutic work with the parents. Their motivation to keep rehabilitation as the social worker's main reason for coming to see them may deflect us from the therapeutic task which we see as the priority. Inexperienced workers may unwittingly collude with this deflection and so avoid the central issues.

The parents are highly motivated to appear to have made progress and so qualify for the child's speedy return. There is a danger that the worker will interpret superficial progress as a real modification of the underlying problems, for changes in attitude towards the separated child are difficult to evaluate with any degree of confidence. The distance that has been created between parent and child reduces the stress of parenting and sometimes creates the impression of change and that the parents can now enjoy the child. But what is sometimes observed is the product of stress-reducing separation rather than any real change of perception and attitude towards the child. A period of residential assessment would be of great help in some cases.

A child removed on a care order must not be returned to a situation that is basically unchanged. Sometimes the original injury occurs in the context of family difficulties which are specific to that time and not necessarily self-repeating. The parents' personalities would not normally be so vulnerable. One young married couple lived in one room of the paternal grand-parents' home. The mother, aged 18, depressed after birth, tense and fearful of showing her "in laws" her depression and lack of confidence and knowledge of baby-care, was possessive of her baby and jealous when her mother-in-law held the baby. She was unsure of her own influence over her young husband, compared with his mother's. Although this couple were never able to admit to fracturing the child's leg, when they moved in to a house of their own, the mother's depression passed, and she recognized her general vulnerability, readily accepting birth control in order to postpone another baby for some years.

On the other hand, when the emphasis is on the parents' seriously disturbed personalities, we would want to see real changes before returning the child. Two things are crucial: that the parents have been able to make a truly dependent relationship with us, as distinct from mere compliance; and second that they are not so highly defended psychologically that they cannot foresee a crisis (Court, 1969). These two factors combine so that the parent is able to take effective avoiding action to forestall crisis, if only by calling the social worker. Implicit in this would be for the parents to have sufficient psychological integrity to perceive and admit to some part of the problem areas of their life without excessive denial and distortion of reality.

Positive planning for rehabilitation assumes that the parent positively wants the child and does not see the child from a completely egocentric point of view. A parent may declare adamantly and repeatedly that he or she wants and loves the child, but, by their actions, they may demonstrate a massive ambivalence or even rejection of the child.

Normally, we would want the recommendation for rehabilitation to be made by a case conference, from which the original recommendation for care would have originated. It is always a phased and carefully monitored process over a period of time in which child-parent contact slowly increases. This period is used by us to validate the prognostic factors that are crucial for appropriate rehabilitation.

We are likely to be heavily involved with the family at this time; their desire to succeed may add to the burden of anxiety, mitigating against spontaneity and calling for our reassurance and support. Characteristically, this sort of regression might be expected to occur when the child first sleeps at home over one night. Progressively regular weekends at home lengthen until total rehabilitation is effected.

For a child to be on a care order but living at home on trial provides for by far the most effective form of supervision in the home. The local authority retains the legal right to remove the child should progress fail; and this sanction gives to the social worker a far greater degree of control than a supervision order would provide. Arguably a care order with speedy home on trial could be used more freely as an alternative to a supervision order, in those cases which call for rather more explicit sanction than that order allows.

In our opinion, where a court under the Children and Young

Persons Act 1969 places a responsibility on the social worker to "advise, assist and befriend" a child (Section 14), it should also invest in the worker the power to do so. We would like to see conditions attached to supervision orders which would give the social worker the right of access to the child, the right to require the child to be medically examined and the right to require the child to attend such community provisions that are considered to be of benefit to the child. We particularly have in mind children under five who may benefit from attendance at a day nursery and who should regularly attend their child health clinic. The present powers to include requirements in supervision orders (Section 12) are inadequate for the proper supervision of the young abused child and in our view were never intended for these children.

Ultimately, after rehabilitation, and if progress is sustained, a joint application can be made by parents and the local authority for the revocation of the care order. This, when justified, indicates a very successful outcome.

Conclusion

Any attempt to evaluate the efficacy of our case management and therapeutic involvement with the families must be highly subjective. We hope to develop an authentic and quantified evaluation of progress in our families during the next year or so. Given the implicit weakness of unvalidated evaluation, we believe that we have probably been effective in reducing the incidence of repeated non-accidental injury to the children in our families, in most cases to the point where physical violence would be used towards them barely more than society generally accepts.

With less certainty, we believe that, with the less seriously disturbed parents, we have marginally assisted maturation to the point where they can exercise increased self-control in some areas of life. Our involvement has at least eased them through a phase of their family-life span which was particularly difficult but not self-repeating.

One fairly definite observation we can make concerns the differential progress we cause between two parents. Where we are able to work to some effect with one partner, a disparity grows between husband and wife and we are not able therefore to demonstrate effective intervention in those families fraught with marital disharmony, at least in this aspect of their functioning.

We are not able to demonstrate in many cases that the overall qualitative life-experience of the chidren or the quality of their parenting improves. It may even be that the form of abuse changes to more subtle and emotional forms. The corollary is that we are unable to demonstrate essential change in the personalities of the parents, and this includes the basic constellation of their projections, misperceptions and dissociations.

The two directions in which social work should therefore follow in parallel are these. The first is to devise and implement more precise evaluative techniques in association with the disciplines of child and family psychology and psychiatry. The second is to widen the range of therapeutic modalities (Kempe and Helfer, 1972; Bean, 1971; Goldstone, 1973; Ten Broeck, 1974; Belluci, 1972). We are now planning, at the Special Unit, a number of interrelated programmes as a supplement to the process we have already described. These include parent education regarding child health and development, both in the context of intensive health visiting and as a part of increased group work with parents. The latter would be part of a day-care programme for parents in association with a day nursery for the children. This would be based on a closer involvement of the parents with the day nursery regime and therapy aimed at the children. A clear identification of the parents with the nursery staff and activities, for example, may make it easier for the parents to learn. The extension of play therapy as a domiciliary service is another possibility. We suspect that as social caseworkers we will only be more effective in reaching both parents equally by a consistent use of co-workers, particularly in families where there is a serious marital problem.

There are two main obstacles to the implementation of a wider range of treatment modalities. The first is the availability of resources, both of finance and of personnel who have the maturity and commitment to work in a setting/context, that is demanding both by virtue of the nature of the problem and the implications of close teamwork. Second, there is little provision in this country (for the professionals or families) for a more contractual basis for social-work intervention. The absence of specific conditions attached to supervision orders made in the juvenile court illustrates this unfortunte problem.

The extent to which we are able to develop, on any scale nationally, such a constellation of therapeutic provisions, as we have described, will be an index of the extent to which our society is prepared to be committed to the qualitative improvement of life as a whole for coming generations.

References

Baher, E., Hyman, C., Jones, C., Jones, R., Kerr, A. and Mitchell, R. (1976). "At Risk: an account of the work of the Battered Child Research Dept., N.S.P.C.C.". Routledge, Kegan Paul, London and Boston.

Bean, S. L. (1971). The Parents' Centre Project: a multi-service approach to the prevention of child abuse. *Child Welfare* 50.

Belluci, M. T. (1972). Group treatment of mothers in child protection cases. *Child Welfare* 51, 110–116.

Castle, R. L. and Kerr, A. M. (1972). "A Study of Suspected Child Abuse". N.S.P.C.C.

Court, J. (1969). The battered child 2. Reflections on treatment. *Medical Social Work* 22, 11–20.

Court, J. (1970). Psycho-social factors in child battering. *Women's Federation* 52, 99–104.

Court, J. (1974). Characteristics of parents and children. *In* "The Maltreated Child". Ed. J. Carter. Priory Press, Chicago.

David, C. A. (1974). The confrontation technique in the battered child syndrome. *Amer. J. Psychotherapy* 28, 543–622.

Davoren, E. (1974). The role of the Social Worker. *In* "The Battered Child" (2nd edn). Ed. R. E. Helfer, and C. H. Kempe. University of Chicago Press, Chicago.

Day, B. (1965). Supportive casework in an authoritative setting. *Case Conference* 11, No. 9.

Erikson, E. H. (1970). "Childhood and Society". Hogarth, London. (1963). (2nd edn). Norton, New York. (1965). Penguin, Harmondsworth.

Fox, F. E., Nelson, A. M. and Bolmar, M. W. (1969). The termination process: a neglected dimension in social work. *Social Work* 14, No. 4.

Garner, H. H. (1959). A confrontation technique used in psychotherapy. *Amer. J. Psychother.* 8, 18.

Garner, H. H. (1961). Passivity and activity in psychotherapy. *Arch. Gen. Psychiat.*, 5, 411.

Garner, H. H. (1966). Interventions in psychotherapy and confrontations technique. *Amer. J. Psychother.* 20, 391.

Gil, D. G. (1970). "Violence Against Children". Harvard University Press, Cambridge, Mass.

Goldberg, G. (1975). Breaking the communication barrier — the initial interview with an abusing parent. *Child Welfare* 54, 274–282.

Goldstone, R. (1973). Preventing the abuse of little children. Paper presented to the Annual Meeting of the American Psychiatric Association.

Goode, W. J. (1971). Force and violence in the family. *J. Marriage Fam.* 33, 624–635.

Guntrip, H. (1968). "Schizoid Phenomena Object Relations and the Self". Hogarth, London.

Hyman, C. (1976). Personal communication.

Jones, C. and Jones, R. A. (1974). Treatment: a social perspective. *In* "The Maltreated Child". Ed. J. Carter. Priory Press, Ilinois.

Jones, R. A. (1973). Battering families. *Health and Social Services Journal* February 10th, 1973.

Kempe, C. H. and Helfer, R. E. (1972). Innovative therapeutic techniques. *In* "Helping the Battered Child and His Family". Ed. C. H. Kempe and R. E. Helfer. Lippincott, Philadelphia.

Klaus, M. H., Jerauld, R., Kreger, N. C., McAlpine, W., Steffa, M. and Kennell, J. H. (1972). Maternal attachment: importance of the first post-partum days. *New Engl. J. Med.* 286, 9, 460–463.

Lynch, M. (1975). Ill health and child abuse. *Lancet* No. 7929, 317–319.

Morris, M. G. and Gould, R. W. (1963). Role reversed: a concept in dealing with the neglected battered child syndrome. *In* "The Neglected Battered Child Syndrome", pp. 26–46. Child Welfare League of America, New York.

Oliver, J. E., Cox, J. Taylor, A. and Baldwin, J. (1974). Severely Ill-Treated Young Children in North-East Wiltshire. Oxford Regional Health Authority.

Owtram, P. J. (1975). N.S.P.C.C. Special Units, Social Service.

Pickett, J. (1976). The management of non-accidental injury to Children in the City of Manchester. *In* "Violence in the Family". Ed. M. Borland. Manchester University Press, Manchester.

Polansky, N. A., Borgman, R. D., De Saix, C. and Sharlin, S. (1971). Verbal accessibility in the treatment of child neglect. *Child Welfare* 50, No. 6.

Pollock, C. B. and Steele, B. F. (1972). A therapeutic approach to the parents. *In* "Helping the Battered Child and his Family". Ed. C. H. Kempe and R. E. Helfer. Lippincott, Philadelphia.

Reiner, B., S. and Kaufman, I. (1959). "Character Disorders in Parents of Delinquents". Family Service Ass. of America.

Richards, M. P. M. (1974). Non-accidental injury to children in an ecological perspective. *In* "Non-accidental Injury to Children". H.M.S.O., London.

Richards, M. P. M. and Bernal, J. F. (1972). An observational study of mother–infant interactions. *In* "Ethological Studies of Child Behaviour". Ed. N. Blurton Jones. Cambridge University Press, Cambridge.

Rose, R., Owtram, P., Pickett, J., Marran, B. and Maton, A. (1976). Registers of Suspected Non-Accidental Injury: a report on registers maintained in Leeds and Manchester by N.S.P.C.C. Special Units. N.S.P.C.C. Casework and Developments Dept.

Skinner, A. E. and Castle, R. L. (1969). "78 Battered Children: a retrospective study". N.S.P.C.C.

Smith, S. M. and Hanson, R. (1974). 134 Battered children: a medical and psychological study. *Brit. Med. J.* No. 5932, 666–670.

Spencer, C. (1970). Support as a key problem in social work. *Social Work Today* 3, 4–27.

Steele, B. F. and Pollock, C. B. (1974). A Psychiatric Study of Parents who abuse infants and small children. *In* "The Battered Child" (2nd edn). Ed. R. E. Helfer and C. H. Kempe. University of Chicago Press, Chicago.

Stevenson, O. (1975). The Social Worker's Responsibility to the child. A paper presented at a British Assoc. of Social Workers Conference, Manchester.

Ten Broeck, E. (1974). The extended family centre. *Children Today* 3, 2–6.

Underhill, E. (1974). The strange silence of teachers, doctors and social workers in the face of cruelty to children. Chronicle — The Child — his surroundings, pp 16–21.

Wasserman, S. (1967). The abused parent of the abused child. *Children* 14, 175–179.

Winnicott, D. W. (1965). "The Maturational Processes and the Facilitating Environment". Hogarth, London.

Discussion

(Chapter 5 and 6)

The discussion centred first round the part which could be played by the psychiatrist. In diagnosing psychopathic disorder he was invaluable. Everyone accepted that, for some families, the only safe intervention was the permanent placement of the child out of the home and in long-term fostering or through adoption. Parental rights should be permanently removed and voluntary sterilization encouraged. Compulsory sterilization was considered to be an unwise practice. The psychiatrist would naturally as a doctor use a medical model and his case might be differently presented depending on whether he was only giving an expert opinion or taking the responsibility for further treatment. In the absence of psychiatric illness, he was no more "expert" than anyone else, although he might provide an explanation of the client's actions. His use of the medical model was not always appropriate, and certainly the psychiatrist should not be regarded as the provider of solutions. Not all psychiatrists were familiar with child abuse, and the psychiatrist who lacked the developmental approach might well be unsuitable to play any part in the case.

The court could be misled unless the differences of psychiatric approach were understood. Should a suitable psychiatrist sit with the court as an assessor? His approach would become known to the court in the same way as that of the welfare officer. The judge or the magistrates would really benefit from hearing all parties and needed to hear opposing views. These would be based primarily on the facts of the child's present situations, although the theory held by the psychiatrist was bound to influence the selection of facts to be brought forward. Evidence would also be admissible about the previous behaviour of the parents if this helped the court to assess the safety of the home. This was something that the solicitor should know, as well as the clerk to the justices, so that the proper questions could be asked. Although much could be said in favour of the wider use of the wardship of the court procedure, the numbers would always be a limiting factor.

In gathering information about the family and the home, the probation officer was the most experienced. A check list of the more important observations to make could be a great help. Perhaps the health visitor could play a larger part. Disadvantages were that home visits could be deceptive and the health visitor had no right of access. To take a member of the police force with her in order to gain admittance would not improve the chance of making a happy relationship. Her suitability was questioned on two important grounds. First, was she fully instructed in current views about family interactions and relationships, and second, was her training intended to enable her to instruct parents, especially young mothers, so that her approach was almost bound to be authoritative in order to be effective?

Until recently most of the therapeutic work was done by social workers on the adults, in the hope that dealing with their unmet needs would improve parenting skills. A difficulty arose over the dual function of exercising control while discouraging dependence in favour of maturation. Once the element of control was established, a volunteer might succeed more than a professional whose caring might be suspected, while only a caring person would volunteer for this work.

Certainly, much could be said in favour of using more than one worker, so that the client who was distressed about one could fall back on another. With present case loads, social worker help might have to be withdrawn at a critical time, for example of depression, while working through the grandparents' failure of parenting.

The clients should know that care orders can be rescinded. The suggestion had some support that a further episode of abuse should lead to removal of the child, either to a day centre or permanently, on the grounds that the child was being emotionally deprived. The need for more active therapy for the child was stressed, to replace the present pre-occupation with the adults. Although not all abused children were rejected and abused, children were far from rejecting their abusers; perhaps the law as well as social policy should make the giving up of children easier and more acceptable.

In the discussion so far, the assumption was that abuse was definitely established. Suppose that there was no more than strong suspicion. Should the family be explicitly told of the nature of the suspicion? Labelling was inclined to be self-fulfilling and denial might be necessary to integrity. On the other hand, is it possible really to help the family without explicit acceptance of the situation? The question remains open.

7. Parents and Children and Child Abuse

Martin Richards

Child abuse, at least in the sense being considered in this symposium, takes place in the context of relationships between caretakers and children. In this paper I will suggest that abuse of children should be considered as an aspect of such relationships, albeit an unusual and highly undesirable aspect. I want to contrast this view with one that is probably more generally held that child abuse constitutes a special problem or syndrome that can be considered in isolation from more usual parental behaviour. The disjunction between much of the discussion of child abuse and that of normal parental relations is hardly surprising, because the dominant views of the nature and growth of such relationships deal almost exclusively with their positive aspects and have little or nothing to say about the universal features such as anger and frustration, let alone violence. This theoretical inadequacy has led to the suggestion that abuse occurs when there is a complete absence of a relationship between parent and child, and is due to a "bonding failure". But this view misses the central point. We are not dealing with an act of malevolence or violence between strangers but almost always with one that happens where there is a long-lasting and very intimate association of two partners, a child and a caretaker (generally the social parent, though sometimes not the biological parent). Of course, these relationships may be deeply unsatisfying to all concerned, but they are relationships none the less. Thus the nature and varieties of parental relationships become central to the understanding of child abuse. I would submit that, until we have better models of parental attitudes and behaviour to guide our strategies of intervention and prevention, our efforts are unlikely to be very successful.

In the first part of this paper, I outline some of the deficiencies of current theories of parental relations with children and then sketch out an alternative perspective which I believe might serve us better. The second section will be devoted to a consideration of some of the implications of the alternative perspective for the aetiology and prevention of child abuse, with special emphasis on non-accidental injury.

Parent–child Relationships

I must begin with a warning to prevent possible misunderstandings. The dominant conception of parent-child relationships described below is not intended to represent the view of any theorist or group of theorists, but is an attempt to describe the explicitly and implicitly held theories which those professionally involved with children use to determine and rationalize their actions. The gap between these "theories in action" and the formal statements of social scientists is often wide since the latter are usually modified (for better or worse) to a considerable degree as they are handed on through writing and teaching and reconciled with the exigencies of practical activity. When we are discussing practical activity, it is obvious that the "theories in action" should be our concern, and criticisms of these cannot be dismissed simply because they are shown to diverge from the statements of theorists.

Attachment Theory

The general concept of parental relationships is that some process of "attachment" or "bonding" occurs in days or weeks after birth. These terms tend to be used to describe both the physical and emotional closeness of parents to their children. At least in the first year of life, the securely attached child is one that, during the waking hours at least, remains in physical proximity with the mother and is likely to protest at physical separation. I use the term mother rather than parent here, because, though a certain amount of lip service is paid to the role of fathers, their prime function is usually not considered to be through their direct relationships with their children. The father is thought of as financial provider for the family and a source of emotional support for the mother. The mother of the well attached child is described as showing high levels of positive feeling which are

---

* An irony worth noting here is that, in several situations, higher levels of these sorts of behaviour patterns are often seen with fathers rather than mothers (e.g. Lamb, 1976). This is presumably because infants are more interested in the less familiar parent who, anyway is often playing little of a caretaking role, so that a greater proportion of his contacts with the child are playful and "purely social". This has led attachment theorists (e.g. Bretherton and Ainsworth,

generally indexed through such criteria as smiling, talking, close body contact and so on.*

The determinants of a successful attachment are seen to reside in both the child and the mother. Some babies are described as having difficult or unrewarding behaviour which makes it hard for the mother to read the cues thought necessary for phasing her behaviour with that of the infant to produce a truly interactive relationship. Mothers too are sometimes held to be deficient by being unresponsive to their infants and to the usual or "natural" stimuli, like crying, which the infant is thought to use to evoke maternal responses.

Physical separation, especially if it occurs in the early stages of the relationship, is said to delay or disrupt the growing attachment. In some versions of this theory, it is suggested that there is a sensitive period for the formation of attachments in the first post-partum hours or days. If separation occurs during this time, it has been claimed that bonding may not happen at all. Separation after the formation of the attachment is also seen to be upsetting and damaging for the child. This is usually considered to be particularly disruptive when separation is compounded with the removal of a child to a strange place such as a hospital or children's home, but it has also been suggested that recurrent short-term separations, as when a child attends a day nursery, can have damaging effects in the first two or three years of life.

It is not my intention to review the experimental evidence for and against this general proposition which has recently been discussed by Rutter (1972), Douglas (1975) and Richards (1976) among others, but rather to point out some of the most general assumptions embodied in these concepts.

The attachment theory has been rightly criticized for being a "desert island" view of human relationships. The mother and child are considered as a unit detached from the rest of the world. If this world impinges at all, it is as a set of distant "social factors" which may push the "natural" development of attachment off its true course. Attachment is viewed as the product of the biological nature of the mother and infant. Each, if correctly functioning, brings a set of responses to the situation independent of the social conditions. These responses are seen as inevitable products of biological organization which have been shaped through the process of evolution. Those who hold these views often consider information about animal species to be of direct relevance, and many discussions of attachment devote more attention

---

1974) to draw a distinction between filial and attachment behaviour, and to suggest that infants only reveal their "true attachments" in their preferences for a particular caretaker, usually the mother, under situations of stress. If one accepts this line of theorizing, it means that the kind of everyday interchange of mother and infant, that has been described by many observers in recent years, may be unrelated to the quality of the child's attachment.

to the doings of chickens, goats and macaques than to the predica-
ment of parents in our own society.

If we are to conceptualize parental relationships more adequately,
we must bring the mother and baby ashore from their desert island
and place them in the more familiar world of four-hourly feeds,
disturbed nights punctuated by crying, wet nappies and visits to the
local Welfare Clinic. At the same time, it must be understood that
social relationships are inherently and fundamentally of a social
nature. They are products of our social world, and, for practical
purposes at least, their social origins outweigh the consequences of
our biological evolution.

Social Determinants

Human parental behaviour has strong social determinants. What a
mother does with her baby is a product of what she has been led to
believe is expected of her as a mother by informal and formal learning
and the degree to which her baby may or may not conform to her
expectations. Very few mothers in Britain have much practical
experience of caring for young children before their own are born
(Richards, 1974a), but this is not to say that they do not have highly
developed ideas of what is expected of mothers and of the role they will
play in bringing up their children. Throughout all our lives, we build
up our conceptions of parenthood from many sources. In the period
just preceding the birth of a child, there is often a very rapid
development of these concepts through a heightened interest in other
people's children, formal parentcraft classes and the reading of books
and magazine articles. Usually, where the mother takes responsibility
for her child soon after the delivery, her "theoretical" picture of
motherhood and child care is rapidly modified by the practical
realities as she adjusts to the new role and to the individual
characteristics of her baby. These adjustments can take place very
quickly. For the first few days after birth, a primiparious woman often
shows a degree of inco-ordination with her baby, but this is short-lived.
By about the tenth day, there are minimal differences between a first
mother and one that has had a previous child (Dunn and Richards,
1977). The pattern of interaction that emerges is strongly influenced by
the behaviour of the baby. This is not so only on a minute-to-minute
basis as the mother reacts and interacts with what the baby does, but
also in a longer term way as she comes to learn her baby's
characteristics and is better able to predict what he or she may do next.
However, a mother's responses to her baby are not driven by any
inbuilt biological imperatives, they are formed socially. Responses to a
crying baby depend on how a mother interprets the crying and what it

means to her (Richards, 1974b), and these are matters of social learning and understanding. In the early weeks, at least, the probability of a mother responding to her baby's cries seems to depend largely on the timing of the cry in relation to the feeding schedule. A cry at an expected feeding time is likely to lead to the baby being picked up and fed while at other times it may be ignored or dismissed as naughtiness. In our work in Cambridge (Bernal, 1972), we found that responding to crying was organized around four-hour periods, corresponding to the local professional view of a correct feeding schedule. Four-hourly feeding, far from being biologically determined and a product of our evolutionary history, is a social custom that has grown over the last 50 years with the development of protein (over)rich artificial infant foods.

We live in a society that places high value on technique and formally-defined bodies of knowledge produced and distributed by "experts". Not surprisingly, this has led to a shift in the source of values for child care from the craft skills and attitudes that were handed on from generation to generation to the information provided by professionals (Wright, 1976). This shift has probably led to child rearing becoming more problematic and anxiety-provoking for parents, because the existence of professional experts suggests both that there are complex and difficult problems to be faced and that problems are ultimately solvable in terms of the technical considerations with which the experts tend to deal. Thus a mother who feels angry with her baby because it cries a lot at night is likely to receive a lot of information about feeding regimes, but her anger is often ignored. This can have the effect of making her feel even more inadequate and guilty about her role as a parent and confirms her feelings of abnormality and failure.

It has often been pointed out that parents get confused by varying advice received from different quarters. However, though advice may diverge in specific detail, there is a widespread assumption that early experience is of particular importance in a child's development. So, for the parent, there is the alarming possibility that, if they do not do the "correct" thing with their child, there will be long-term repercussions. When difficulties do arise with the child, the message parents often get, if they seek professional advice, is that the child's misbehaviour stems from their mishandling. If we look at the paediatric literature on night waking in children, for example, we find widely divergent opinions about its origins. However, with few exceptions, writers are agreed that the problem stems from some form of "incorrect" parental handling. In our present-day society, it is difficult to feel successful as a parent. Often all that parents do with babies is coloured by a concern that they are doing the right thing, and there may be a constant struggle to maintain a sense of adequacy.

Today, as perinatal mortality rates have fallen to very low levels, the probability that any pregnancy will lead to the birth of a live and normal baby is high. However, a doubt still hangs over the outcome of any pregnancy. At a delivery, the first thing a mother usually asks her attendants is whether the baby is normal and not, for example, its sex. In the first periods of contact with a baby, the mother typically explores the baby's body often undressing him to check that the whole body is complete and normal. If a delivery goes badly and a baby has medical problems, the parents' worst fears seem to be realized. If one assumes that any admission to a special or intensive care unit is likely to confirm the parents' fears, about one in five of all deliveries goes badly wrong from the parents' perspective. As studies have shown (Seashore *et al.*, 1973), the partial or total separation that a special care admission generally entails reduces a mother's confidence in feeling able to cope with the baby when they both are discharged. Similar effects have been documented (Greenberg *et al.*, 1973) with hospital regimes that regulate and restrict contact between mother and child.

It would, of course, be wrong to paint too black a picture of the situation in which parents begin to form their relationships with their children, and we must not forget the joy, pleasure and satisfaction that accompany many deliveries. However, I have tried to emphasize some of the complexities of becoming a parent and to show how far reality may diverge from the fairy story in which the mother gazes into the baby's eyes as the cord is clamped, a bond is formed and both live happily ever afterward in a world of mutually satisfying and pleasurable interaction.

We have hardly begun to analyse parent-child relations as a socially-defined and constructed phenomenon. We know little, for example, of the relative importance of different kinds of situations and events in forming attitudes and perceptions, or how parents, with varying experience, view babies with differing characteristics and behaviour. The most important fact in the context of this meeting is that we have little understanding of how most parents cope with the frustrations and discomforts that all children, at least occasionally, provide and why a very few allow their anger to overwhelm them and become directed in physical violence towards their children. If we are to answer these questions, we need to concentrate much more on what it feels like to be a parent and rather less on what parents can be seen to be doing.

Non-Accidental Injury

In describing some of the implications of the view of parent-child relations that has been outlined, I will only consider non-accidental injury to children. This is partly because most of the recent concern about child abuse has been confined to this problem, but more fundamentally because the range of phenomena included under the term child abuse is so wide that all generalizations are dangerous. As will be described, even the restricted category of non-accidental injury covers such a heterogeneous set of events that its value in any social analysis is severely limited.

Problems of Definition

Research on non-accidental injury is beset by two major problems. First, the phenomenon tends to be defined in terms of the severity of physical injury to children and several difficulties stem from this. Perhaps the most important of these is that an apparent homogeneity is given to a divergent range of parental actions. Not only will there be an enormous variety of situations that lead parents to inflict what on medical examination appear to be similar injuries but, in similar situations, parents may cause injuries of a widely differing nature and severity. If it is the parental actions in which we are interested, we are only likely to be misled if we use any classification based on the nature of the injuries. As yet, there is almost no research work which has not used the children's injury as the basic defining feature of the families that have been studied. Defining a sample in terms of reported injury has the further disadvantage that we have no means of knowing how representative of all injuries the reported cases are.

The second major difficulty is that we have very few certain grounds for defining the outer limit of the phenomenon — where do we draw the line between the bruises that almost any parent inflicts on his child sooner or later and injuries that demand intervention and treatment? A decade ago when non-accidental injury was widely ignored and mis-diagnosed, concentration on the cases of serious injury was natural and proper. Now there are grounds for believing that awareness and diagnostic accuracy have greatly improved. With serious injury, the problem is relatively straightforward — how did the child acquire the injury? But what about a thriving child who is found to have a single bruise on his arm when being presented for inoculation? Should any action be taken? If so, what action? Now that risk registers are widely established, how are we to ensure that they do not become over-burdened with trivial cases? It is worth remembering the problems of the risk registers for developmental abnormality that were in vogue a few years ago. If anything, their criteria were somewhat better defined than is currently possible for non-accidental injury, but yet, in several areas, a majority of the population of children ended up on the registers and the prevalence of handicap hardly differed between those on and off the lists.

From the standpoint of practical intervention, one cannot recommend anything more satisfactory than common sense as an answer to the problems of definition. But for research and a longer-term perspective, this cannot suffice. The inherent problems of definition merely serve to give added weight to the arguments presented earlier, that the whole problem must be considered as an aspect of the social dynamics of parent-child relationships. This is where we need to concentrate attention and must analyse much more thoroughly the variety of parental attitudes and behaviour, paying particular attention to factors that are associated with frustration and anger directed at children.

We already know that situations that add to stresses and burdens for parents, particularly mothers, are more common than usual in the case histories of non-accidental injury (Gil, 1970). Many of these situations could be alleviated by appropriate measures which not only might help to reduce the incidence of non-accidental injury but would help to ease the lives of a great many parents. The remainder of the paper will be concerned with a discussion of a few of the measures that we could take.

There is one very important point that must be borne in mind in considering any intervention in child-rearing practice: these practices are socially determined. This means that they will vary between different sections of the community so that we cannot draw up a universally applicable list of acceptable and relevant intervention methods. These must be tailored to varying needs of different social groups. Much, but not all, of this variation may be subsumed under the rubric of social class and much research (Newson and Newson, 1968) has demonstrated the wide variation in child-care practice and attitudes that can be found in one small geographical area across the social-class groups. Here we are not simply dealing with different practices but also with profoundly varying responses to the same events, including the raising of children itself. This can be illustrated by a population survey of psychiatric disturbance in married women carried out by Brown (1976). As may be seen in Fig. 1, working-class women have higher rates of psychiatric disturbance than other women, and rates rise with the arrival of babies. However, what is perhaps even more important is that while working-class rates decline as the children grow up, the opposite is true in the high-class sample. The implication for where to concentrate preventive services is clear. Another indication of the importance of social context is given by studies of perinatal mortality (Chamberlain *et al.*, 1975) which show a doubling of the rate for married women (20.2./1000) in those

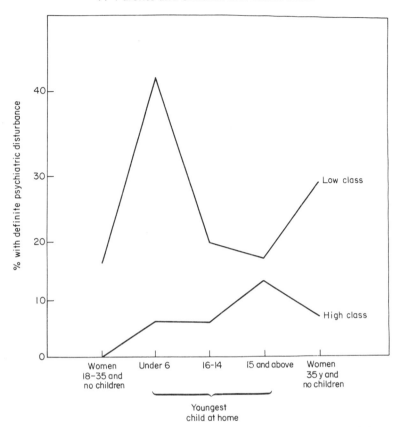

Fig. 1   *Psychiatric disturbance in women as a function of their age, social class and the presence of children at home* (Brown, 1976)

separated from their husbands (41.9/1000) and an almost equally high rate in single women (36.4/1000). Survey of the literature on non-accidental injury demonstrates a comparable relationship with the social position of the mother (Gil, 1970; Spinetta and Rigler, 1972).

Hospital Relationships

For most parents in Britain today, their social relationships with their children begin in a hospital. It is here that the expectations, hopes and fears of pregnancy are realized and the sometimes traumatic conversion to parenthood takes place. These are important events in any life, but how far can we claim that hospitals provide a suitable setting for such important experiences? Even a brief review of the writings of consumers suggests a profound dissatisfaction, and it is noteworthy that there are more complaints about maternity services than any other section of the National Health Service (Robinson, 1974). Hospitals are places of hierarchy and routine and are understandably concerned with the medical and technical problems of child care. but these features stand in opposition to what is desirable as a setting for a developing human relationship. Mothers who may want privacy to explore and get to know their newborns are likely to find their contacts severely limited by routines. Any attempt to undress their child will usually bring a nurse hurrying over to see what is "wrong". Human relationships have a timeless quality and it is very hard to learn to know and love someone whom you see for only 20 minutes every 4 hours.

In hospital it is difficult for a mother to feel that her child belongs to her. All responsibility is removed from her and important decisions are made by others. Fathers are often made to feel even more peripheral to the process. Attempts to teach child-care techniques are often made in hospital, but how many mothers find them of much value? This is partly because the basic problems of caring for a new child are not ones of technique; few parents, for example, come to grief because they are unable to put on a nappy but because of emotional and social reasons related to the radical changes in their lives that a child may often bring. Also the techniques taught in hospital may sometimes have only marginal relevance to the situation in the home.

Many mothers approach delivery with little confidence that they will be able to cope with the demands of motherhood. Hospitals frequently add to these fears. Here it is often the unintended remark or action rather than structural features or policies that do the damage. For instance, I have seen a mother who had just put on a nappy for the first time reduced to tears by a nurse who, without saying anything, removed the nappy and replaced it folded in the "correct" hospital manner. For many mothers much nursing practice operates as a kind of judiciary over their competence and by the nature of the system it is the mother who most often loses out. Always hanging over the mother's head is the risk that she may be labelled as a "difficult" patient, so that the pressures to conform to the system are very strong, however absurd she may think the hospital routines may be. Sometimes a sort of underground movement grows up among the mothers on a lying-in ward and they are able to support and encourage each other by their common criticisms and their resistance to the system. But all too often, a mother arrives home exhausted and demoralized and feeling quite unable to cope with her baby.

With almost universal hospital confinement and the continued long lengths of stay (still almost a week on average), the role of the district midwife in providing effective support has been much reduced. Potentially, midwives can provide effective help and support as this is given in the context of the home. However, the days are almost gone when the midwife becomes a familiar figure during pregnancy and pays daily visits throughout the crucial first 10 days. With the falling midwifery work-load, it would seem to be desirable to consider extending visiting beyond the first 10 days so that mothers returning from hospitals can be given a reasonable period of support. This is an area where it seems essential to strive for a genuine "continuity of care".

The problems for parents during the lying-in period are greatly increased if the birth is difficult or the baby is found to have medical problems. In 1974, 16.8% of all newborns were removed from their mothers and admitted to special care nurseries. The evidence is rapidly accumulating (Richards, 1977) of the anxieties and fears that can be engendered by these admissions, and there can be little doubt that many of them do not serve the child's best interests. Too often, all the medical and nursing attention is devoted to the sick baby and parents' needs are ignored. The mother may be left in a ward surrounded by other women who have their babies with them and only provided with minimal information about her baby. Visiting is still severely restricted in many special-care nurseries. The demoralizing features of the ordinary lying-in ward can be greatly intensified for the mother whose baby goes to a special-care nursery. Implicitly, she is being told that she is incapable of looking after her own child and there is the constant worry of long-term developmental consequences of the baby's problems. We should hardly be surprised that the birth of a preterm baby is seen as a severe emotional crisis (Caplin *et al.*, 1965), or that children who have received special care are particularly likely to be abused (Lynch, 1975).

Present-day obstetric and neonatal paediatric policies have been formed on the basis of very narrow medical considerations. They have brought profound changes for parents and not all of these have been for the better. Today, because of the falling birth rate, this sector of the Health Service is in a uniquely favourable situation and there is time and space for a radical reconsideration of present policies. The central point here is to try to view the system from the parents' point of view. Many medical decisions may seem straightforward, but a lightly taken routine decision can have devastating consequences for parents. An example here is phototherapy for jaundice. It might seem unproblematic to order phototherapy when bilirubin reaches a critical level, but it is not so simple for a mother when her baby is suddenly taken away and is next seen naked with eyes bandaged under bright lights. In situations like this, a full explanation to the parents of what is being done, and why, and attempts to involve them in the care of their baby can make all the difference.

Needs and Services

I have only been able to touch on a few of the features of maternity care that can create problems for parents, and many of the issues are much more complex than I have made them sound. But the problems of the first year of life are even more wide-ranging and difficult. Few who have examined the current situation can be convinced that the professional support available — health visitors, welfare clinics, social workers, G.P.s and hospitals — meets much more than the needs of a few.

Needs in the early months of parenthood can be divided into technical, emotional and social. The health visitors, welfare clinics and G.P.s have primary responsibility for meeting technical needs — problems of feeding, medical difficulties, sleep requirements, etc. Several factors reduce the effectiveness of these potentially valuable services. The most obvious is that advice given to parents is all too often misleading and unhelpful. We have to remember that many of the feeding practices deprecated by the recent D.H.S.S. Expert Committee, such as the too-early feedings of solids, are ones that have been actively propagated by health visitors and welfare clinics.* The recent government consultative document on the health service has suggested that expansion of the health visiting service is an urgent objective. Let us hope that this will be accompanied by much more effective primary and in-service training.

Another important factor is that all worries and problems tend to be reduced to technical questions. A mother may seek advice on persistent crying and receive information about feeding routines. However, not too far beneath the surface she may be saying that she is finding the crying intolerable and is feeling less and less able to control her more violent impulses. The problems are left untouched by the usual advice.

Like hospital staff, health visitors and welfare clinics are often seen as standing in judgement over a mother's parental competence. Visits may become empty routines in which the mother may do all she can to present an image of control and competence when, in fact, her life may be beset with difficulties. Here I think we may be over-optimistic about the possiblities of what can be achieved with professional workers. It is easy to ask for more training, but what is there that we can teach that

---

* They still are in some cases. Recently, a mother took her thriving two-month-old baby to a welfare clinic. She happened to mention that he was waking regularly at night and was advised to add an extra scoop of milk powder to the last feed in the evening. When the mother said something about over-concentrated feeds she was told that this was simply "government propaganda" and demonstrated "how little the government knows about babies"!

Another mother was advised to spoon-feed brown sugar to her two-week-old as a cure for diarrhoea.

can break down the barriers? After all, we do not have a technology of human relationships that can be passed on in training. Relationships, even those between client and professional involve sympathy, empathy and shared values. Certainly, we can draw attention to the problems, but time and experience are probably far more important than anything that can be imparted in training.

The emotional needs of parents, particularly mothers, are probably those that are least often effectively met by present day services. The pressures of 24-hour child care can be enormous, and loneliness and depression among mothers with young children are very widespread; it should not be necessary to argue once again the case for improved and expanded day care for children. However, there are probably many situations that cannot be alleviated in this way, and here it often falls to social workers to do what they can; but this can be very limited. Though we must be cautious in importing evidence from other communities where the situation may be very different, I think we must take seriously Kempe's view that case work is ineffective in modifying child-care practices. Indeed, if our ideas about the ways in which social behaviour develop and is modified are anywhere near reality, it would be odd if social workers with the very limited time at their disposal had much impact. Again following Kempe, it seems reasonable to suppose that, given time, much valuable help can be provided for mothers by people without any professional training. It does not require training to talk over a mother's frustration with her, to chat while she feeds her baby, to go out shopping with her or take her child off her hands for a few hours. The Colorado workers make high claims for the success of their foster grandparents scheme, and in Britain we have the self-help model of the battered wives organizations. This is an area in which we need imaginative experimentation. The case-work skills that may serve so well in other situations are not the only answer. In other social work fields, such as youth work, social workers already undertake an "enabling" role by providing a framework in which volunteers and self-help groups can operate. From this sort of position the statutory duties could still be carried out, but most face-to-face contact would not be complicated by the judicial role.

Another American scheme, that has not yet been tried in Britain on any scale, is a crisis telephone — much on the same lines as the Samaritans operate for depressed people and potential suicides. Again we can see considerable advantages in a service that is operated by well-informed non-professional people. Most parents face at least the odd day or night when the demands of their children seem overwhelming and there appears to be no way out. A sympathetic voice on a telephone could go some way to relieve the immediate tensions and be a source of contacts for longer-term solutions.

As far as social factors are concerned, we have now learnt that new houses and running hot and cold water are neither necessary nor sufficient for adequate child care. This does not mean that improved material circumstances cannot contribute a great deal in certain cases. We know that single parent families are among the poorest in Britain, and this can hardly ease the burdens of child care under circumstances that may be already difficult. Here there is much scope for the professional knowledge of health visitors and social workers to be used to improve situations on an individual basis. For example, many of these families live in rented accommodaton and need advice and assistance in understanding the complexities of the law. Others may be eligible for Social Security benefits they do not take up, or simply may want to make contact with other women in similar situations.

Conclusions

The latter section contains criticisms of some existing services, although I am aware that many institutions and individuals provide a very high standard indeed. If the kind of difficulties described were isolated instances, they would not be worthy of much attention. Many of the difficulties stem not so much from individuals who provide services that fall short of a reasonable level but from the ways in which institutions and professions have defined their goals. In child care, we are dealing with social actions, needs, intentions, motives and emotions, not systems that are amenable to the kinds of techniques that have proved so successful in much of medicine and public health. It is not only relatively easy to reduce infectious disease with clean-water supplies, sewage disposal, inoculations and antibiotics, but the kinds of processes involved can be treated as very simple mechanistic systems.

Social actions are of quite a different order and do not, in general, respond predictably if we treat them as if they were complex machinery. Many of our psychological theories have attempted to reduce our actions to the status of the responses of machines, and it is little wonder that social and psychological interventions based on such assumptions have not been very effective. At least a start has been made in the study of parent-child relations to build more satisfactory alternatives and to use these as a basis for examining and improving current practices. Given a healthy scepticism of traditional views and a willingness to experiment and to take risks, a great deal could be done to reduce the stresses and strains of child rearing. This is unlikely to solve all the problems raised by child abuse and non-accidental injury, but it might go a good way in reducing its incidence.

References

Bernal, J. F. (1972). Crying during the first 10 days of life, and maternal responses. *Develop. Med. Child Neurol.* **14**, 362–372.

Bretherton, I. and Ainsworth, M. D. (1974). Responses of one-year-olds to a stranger in a strange situation. *In* "Origins of Fear". Ed. M. Lewis and A. Rosenblum. Wiley Interscience, New York.

Brown, G. W. (1976). Social Causes of Disease. *In* "An Introduction to Medical Sociology". Ed. D. Tuckett. Tavistock, London.

Caplin, G., Mason, E. A. and Kaplan, D. M. (1965). Four studies of crisis in parents of prematures. *Community Ment. Health J.* **1**, 149.

Chamberlain, R., Chamberlain, G., Howlett, B. and Claireaux, A. (1975). The first week of life. "British Births 1970", Vol. 1. Heinemann Medical Books, London.

Douglas, J. W. B. (1975). Early hospital admissions and later disturbances of behaviour and learning. *Develop. Med. Child Neurol.* **17**, 456–480.

Dunn, J. F. and Richards, M. P. M. (1977). Observations on the developing relationship between mother and baby. *In* "Interactions in Infancy". Ed. H. R. Schaffer. Academic Press, London and New York.

Gil, D. (1970). "Violence against Children: physical child abuse in the United States". Harvard Univ. Press, Cambridge, Mass.

Greenberg, M., Rosenberg, I. and Lind, J. (1973). First mothers rooming-in with their newborns: its impact upon the mother. *Amer. J. Orthopsychiat.* **43**, 783–788.

Lamb, M. E. (1976). Effects of stress and cohort on mother– and father–infant interaction. *Develop. Psychol.* **12**, in press.

Lynch, M. A. (1975). Ill-health and child abuse. *Lancet* **3**, 317–319.

Newson, J. and Newson, E. (1968). "Four Years Old in an Urban Community". Allen and Unwin, London.

Richards, M. P. M. (1974a) (Ed.). "The Integration of a Child into a Social World". Cambridge Univ. Press, London.

Richards, M. P. M. (1974b). First steps in becoming social. *In* "The Integration of a Child into a Social World". Ed. M. P. M. Richards. Cambridge Univ. Press, London.

Richards, M. P. M. (1977). Possible effects of early separation on later development of children. *In* "Early Separation and Children in Special-care Nurseries". Heinemann Medical Books, London.

Robinson, J. (1974). Consumer attitudes to maternity care. *Oxford Consumer* **50**, May.

Rutter, M. (1972). "Maternal Deprivation Reassessed". Penguin, Harmondsworth.

Seashore, M. J., Leifer, A. D., Barnett, C. R. and Leiderman, P. H. (1973). The effects of denial of early mother-infant interaction on maternal self-confidence. *J. Pers. Soc. Psychol.* **26**, 369–378.

Spinetta, J. and Rigler, D. (1972). The child-abusing parent: a psychological review. *Psychol. Bull.* **77**, 296–304.

Wright, P. W. G. (1976). The birth of child rearing as a technical field and its importance as a form of social control. Paper presented at the British Sociological Association Conference, Manchester.

For Discussion see p 157.

8. Deprivation Dwarfism Viewed as a Form of Child Abuse

Dermod MacCarthy

Is material rejection to be regarded as a form of child abuse or metaphorically "a form of battering"? The "battered child syndrome", as it was first called, and the syndrome of "emotional deprivation", "maternal rejection", "stunting of growth and deprivation dwarfism" or "intrafamilial hospitalism" (MacCarthy and Booth, 1970) can be separately described. The description of one would not do for the other, but there is a certain amount of overlap. Many battered children are indeed also suffering from emotional deprivation; some but not many deprived children come in for physical abuse, usually not very severe. Both syndromes have many fringe cases.

Deprivation and Rejection

In a symposium on child abuse, it is as well that deprivation and rejection should be discussed, for it is a cycle which perpetuates itself and which it may sometimes be possible to break.

Many children suffer intermittently the stresses due to poverty, maltreatment, neglect and malnourishment, but because of their innate resistance, toughness, aggressiveness and ability to play, they survive it without severe bodily effects. When there are such effects, especially stunting of growth, we may be sure that a continuous deep psychological stress has been present for a long time; this is the essence of the deprivation syndrome. We could, however, postulate that a special vulnerability to being rejected, scapegoated, discriminated against, hated or despised is present in the child, which exaggerates his reaction; whereas a child with no special vulnerability survives without physical symptoms.

The Evidence

The health visitor, welfare clinic doctor, general practitioner or anyone really familiar with young children will note two factors.

The first is an absence of the signs of good mothering, which are skin warm, clear and without blemishes, visual alertness, the child noticing things all the time, the head and body moving in response to what the eyes are seeing (the opposite of this is "frozen watchfulness") and muscles strong. The normal child will explore everything and will make plenty of noise if it is feeling secure. Obvious attachment to mother is shown when put out by strangeness or strangers.

Second, some disquieting physical signs are noticed.

1. The child is strikingly small. The head and the facial features are appropriate for the age; the small stature gives quite a shock (Frontispiece).

2. Undressed, the child of 3–5 years has the proportions of a younger toddler, the legs especially being short.

3. There is a pot belly (not invariable).

4. The skin is cold, dull, dappled and blemished here and there by little cuts and abrasions, healing poorly, and perhaps there are more minor bruises than the expected ones on the shins and other places.

5. The hair is thinning out on top of the head or at the back, or alopecia patches may exist, which are accepted signals of emotional stress.

6. The hands and feet are very cold, dusky red and if also sweaty may show tiny pitted ulcers on the soles of the feet. The appearance rather resembles that of acrodynia (pink disease), a now forgotten children's disease due to ingestion of mercury from calomel or other sources. The reason for mentioning this is that the child may also have severe mental symptoms consisting of sleeplessness, lethargy, anorexia and utter misery; a state that has been described as "acute nervous breakdown" (Franklin, 1975). We also could put the question, "was the pinkness of the hands and feet due to the effect of mercury or to the nervous depression? Cold extremities are common in anorexia nervosa, mental subnormality and in children at boarding schools, in all of whom winter exaggerates the condition. But it is also seen in children with none of these background stresses and it is not, therefore, a truly specific sign. In babies, a striking degree of pinkness and coldness of the feet and hands is an alerting signal, for they are at least as prone to "depression" as toddlers and older children.

Chilblains may occur, which blister or ulcerate, and possibly oedema. A psychosomatic condition of the 19th century, consisting of coldness, oedema, ulceration, cyanosis and immobility of an arm (for which amputation might be advised) was known as "Charcot's blue oedema".

7. The child is underweight, even for the small stature; but, if not underweight, it must be borne in mind that a deprived child temporarily relieved of the stress of rejection may quite quickly turn into one of Talbot's "well nourished dwarfs" (Talbot *et al.*, 1947).

8. The child looks sad, dejected, apathetic, indifferent. This can be quite an objective assessment by an experienced worker.

9. Katatonia is observed. Place the child on a couch, on the floor or in a chair, anywhere in fact in a set position with a leg or arm raised against gravity and leave him or her there while continuing to talk to the mother. The statuesque pose is held fixed by the child for several minutes, with only a very gradual subsidence, something no normal child will do. It appears to denote extreme passivity or extreme obedience. Under clinical examination also, there is a strange passivity and malleability about the child.

10. A lack of normal aggression seems to go with it, and such children are apt to be persecuted by others, bullied and sat on, having no powers of counter aggression.

Third, inquiry into symptoms and behaviour may reveal the following peculiarities.

1. Disturbance of appetite and feeding perversions are found. Anorexia may predominate, "he eats nothing; can't eat; won't eat" or the reverse "eats a lot, always hungry; eats more than the others". Then instances of gorging on stolen food are given or scavenging from dustbins or eating grass, leaves or rubbish, as the mothers may deduce from finding particles of these in the stools, pet's food or scraps on plates. This is not quite the same as "pica", in which children with iron deficiency sometimes eat dirt, earth, gravel, cement or anything mineral.

2. Coeliac type stools and a pot belly make that diagnosis seem probable but investigation disproves it.

3. Two types of eating behaviour are reported: holding food in the mouth for ages without swallowing, or gulping food whole like a dog.

Fourth, strange behaviour traits are reported.

1. These children cannot play either alone or with others. They drop out and remain solitary, doing nothing or fiddling aimlessly.

2. They are indifferent about being taken away from the mother.

3. When they are taken into hospital or into care they do not overtly fret. They soon become over-familiar with strange adults, shallowly affectionate, prone to temper tantrums and demanding, indeed attention *needing*, but seeking it indiscriminately and then often rejecting it.

4. At meals, they are really greedy, seemingly insatiable; one cannot help wondering whether they have been starved.

Discussion of the Eating Behaviour

The mother's story of eating a tremendous lot seems to be borne out by the behaviour in hospital, but there is a difference. In hospital, they put on weight very quickly and fatten almost visibly. A bit later growth is found to have started. It accelerates and so called "catch-up" growth is seen. At home on the other hand, they were not growing and not gaining weight. Was it a lie that they ate prodigiously? Or was it perhaps the exaggeration of an occasional event, when they got the chance from being predominantly under-fed and discriminated against in matters of food? If it is true that a deprived child can be eating more food than his sibs at home and still failing to fatten or to grow, then what is the mechanism? Widdowson's (1951) much quoted article Mental Contentment and Physical Growth may be invoked, though it does not explain what happens. In it, orphanage children are described who failed to benefit from a considerable supplement to their diet because, along with it, there arrived a harsh new Matron, who made them all unhappy. The phenomenon is well known in babies under impersonal handling in institutions. Is it "indigestion" or indigestion plus impaired absorption or altered metabolism? A functional pituitary insufficiency with growth hormone depression has also been postulated (Gardner, 1972; see below).

Failure to thrive in infancy is a complex subject. As a world problem, it is mostly to do with chronic disease and food shortage, but also with the cycle of under-stimulation and lack of feed-back between low-vitality mothers and infants (Cravioto *et al.*, 1966; Pollit, 1975). Failure to thrive is a form of maternal deprivation, environmental rather than sociopathic. In this country, there is no food shortage and poverty alone cannot be (at least should not ever be, under the Welfare State) a cause of failure to thrive in early childhood. When it occurs, we start to look for a cause in the mother's inadequacy, whatever form that may take: lack of intelligence, lack of concern, a story of deprived childhood herself, depression or other mental illness, preoccupation with life problems or "character disorder". It is the last, character disorder, which is the most destructive of the mother–child relationship.

Before coming to the pointers to "character disorder" for the health visitor, social worker, G.P. or paediatrician, we must look at that type of case in which it is certain that we are up against something more than those temporary difficulties which commonly bring babies under medical care. Rare though they may be, there are some instances of mothers literally starving their babies through lack of concern, tantamount to deliberate abuse, although the accusation cannot be made as simply as with the infliction of injuries. Not so rare are the slightly older children described above, who are undernourished and dwarfed. Their tiny stature is not usually noticed till they are old enough to run about and mix with other children of normal height. What has been happening to them?

They have probably been very short of calories for a long time. The velocity of growth is extremely high in fetal life and, though slowing, is still very fast during the first year. Shortage of protein and, above all, of total calories, at this time of high demand, leads to growth failure. This is well known in the raising of farm stock, but many instances can be found of babies failing to grow on an inadequate intake from whatever cause who subsequently exhibit catch-up growth when the cause, whether organic, environmental or purely nutritional, is corrected (Fig. 2). Measuring babies length is therefore a more sensible

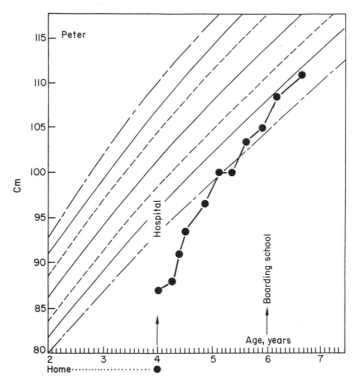

Fig. 2 *Rejected from infancy, severely dwarfed and finally battered, this child was admitted to hospital aged 4 years. During the next 2 years in hospital and children's home, catch up growth is seen. At boarding school his growth rate appears to have settled on the 25th percentile.*

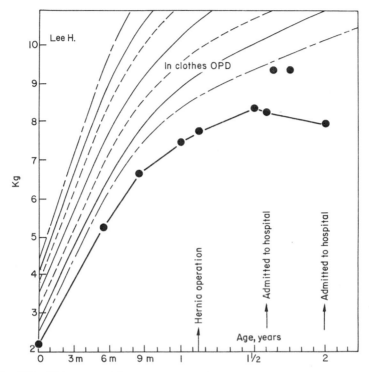

Fig. 3 *This child's poor weight progress was probably thought acceptable, owing to low birth weight; but see Fig. 4.*

exercise than weighing them, and in the long run length is a better arbiter of health and nutrition than weight. Poor weight at a certain age may be less serious in the light of a good measurement for length. But persistently poor linear gains may be sinister (Figs. 3 and 4). Children with deprivation dwarfism have escaped such detection.

Short periods of severe malnutrition do not appear to affect the attainment of normal height in later childhood. Prolonged under-nutrition does affect stature, at any rate under 5 years, and perhaps, because of the slowing of cell replication at a critical age, may lead to a short stature in adult life. This is the case with experimental animals and farm stock. There is suggestive evidence of a hormonal cause of the growth failure, and there are tempting theories of pituitary insufficiency (a so-to-speak emotional "hypophysectomy") due to depletion of growth-hormone releasing factor or failure of the releasing centre due to disturbance of the hypothalmus which is influenced by the child's depressed state; but food has as much to do with growth as hormones or even more, and the evidence for the nutritional cause appears to be the stronger (MacCarthy, 1974a).

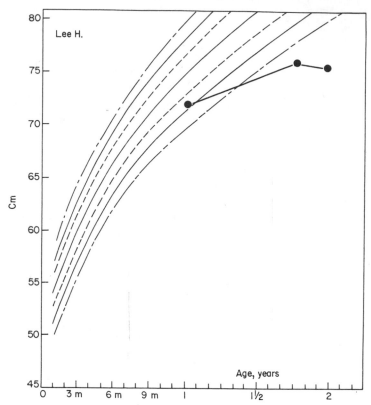

Fig. 4   *This is the same child as Fig. 3. At one year length for weight was good, but 9 months later measurement of length shows that growth has seriously slowed down.*

Deprivation Dwarfism: The Result of Being Underfed

The Evidence

1. The Newcastle Thousand Families study showed that for boys and girls with feeding neuroses, food fads and food battles were significantly shorter (within the normal percentile ranges), than controls with normal appetites when aged 3, 5 and 9 years (Brandon, 1970).

2. A study in Bristol, with the help of psychiatric social workers and dieticians and judging by the food inventories they were able to compile, showed that children with dwarfism without endocrine and other disease had a caloric consumption of a little more than half that expected for their age (Apley *et al.*, 1971).

3. Mothers' statements about what the dwarfed child eats have been shown to be untrue, through either deliberate fabrication or self-deception.

A very detailed study (Whitton *et al.*, 1969) of 13 emotionally deprived children aged 3–24 months showed first that, when given food on a schedule of 140 calories per kg of ideal weight for length, these babies gained at normal or at accelerated rates, in spite of remaining under "depriving" conditions. This kind of study is not likely to be repeated, so it is important that the findings of its authors should become widely known. During the period of study, the children were kept in windowless rooms, they had no toys, they were not picked up, except where feeding actually required it, and they were not spoken to, played with, fondled or smiled at, except by visiting parents who could do so if they wished. This rather harsh sounding treatment was justified as being merely a continuation in hospital of the daily life the children were having at home anyhow. Nine of the children made twofold to sevenfold increases in the rate of weight gain during 2 weeks. They ate well and did not show any outward reaction to the emotionally isolating conditions. Although this is cited as evidence that they only needed the requisite calories and not "nurture" (affection, stimulation, activity, etc.) to make them thrive, there is a possible factor unaccounted for here, namely that when removed from home they were relieved from the constant stress of living with a rejecting parent.

One would not wish to carry out the necessary complementary study, with its ethically more uncomfortable associations, which would be to continue the presumed nutritional deprivation of the home life in the hospital while providing warm, human contact, tenderness, cheerfulness and play; in a word good mothering. Would the babies then gain weight on their meagre food supplies? Probably they would, but inadequately. One effect might be a revival of appetite and crying for more food, in which case it would be impossible to continue the study. If the key to the situation could really be found it might be that the main effect on an infant of a rejecting mother is lack of appetite and apathy, hence malnutrition, low vitality and a cycle of un-derstimulation between mother and child. A continuation of the same study gave evidence in support of this.

Four of the original 13 babies, aged 6–12 months, had food brought to them in their own homes by a professional worker. The feeds provided adequate calories for weight gain. The mothers were told this was to help to understand the reason why their babies were failing to thrive. The workers merely observed the feed being given and took away for measurement anything that was left over. All the babies made spectacular weight gains. But two weeks after the observer and the imported meals were withdrawn, they relapsed to their original very slow rates.

Three more children, who had not been through the hospital study, presenting the same picture of emotional deprivation and failure to thrive, aged 11–23 months, similarly had meals taken to the home. The mothers had been asked to say what their children were eating at each meal. The meals brought by the observer, who watched while they were eaten, were exact replicas of what the mother had described. Excellent weight gains were recorded during the two weeks of this experiment. Later, one child was found to be still gaining spectacularly, the other two could not be traced.

The authors' comments on these findings are very important.

The home feeding program embarked upon as an investigative tool unexpectedly had some therapeutic value. The relationship between the improved weight gain and being fed an adequate diet by the mother was so unequivocal that two of the three mothers whose infants were not hospitalized spontaneously verbalized, after the home feeding program, that they were now aware that they previously underfed the infant and were resolved to correct this. They volunteered that they had slept through meals, permitted the infant to sleep through meals, at times had given them a cookie instead of a meal, etc. Each had previously claimed a consistently adequate intake and had attributed the growth retardation to constitutional factors.

The mother of a child with stunted growth generally reacts in the same way, attributing the condition of the child to having "something wrong with him" and pointing to other well grown children of hers as witnesses to her good mothering, while repeating that the dwarfed child eats as much as they do or more.

The Effects of Under-nutrition

One effect of chronic calorie insufficiency, with or without severe protein deficiency, is dwarfism, as described; the other is on the mother/child relationship. The fact that this would be impoverished rather than be intensified is not unexpected. There is in fact a vast amount of recorded observation of the mother/child feeding situation, much careful measurement and many statistical appraisals of such observations. A recent symposium of the American Institute of Nutrition (Chavez *et al.*, 1974) dealt with the effects of nutrition on maternal-infant interaction. The papers reaffirm the concept that in the cycle of stimulation of each other by baby and mother, food of adequate calorific value supplies the energy of the cycle, and, as the energy increases or falls according to food consumption, the child's development, his responsiveness, "intelligence" even and personality prosper or dwindle.

Assessement of the Mother Whose Child is Failing to Thrive

There is no standard mother. There are superlative mothers and poor mothers, and some between the two; all are normal. All need help at times and help of different kinds. Organic causes of failure to thrive are very common. The diagnosis that an infant is being affected by a mother's rejecting attitude, which may be only a bit of her and only a partial rejection, is set about with pitfalls. But, as stated at the outset in this paper, there are many fringe cases who without help may get worse. So the diagnosis must not be missed. Rejected children appear to have a passive acceptance of being half starved, though the grim possibility of unanswered cries of hunger remains in our minds.

Some of the criteria used as aids to identifying parents whose children are at risk of non-accidental injury are applicable and, with additions, the following list may prove helpful.

1. The mother herself had a very depriving background as a child, or all her life.
2. The paternity of child is in question.
3. The child is not of the marriage or of the co-habitation.
4. The child was not wanted in the first instance (termination refused or asked for too late).
5. The child is not of the wanted sex.
6. The mother is isolated from her relations and friends.
7. Crisis (financial, eviction, renewed pregnancy etc.) may precipitate physical injury to the child on top of the syndrome of deprivation; but this is a single event, whereas emotional deprivation and rejection are continuous.
8. The mother speaks about the child in a disparaging tone and denigrates him on all counts.
9. There is a character disorder in the mother (see below).
10. The child is scapegoated by the mother. The reasons for this are not easily accessible and lie deep in the mother's character (see 9).

The assessment of the mother's character disorder is not usually within the competence of workers outside the psychiatric discipline, even though in some cases the rejection is conscious and openly admitted. The following quotation from MacCarthy (1974b) gives some of the points.

The mothers of children with non-organic dwarfism have severe personal problems; yet they may be succeeding reasonably well with all their children except one, whom they reject. The rejection may have existed from the moment of conception. If not, then the mother's failure to respond to her baby may go back to the first few days, the first hours or even the first moment of seeing the newborn baby — a moment of truth for all parents, in which there are no defences against the impressions that reach the eye or ear and which may take instant and permanent root in the mind. Feelings of rejection at such a moment may be ineradicable.

The child may also at any time become a scapegoat in the mother's eyes because he reminds her of what she regards as bad or to be rejected in herself, in her husband or in the father of the child who is not her husband. Further reasons for hostility may be the child's responding better to the husband than to her, his mothering of the child becoming better than hers.

Mothers with character disorders have disturbed early histories and have often been rejected or ill-treated by their own mothers. They have an intense need to be taken care of. They have literal concrete thinking patterns and poor capacity for abstraction or looking into the future. A verbal approach is not useful in trying to help them; they feel criticized. Psychoneurotic mothers on the other hand are easier to help because they have insight. (Fischoff *et al.*, 1971).

Penetrating psychological exploration of a few mothers with children showing non-organic failure to thrive (Togut *et al.*, 1969) have shown in all of them the expression of profound emotional and physical deprivation, apparently extending back through their own early childhood. Also inability to perform on a level commensurate with their intelligence and "a self concept which is that of an extremely damaged and deprived individual, unworthy of the attention of others, seeking the support and approval of significant adult figures in their lives". They tend to fuse together sexuality and aggression and are concerned about the status of themselves in the eyes of their own parents, again harking back to their childhood. Contributions of the husbands of these women to family life were minimal.

On the other hand, fathers may show a deep feeling for the child. Why cannot they prevent what is happening? Perhaps because their contact with the child and opportunity for giving affection is too intermittent, or perhaps because they themselves are in a position of too great a dependence on this mother.

References

Apley, J., Davies, J., Russell Davis, D. and Silk, B. (1971). Dwarfism without apparent cause. *Proc. Roy. Soc. Med.* **64**, 135–138.

Brandon, S. (1970). Epidemiological study of eating disturbances. *J. Psychosomat. Res.* **14**, 253–257.

Chavez, A., Martinez, C. and Yaschine, T. (1975). Nutrition, behavioral development and mother–child interaction in young normal children. *Fed. Proc.* **34**, No. 7 (June).

Cravioto, J. and Delicardie, E. R. (1966). Nutrition, growth and neurointegrative development. *Pediatrics* **38** (suppl.), 319–372.

Fischoff, T., Whitton, C. F. and Pettit, M. G. (1971). Psychiatric study of mothers of infants with growth failure secondary to maternal deprivation. *J. Pediat.* **79**, 209–215.

Franklin, A. W. (1975). Personal communication.

Gardner, L. U. (1972). Deprivation dwarfism. *Scientific American* July, 76.

MacCarthy, D. (1974a). Physical effects and symptoms of the cycle of rejection. *Proc. Roy. Soc. Med.*, **67**, 35–39.

MacCarthy, D. (1974b). Effects of emotional disturbance and deprivation on somatic growth. *In* "Scientific Foundations of Paediatrics". Ed. J. A. Davis and J. Dobbing. William Heinemann Medical, London; Chapter 5, p 65.

MacCarthy, D. and Booth, E. M. (1970). Parental rejection and stunting of growth. *J. Psychosom. Res.* **14**, 259–265.

Pollit, E. (1975). Failure to thrive; socioeconomic, dietary intake and mother–child interaction data. *Fed. Proc.* **34**, 1593–1597.

Talbot, N. B., Sobel, E. H., Burke, B. S., Lindeman, E. and Kaufman, S. B. (1947). Dwarfism in healthy children: its possible relation to emotional, nutritional and endocrine disturbances. *New Engl. J. Med.* **263**, 783–793.

Togut, M. R., Allen, J. E. and Lelchuck, L. (1969). A psychological exploration of the nonorganic failure to thrive syndrome. *Develop. Med. Child Neurol.* **11**, 601–607.

Whitton, C. F., Pettit, M. G. and Fischoff, J. (1969). Evidence that growth failure from maternal deprivation is secondary to undereating. *J. Amer. Med. Ass.* **209**, 1675–1682.

Widdowson, E. M. (1951). Mental contentment and physical growth, *Lancet* **1**, 1316–1318.

For Discussion see p 157.

9. The Fate of Abused Children

Assessing the effects of the physical trauma,
the abusive environment and the
consequences of professional intervention

Carolyn Okell Jones

> Even without damage from trauma, even without the associated effects of poverty,
> parental mental illness, neglect, under-nutrition or deprivation, the child cannot be
> expected to thrive in a home in which fear of bodily harm is an unrelenting spectre. It
> has long been recognized that imagined fear of physical harm affects the developing
> psyche. Abused children live with a continual fear of harm, that is not a fantasy but an
> ever present reality. (Martin, Beezley, Conway and Kempe, 1974)

When we survey the rapidly increasing volume of world literature on
child abuse, it is striking how relatively few publications have focused
on the experiences and development of the surviving affected children
and their treatment needs. Yet, on reflection, it is very understandable.
In the decade following the publication of Kempe's (1962) classic
article on The Battered Child Syndrome, which drew attention to its
high mortality rate and the associated brain injury, the main concern
was to protect the child from lethal physical harm, and the main thrust
of professional intervention was directed towards life-saving procedures. Emphasis was placed on clinical manifestations in order to
improve diagnosis, on the dynamics of the abusive parents in relation
to the type of psychiatric and social work treatment that they could use
with benefit, and on the complex legal issues. Regarding the children,
the tendency was to make theoretical generalizations about their
development and to stereotype them in terms of their characteristics
and behaviour on the basis of early anecdotal data. Although clinical
observations suggested that many of the children were considerably
damaged, emotionally as well as physically, by the time they came to
professional attention, direct work with the children was, in the main,
neglected. Also overlooked, when their physical safety was so much at
stake, was the potentially damaging effect on the children's personality
and emotional development, of separating them from their parents,

placing them in hospital often for extended periods and moving them from one caretaker to another.

Some Follow-up Studies

It is only now, in the second decade of child-abuse research, that professionals have begun to ask, "for what are we saving these children and what is the quality of their subsequent life?" The depressing data from follow-up studies on the neurologic, cognitive, social and emotional development of abused children have prompted us to acknowledge that there is an urgent need to broaden our therapeutic goals.

The literature shows that common sampling problems have been met by most of the researchers conducting follow-up studies of children diagnosed as abused. Abusive families are difficult to trace because of their frequently high mobility rate; parents resist evaluation of their children; the children may have died or been placed far away from their families of origin in institutions or adoptive or foster homes. While the morbidity in children who are traced has been shown to be serious, one feels even more pessimistic about the fate of many of the other children, who were not available for study, as they are likely to be living in considerably worse environments with minimal or no professional intervention.

Other methodological problems associated with the follow-up studies include failure to employ matched comparison groups, so that the findings may be skewed by uncontrollable variables such as social class, and failure to document the type of intervention the families have received. Methods of assessing the children vary from study to study, some researchers having used a range of formal psychological and developmental tests, whereas others have relied mainly on clinical impressionistic data.

This paper gives an overview but no detailed consideration of the follow-up studies of abused children. Some of the complex issues inherent in assessing the consequences of physical abuse and the need to scrutinize our therapeutic options in terms of their effect on the children's development will be examined. A masterly review of much of the existing literature on the development of abused children has been made by Martin and his colleagues (1974) and reported together with their own findings on the physical and intellectual functioning of 58 children, a mean 4.5 years after identified abuse.

Available data clearly show that abused children are at high risk for damage to the central nervous system and maldevelopment of ego function. Severe brain damage, mental retardation, speech problems growth failure and emotional disturbance are documented with depressing frequency (Elmer, 1967; Elmer and Gregg, 1967; Birrell and Birrell, 1968; Johnson and Morse, 1968; Terr, 1970; Martin, 1972; Martin and Beezley, 1976; Sandgrund *et al.*, 1974; Morse *et al.*, 1970; Baldwin and Oliver, 1975). However, there are conflicting findings on the extent to which such physical or developmental deviations antedate abuse and are of a congenital nature or are the result of rearing in an abusive environment.

The hard data from follow-up studies relate chiefly to mortality and significant intellectual and neuromotor handicap, whereas the psychological damage sustained by the children has in the main been the subject of speculation. For example, Green (1968) postulates that early physical abuse which occurs in a matrix of overall rejection and stimulus deprivation may enhance the development of pain dependent behaviour. The children may become accident prone, indulge in self-destructive behaviour or establish a pattern of inviting harm and playing the victim. Other writers have emphasized the tendency of the children to identify with aggressive parents and pattern themselves on the parents' behaviour. Clinical experience suggests that the young child, physically-abused at a pre-verbal stage of development, is particularly prone to develop violent behaviour as a character trait (Galdston, 1975). The most detailed study of the emotional development of abused children to date has been completed by Martin and Beezley (1976). The nine characteristics and behaviours noted with impressive frequency and intensity in the 50 children studied, included:

1. impaired ability for enjoyment,
2. behavioural adjustment symptoms,
3. low self-esteem,
4. withdrawal,
5. opposition,
6. hypervigilance,
7. compulsivity,
8. pseudo-adult behaviour,
9. school learning problems.

Over 50% of these abused children had poor self-concepts, were sorrowful children and exhibited a number of symptomatic behaviours which made peers, parents and teachers reject them.

A few studies of the siblings of the presenting children indicate that they are also at risk of physical abuse, be they older or younger, and they often appear as deviant in their functioning as the child identified as abused (Johnson and Morse, 1968; Skinner and Castle, 1969; Baldwin and Oliver, 1975; Smith and Hanson, 1974; Baher *et al.*, 1976). The children seem to have few healthy ways of adapting to the abusive environment, but variations in the inherent equipment of the child, which determines his capacity to adapt to these stresses, warrant further exploration.

Malone (1966) has noted that children living in dangerous environments (including danger of abuse from their parents) have certain areas of "hypertrophied" ego functioning, areas of advanced ability. These include role reversal with parents, such as making decisions for them or taking care of younger siblings. Such "precocious" behaviour is reinforced by the parents. While the child's ability to cope and his areas of hypertrophied ego strength are highly adaptive and assets to survival, they are weaknesses insofar as they contribute to the child's literalness and inflexibility. Similarly, Martin and Beezley (1976), out of their total sample of 50 abused children, identified a group of 10 pseudo-adult children who demonstrated marked compulsivity. Both groups tended to have a high frustration tolerance and were attentive and cooperative in the testing situation. Martin and Beezley stress that, although these behaviours appeared to be more successful modes of adaptation, they are not necessarily healthy ways of coping.

The compulsive and pseudo-adult children were locked into styles which are not conducive to age appropriate enjoyment or flexibility. Compulsivity, by definition, connotes rigidity and inflexibility. The pseudo-adult child has forfeited his right to feel and act like a child, planning his life instead for the pleasure of adults rather than for himself.

The above examples describe the behavioural characteristics of a small group of children who appear to have learnt certain adaptive coping mechanisms in order to survive in dangerous environments, but at considerable cost to themselves. However, we can no longer assume that the abusive environment results in either a specific personality or a neurologic profile. Too much variation between abused children has now been shown for such a simplistic cause and effect relationship to be accepted. Some abused children have been observed to be passive, withdrawn, unresponsive and apathetic, while others present themselves as being hyperactive, aggressive, attention seeking and extremely provocative (Baher *et al.*, 1976; Martin and Beezley, 1976). Some, with extremely high intelligence, do well at school, but they more commonly have school learning problems (Martin *et al.*, 1974; Martin and Beezley, 1976).

The Sequelae Analysed

Apart from continuing to identify common sequelae of abuse, the researcher's main present task is to ascertain to what extent these are sequelae:

1. of the physical trauma *per se*;

2. of other malevolent environmental influences of the kind frequently associated with abuse, each of which is already known to have the potential to impair and disrupt the growing child's development. These include under-nutrition, emotional and physical neglect, social and/or economic disadvantage, emotional disturbance in the parents and family instability;

3. of professonal intervention and treatment planning.

The following discussion illustrates how difficult this identification is.

Physical Trauma

Physical trauma may itself be the cause of the child's neurological handicap. Considerable variation has been noted in the type and severity of neurologic damage sustained by abused children. Martin *et at*. (1974) report that, as expected, neurological dysfunction is highly related to I.Q. and a history of head trauma. However, he emphasizes that some children with serious head injury were not retarded and that significant neurologic dysfunction occurred in 16 children with no explanation of the cause and no documented history of head trauma. They offer three possible explanations: (a) that, as indicated by the study of Baron *et al*. (1970), neurologic findings that quickly disappear after hospitalization suggest that neurologic dysfunction may be an adaptation to the abusive environment; (b) that there may be undetected trauma to the cranium after repeated assaults for which the child has never received medical attention; and (c) that, as reported by Caffey (1972), the child may have been shaken violently, with swelling of the brain or scattered petechiae as the end result, but no skeletal abnormalities or subdural fluid collections. Caffey (1974) further states that habitual and prolonged whiplash shaking of an infant may produce a syndrome which is first noticed

at school age when minor idiopathic cerebral motor defects are first detected along with minor idiopathic mental retardation. Permanent impairments of vision and hearing may also be identified at this time for the first time when the children are 5–6 years of age.

The physical trauma itself may affect the children's subsequent emotional development. Martin and Beezley's data (1976) do not confirm any relationship between the type of injury nor the age at which it was inflicted with subsequent emotional development. On the other hand psychiatric symptoms were significantly correlated 4.5 years after abuse with environmental factors such as the impermanence of the subsequent home, instability of the family with whom the child was living, punitiveness and rejection by caretakers, and the emotional state of the parents or parent surrogates.

Other Malevolent Environmental Influences Frequently Associated with Abuse

Undernutrition   Undernutrition was present in approximately 30–35% of abused children at the time abuse was recognized (Elmer, 1967; Birrell and Birrell, 1968; Martin, 1972). Martin *et al.* (1974) refer to convincing evidence that undernutrition during the first year of life can and does result in permanent effects on the nervous system, including motor dysfunction and mental impairment; and in older children may reduce the child's ability to focus on, orient to or sustain interest in learning tasks. Irritability, fatigue, lassitude and perceptual deficiencies have also been documented in undernourished children. Martin's (1972) report of 42 abused children as well as Elmer's (1967) report indicate a significant difference in intellectual prognosis when undernourished, abused children were compared with well nourished, abused children. It appears that children who are undernourished as well as physically abused have a much poorer prognosis in terms of mental function and neurological integrity.

Social and economic disadvantage   While child abuse occurs in all social classes, low socio-economic families predominate. Elmer's recent (1975) follow-up study of abused and accidentally injured children 8 years after their referral to the X-ray department of The Children's Hospital, Pittsburgh, strongly suggests that lower-class membership, with all its concomitant disadvantages and stresses, is more potent than abuse for the subsequent development of the children. The majority of the children came from social classes IV and V and a matched comparison group was employed. When pertinent demographic variables were taken into account, few overall differences were found between abused, accident and comparison children. Among the characteristics examined were health, language development, intellectual status in school, self-conception and behaviour. The majority showed some degree of emotional disturbance and many had language difficulties, and the incidence of allergies in the total sample was unexpectedly high. The abused children differed significantly from their peers only in weight (they were heavier) and in some measures of impulsivity and aggression. Clinical impressions supported the absence of substantial differences between the abused children and their matched comparisons. No one group of families stood out; the majority appeared chaotic and poorly organized, many parents relied upon drugs or alcohol, and most were living in circumstances of daily violence. Overall the children had an air of depression, sadness and anxiety. In many spontaneous stories told to the examiners, the children showed greated concern that they might become the victims of attack. Unlike most children of their age, they linked their fears of injury or mutilation to real persons (such as parents, older children or school teachers), not to fantasy figures.

Elmer concludes,

the use of matched comparison groups to evaluate the outcome for abused children offers a means to correct conclusions based on the study of abused children alone. Validation of the results of this study await similar controlled investigations, using a larger number of subjects living in other communities.

Professional Intervention and Treatment Planning

Another basis for the varying effects of abuse is related to what happens after physical abuse. Hospitalization, separation from parents, frequent home changes and poor quality foster homes or institutional placements may be more damaging to the child than the physical trauma itself. Martin and Beezley (1974) discuss how professional intervention and treatment planning often contribute to the abused children's difficulty in developing a sense of object constancy or a concept of self. In Martin and Beezley's study (1976), 17 children (34%) had from three to eight home changes from the time of identified abuse to follow up (mean of 4.5 years). The more seriously maladjusted the child, the more likely he was to have had three or more home changes. Similarly the more maladjusted a child was, the more likely he was to have perceived his present home as lacking permanence. They comment,

there is no data to show that any of these study children had been physically injured in foster homes but we know that, in foster care, they are frequently subjected to inappropriate discipline, indifference, rejection or seductiveness. Moreover, efforts to reunite the family may prevent consideration of the optimal home placement for the child in foster care. Many children were placed back with their parents on a trial basis repeatedly.

Baher *et al.* (1976) emphasize the urgent need for information on the relative merits of various types of protective placements for abused children in comparison with the home environment. They describe the difficulties that arise when choice of placement is governed, not only by the extent to which it will meet the child's emotional needs, but also by the extent to which it will encourage and enhance the parent–child relationship. They comment that

with hindsight, we now feel that in several cases, the child's interest might have been better served if the focus of our intervention had been on helping the parents to accept permanent separation rather than on working towards rehabilitation.

Baher *et al.* (1976) also note that disrupted caretaking featured prominently in the childhood of many of the abusive parents studied.

Besides considering the possible damaging effects on the child of professional intervention, what needs examining is the extent to which such intervention is capable of improving the abusive home environment. The intervention by many child protective agencies still seems concentrated on the prevention of recurrence of physical assault with little attention to improvement of the home environment. As soon as the initial investigation is completed and the home seems reasonably safe from the standpoint of physical abuse, professionals tend to decrease their visits and support. However, the few studies that have attempted to evaluate progress in families in relation to the type of therapeutic intervention, that they have experienced, suggest that even intensive long term treatment programmes have had little impact so far on what could be termed the emotionally abusive home atmosphere and relationships which exist in many cases.

In 1970, Morse *et al.* reported a follow-up study of 25 children who had been hospitalized 3 years previously for injuries or illnesses judged to be sequelae of abuse or gross neglect. During that 3 year period, one third of the children were again neglected or abused. The data from this study are discouraging. Only 29% of the children were within normal limits, intellectually and emotionally, at the time of the follow-up; 42% were considered mentally retarded and 28% were significantly emotionally disturbed. Ten out of 19 children were below the tenth percentile in height and weight. The study attempted to relate the degree of agency intervention to the status of the abused children at the time of the follow-up study. No pattern of relationships could be found. The authors comment that "neither the amount of time nor skill expended by agency workers and nurses was predictive of how well the children progressed." In fact the only characteristic common to the majority of children who appeared to be developing normally was a good mother–child relationship *as perceived and reported by the mothers.* Additional data from Morse's study suggest that the milieu of the abused child and more specifically the parents' perception of the child are critical influences on the child's development.

Martin and Beezley (1976) also consider the relationship between the therapy received by the abusing parents and the subsequent developmental status of the abused child. They report that almost half of the parents of the 50 children in their study received psychotherapy. Ninety per cent of these parents had their previously injured child home with them at the time of the follow-up. Ten of the 21 children whose parents received psychotherapy were seriously reinjured. The children had been prematurely returned home from the hospital or foster home before an effective psychotherapeutic programme for the parents could be established. The incidence of current excessive physical punishment and/or hostile rejection in these homes remained strikingly high. Even though the children were not being battered in the technical or legal sense, 68% were experiencing rejection, as children who were the usually excessively punished. The authors comment: "It was much easier to assess negative interaction between parent and child than to determine how much positive interaction had taken place at home." Furthermore, almost half of these parents were still unable to provide a stable home for their child. As already stated in this study, instability of the home and punitiveness and rejection by caretakers were amongst the factors relating to the severity and frequency of psychiatric symptoms in the child. Elsewhere, Martin *et al.* (1974) noted that even the intelligence of abused children, when brain damage was controlled for, correlated quite highly with the subsequent stability and punitiveness of the home.

Baher *et al.* (1976) have evaluated the progress made in families referred to the Battered Child Research Department of the N.S.P.C.C., after a substantial period of intensive therapeutic intervention. This was of value to the abusive parents, and improvements in several aspects of family functioning are reported. Also the supportive intensive care provided was, in the main, associated with the absence of rebattering or a reduction in its probable severity. The findings on the cognitive development of the children are encouraging. They show that the Department's system of care helped to restore the child's overall developmental status in most cases, with those in the special therapeutic day nursery showing the greatest improvement of all. However, personality tests on the children administered after a period of casework with their families and nursery care for the children reveal a long term distortion in the child's relationship with the mother, which appears to be less amenable to change. This was substantiated by the fact that only slight positive changes were noted in most aspects of parent–child interaction, leaving many doubts about the effectiveness of the treatment service in improving the quality of parenting. The majority of the children were living in homes where empathy and sensitivity to their needs were still lacking, where inconsistent, harsh discipline remained the mode, where parental expectations remained inappropriately high and where little positive reinforcement took place.

At the time of the final evaluation, four children were described as "pale and deprived looking", generally underweight, undernourished and somewhat lethargic. They displayed varying degrees of withdrawal and anxiety in their behaviour, especially when with their parents. Most of the remaining children seemed to fall into two groups, the introverts and the extroverts.

The introverts were children who at the time of referral had seemed withdrawn, controlled, wary and generally lacking in energy and interest. Now they appeared healthy, but delicate, fairly sprightly and spontaneous, aware of themselves and sensitive to their surroundings and people. A few of these children showed traits of obsessive neatness in their behaviour, wariness of their parents and perhaps an over-eager compliance and willingness to please others. They seemed to be "holding in" their feelings, but the appearance of recurrent problems such as enuresis, food refusal and sleeplessness, suggested that these were highly sensitive and anxious children.

The extroverted group consisted of robust, hyperactive and clumsy children, careless of personal danger in the environment and often prone to accidents. Some were aggressive or destructive, uncontrollable and prone to temper tantrums. They were easily frustrated and distractable and unable to involve themselves with others. Interaction with groups of children or their parents tended to trigger this reckless, violent behaviour which seemed imitative of their parents or siblings. Though many of these children had shown similar characteristics at the time of referral, few developed them at a later stage. Some children were already presenting behaviour problems at school.

In the authors' estimation, only 8 out of 23 children seemed to be making reasonably satisfactory and sustained emotional development. Of the remainder, a few had serious emotional problems which caused grave anxiety about their future development. A few were like weathervanes who reflected the moods of their parents by regressing or displaying disturbances when the home situation was particularly stressful. The authors comment:

". . . we now feel that our dual and interlinked emphasis on treatment of the parents and protection of the children, neglected an important area, the psychotherapeutic treatment of the children, which could well be provided in a day care setting."

Implications for Future Therapeutic Intervention on Behalf of Abused Children

It is apparent from the material presented in this paper that abused children (and frequently their siblings) undergo considerable physical and emotional suffering and that their proper development is impaired in a variety of ways for a variety of reasons. We have far to go in devising methods of intervention that will improve the quality of life for these children. In future, professionals must concern themselves with the needs and rights of the child in a broader context than that of physical safety. We must try to find ways of counteracting other malevolent aspects of home life which result in emotional disorder, inhibited intellectual capacity and a propensity to resort to violence in adult life (Curtis, 1963; Silver *et al.*, 1969; Steele, 1970).

The need for child abuse treatment programmes, to include a comprehensive developmental assessment (including a psychiatric assessment) of all battered children at the time abuse is diagnosed, cannot be over emphasized. Only then can their special needs be recognized and appropriate services be provided. Subsequently, all abused children should be required to be kept under periodic review by medical, psychological and social work staff so that their development can be closely monitored. Longitudinal studies of a cross-disciplinary nature, which such a review would provide, would enable assessment to be made of the long term effects of various types of treatment procedure.

We can no longer cling to the assumption that treatment of the parents will improve the quality of life and relationships for the child. Direct work with the children is essential since their whole personality organization is endangered. Some children may benefit from short term professional help to deal with the immediate stress of physical injury, hospitalization, separation from parents and placement with substitute caretakers. Other abused children will undoubtedly require more intensive therapy to assist them with persistent and deep-seated problems. For example, they may need help in improving their self-concept, in dealing with their own anger, in loosening their inhibitions and in learning to enjoy age-appropriate pleasures, that adults can be trusted and that love is not always conditional on the gratification of adult needs.

Bearing in mind the acute shortage of child psychiatrists and psychotherapists, play therapists and social workers skilled in communicating with young children, we must enlist other personnel, such as experienced nursery nurses and carefully selected, sensitive foster parents, to help meet these children's needs. At the same time, the stress on those workers who become involved in the treatment of the children and are able to share in the horror and pain that many of these child clients have experienced, should not be overlooked. They, in turn, need regular support and consultation themselves.

Ideally, the workers treating the parents and those involved in providing therapeutic day care for the children should be based under the same roof. Galdston (1975), Ten Broeck (1974), Ounsted *et al.* (1975) have discussed the great value of special day or residential family centres in which a multi-faceted treatment programme can be offered. For example, this may include individual and/or group therapy for the parents, parent self-help groups, specific therapeutic attention for individual children in a day-care setting and joint play therapy sessions for parents and children. This kind of setting also helps to facilitate close communication and mutual support between all staff involved in the treatment process.

Dr Ruth Kempe (1975) has compared the merits of individual and group psychotherapy for the pre-school battered child. She describes the difficulties of engaging pre-school children in individual therapy, not the least being parental resistance. She finds group therapy in a therapeutic nursery setting easier to arrange and more appropriate for this age range. Individual therapy is often more suitable for the school-age child for two reasons. First, the school-age child is already used to coping with two environments and making the shift from one to the other. Abused children have also learnt to cope with this difference in structure of their relationships and environment. Second, school-age children are more able to verbalize, are more aware of their difficulties and are perhaps better motivated towards treatment.

The parents also need direct education in alternative methods of child rearing (Paulson and Chaleff, 1973; Savino and Saunders, 1973; Smith *et al.*, 1973), and Baher *et al.* (1976) stress the need for this to follow the establishment of parental trust and co-operation. Jeffrey (1975) reports useful practical techniques for changing parent–child interaction in families of children at risk under three main headings: interventions to change the negative quality of general interaction between children and caregivers, interventions to change attitudes, and interventions to change the child's responses.

Another therapeutic option, which should be considered more frequently than it is at present from the outset in child abuse cases, is permanent separation of the child from his family. One of the provisions of the Children Act 1975, which came into force on 1st January 1976, is of particular relevance, bringing in, as additional ground for dispensing with parental agreement to adoption, that the parent or guardian has seriously ill-treated the child and, because of the ill-treatment, or for other reasons, the rehabilitation of the child within the household of the parent or guardian is unlikely.

While it is impossible to lay down rigorous rules of thumb regarding decisions over permanent removal, the need in some cases remains not only to ensure the child's safety but also to facilitate his development in the broadest sense.

Only if decisions about separation are made early in the casework, can frequent disruptions of caretaking for the children be avoided. Of help here would be the setting up of more residential assessment centres, similar to the one described by Lynch *et al.* (1975), where the whole family could be intensively observed in a safe place over a period of weeks or months. The family's response to treatment and capacity for change could then be evaluated as well as the quality of parent–child interaction.

In conclusion, it has to be acknowledged that the detailed study of the phenomenon of child abuse forces us to consider uncomfortable issues relating to the status and treatment of children in the population at large. Regardless of whether they have been physically abused, many children, who may never come to professional attention are living in sub-optimal environments and experiencing the kind of inadequate parenting described in this paper, which could permanently impair and disrupt their development. Abused children as a group are currently the focus of much public and professional concern in many different countries. It is to be hoped that by devoting considerable attention and resources to them and their families, we shall learn more about preventing the transmission of all kinds of damaging patterns of child rearing from one generation to the next.

Acknowledgement

I would like to acknowledge the work of Harold Martin as an invaluable source of inspiration and data for this paper. I would also like to thank the secretarial staff of the National Children's Bureau for their assistance in preparing this manuscript.

References

Baher, E., Hyman, C., Jones, C., Jones, R., Kerr, A. and Mitchell, R. (1976). "At Risk: an account of the work of the Battered Child Research Dept., N.S.P.C.C.". Routledge and Kegan Paul, London.

Baldwin, J. A. and Oliver, J. E. (1975). Epidemiology and family characteristics of severely-abused children. *Brit. J. Prev. Soc. Med.* **29**, 205–221.

Baron, M. A., Bejar, R. L. and Sheaff, P. J. (1970). Neurologic manifestations of the battered child syndrome. *Pediatrics* **45**, 1003–1007.

Birrell, R. G. and Birrell, J. H. W. (1968). The maltreatment syndrome in children; a hospital survey. *Med. J. Aust.* **2**, 1023–1029.

Caffey, J. (1972). On the theory and practice of shaking infants: its potential residual effects of permanent brain damage and mental retardation. *Amer. J. Dis. Child.* **124**, 161–169.

Caffey, J. (1974). The whiplash shaken infant syndrome: manual shaking by the extremities with whiplash-induced intracranial and intraocular bleedings, linked with residual permanent brain damage and mental retardation. *Pediatrics* **54**, 396–403.

Curtis, G. C. (1963). Violence breeds violence — perhaps? *Amer. J. Psychiat.* **120**, 386–387.

Elmer, E. (1967). "Children in Jeopardy". University of Pittsburgh Press, Pittsburgh.

Elmer, E. (1975). A follow-up study of traumatized children. Paper presented at the Annual meeting of the American Association of Psychiatric Services for Children, New Orleans, Louisiana.

Elmer, E. and Gregg, G. S. (1967). Developmental characteristics of abused children. *Pediatrics* **40**, 596–602.

Galdston, R. (1975). Preventing the abuse of little children. *Amer. J. Orthopsychiat.* **45**, 372–381.

Green, A. H. (1968). Self-destructive behaviour in physically abused schizophrenic children. *Arch. Gen. Psychiat.* **19**, 171–179.

Jeffrey, M. (1975). Therapeutic intervention for children at risk and their parents. Proceedings of the First National Australian Conference on the Battered Child. Mnt. Lawley Teachers College, Perth.

Johnson, B. and Morse, H. A. (1968). "The Battered Child: a study of children with inflicted injuries". Denver Dept. of Welfare.

Kempe, C. H., Silverman, F. N., Steele, B. F., Droegemueller, W. and Silver, H. K. (1962). The Battered Child Syndrome. *J. Amer. Med. Ass.* **181**, 17–24.

Kempe, R. (1975). Individual and group psychotherapy of the pre-school battered child. Proceedings of the First National Australian Conference on the Battered Child. Mnt. Lawley Teachers College, Perth.

Lynch, M., Steinberg, D. and Ounsted, C. (1975). Family unit in a children's psychiatric hospital. *Brit. Med. J.* **2**, 127–129.

Malone, C. A. (1966). Safety first: comments on the influence of external danger in the lives of disorganized families. *Amer. J. Orthopsychiat.* **36**, 3–12.

Martin, H. P. (1972). The child and his development. *In* "Helping the Battered Child and His Family". Ed. C. H. Kempe and R. E. Helfer. Lippincott, Philadelphia and Toronto.

Martin, H. P., Beezley, P., Conway, E. F. and Kempe, C. H. (1974). The development of abused children. *In* "Advances in Pediatrics". Ed. I. Schulman. Year Book Medical, Chicago; Vol. 21, pp 25–73.

Martin, H. P. and Beezley, P. (1974). Prevention and the consequences of child abuse. *J. Operat. Psychiat.* **6**, 68–77.

Martin, H. P. and Beezley, P. (1976). The emotional development of abused children. *Develop. Med. Child Neurol.* (in press).

Morse, C. W., Sahler, O. J. Z. and Friedman, S. B. (1970). A three-year follow-up study of abused and neglected children. *Amer. J. Dis. Child.* **120**, 439–446.

Ounsted, C., Oppenheimer, R. and Lindsay, J. (1975). The psychopathology and psychotherapy of the families: aspects of bonding failure. *In* "Concerning Child Abuse". Ed. A. W. Franklin. Churchill Livingstone, Edinburgh.

Paulson, M. J. and Chaleff, A. (1973). Parent surrogate roles: a dynamic concept in understanding and treating abusive parents. *J. Clin. Child Psychol.* **11**, 38–40.

Sandgrund, A., Gaines, R. W. and Green, A. H. (1974). Child abuse and mental retardation: a problem of cause and effect. *Amer. J. Ment. Defic.* **79**, 327–330.

Savino, A. B. and Saunders, R. W. (1973). Working with abusive parents: group therapy and home visits. *Amer. J. Nurs.* **73**, 482–484.

Silver, L. B., Dublin, C. A. and Lourie, R. S. (1969). Does violence breed violence? Contributions from a study of the Child Abuse Syndrome. *Amer. J. Psychiat.* **126**, 404–407.

Skinner, A. E. and Castle, R. L. (1969). "78 Battered Children: a retrospective study". N.S.P.C.C., London.

Smith, S. M., Hanson, R. and Noble, S. (1973). Parents of battered babies: a controlled study. *Brit. Med. J.* **4**, 388–391.

Smith, S. M. and Hanson, R. (1974). 134 battered children: a medical and psychological study. *Brit. Med. J.* **3**, 666–670.

Steele, B. F. (1970). Violence in our society. *Pharos of Alpha Omega Alpha* **33**, 2, 42–48.

Ten Broeck, E. (1974). The extended family center. A home away from home for abused children and their parents. *Children Today* **3**, 2–6.

Terr, L. (1970). A family study of child abuse. *Amer. J. Psychiat.* **127**, 125–131.

For Discussion see p 157.

10. Deprivation by Neglect of Children Aged 11–16 Years

Joanna Shapland
Anne Campbell

John Wilson, Assistant Commissioner, Crime, Metropolitan Police District, when discussing the figures for crime during 1975, said that one of the biggest problems for the police was the rising incidence of juvenile crime. His message to the families of children in trouble was: "Take a little more care with your property and family. Know where your kids are. The number of parents who turn up at the police station, for the first time, to find that their children are already known to the police, is terrible" (*Guardian*, March 11, 1976). Perhaps one of the greatest social problems in Britain today is the deprivation by neglect of children, and particularly of adolescents. The neglectful parents do not know or do not care what their children are doing, where they are or who they are with. They may not care about their school progress or even whether they are clothed or fed properly.

During our work on adolescents on a housing estate outside a town, we have noticed associations between this syndrome of deprivation by neglect by parents and the behaviour and activities of the children. The causal direction of this interaction is not known, but we have attempted to describe and quantify some aspects of the interaction as seen from the point of view of the child. We have also attempted to find the views of the staff of the school involved, particularly those of the counsellor. The research may only be considered as an exploratory study but, as little systematic work has been published on adolescents' views of their background in Britain, it may produce some hypotheses for more intensive study in the future.

First, we shall describe the area in which the study was done, the samples taken and the methodology used. We shall then describe the activities of the adolescents in the area, including their delinquent activities. Some findings on perceived home background will then be presented and finally we shall consider the view of the school personnel on the subject.

The Area

The housing estate is five miles from the city centre and was built in the early 1960s. At that time it was the only large area of new council accommodation in the city and so was filled mostly by young married couples with small children. It now consists of two fifteen storey tower blocks (comprising 120 flats) set in the middle of a large area of mostly two or four bedroomed houses. It also includes two-bedroomed flats and maisonettes and both private and council accommodation for old people. The estate, however, primarily gains its character from the 1857 houses and maisonettes, a considerable percentage of which are occupied by employees of the nearby car plant. There are also about 15 shops, two public houses, a community centre and an inter-denominational church. Although facilities for young children are quite good, play areas and green spaces being scattered throughout the estate, there are very few facilities for older children. Many complaints have been made about older children congregating outside the small area containing the community centre, shops and public houses and also being rowdy on the younger children's areas and the areas for organized games. This may improve soon as an adventure playground and football pitches are being constructed by the children themselves under the aegis of the community association and the council.

There are three primary and middle schools serving the co-educational school in which the present study was done. This changed from a secondary modern school to a comprehensive upper school (13–18 years) during the period of the study. The remand home used in the present study was situated approximately 5 miles from the housing estate on the outskirts of the town. Its maximum capacity is 12 girls at any one time, the duration of the girls' stay being not in excess of 3 months. The girls' ages range between 14.6 and 16 years. All the girls came from modern housing estates either within the town or in surrounding towns.

The Samples

Over the last three years, we have been looking at the activities of 11–16 year-old children from this area and the way in which their activities are related to their perceived home background. The first author has taken a sample of 54 boys from the first and second years of the secondary school on the estate. They were aged between 11.1 and 12.9 years at the time of first testing and were followed up for a period of $2\frac{1}{2}$

years. This was part of a wider study of personality and delinquency in schoolboys. The second author took an initial sample of 105 girls (average age 16.2 years) from the same secondary school as the boys ($N = 66$) and from a local remand home ($N = 39$).

The Methodology — Self-report Interviews and Questionnaires

Before looking at specific aspects of the life of these children and how this relates to their background and to the decisions made by official agencies about them, it is necessary to discuss the techniques that we have used to investigate them and also to give a general picture of the activities of the children at different ages. The main technique that we have used is self-report semi-structural interviews or questionnaires, in which the children were asked about specific episodes in their life such as delinquent acts or about their reactions to their family and friends. Using this technique, it is possible to compare the child's perception of events with official agencies' perceptions. For example, it is interesting to see whether the agency's perception of a child as in need of care and protection corresponds to the child perceiving his family as neglecting him or being openly aggressive to him. Although official definitions such as criminal convictions or being taken into care might be seen as being more objective and perhaps more valid, we would submit that the use of self-report techniques is more valuable when looking at the activities and home background of children at this age. For delinquency, for example, the number of official convictions that a child may obtain by the age of 15 or 16 is very small, whereas the number of delinquent acts that he admits (acts that would be defined as criminal by a court were he to be prosecuted) may be large. If the problem were only one of too small numbers of convictions to obtain significant results in a study, then we might overcome this by using a larger sample of children. There is, however, considerable evidence that at each stage in the criminal justice system, discretion is employed by the official agencies concerned as to whether the child should proceed further in the system. Hence, the police do not report all offences that they see committed, and whether a child is even questioned on the street has been shown in New York to depend upon his style of dress, manner of walking and way of speech (Piliavin and Briar, 1964). The social class of a youth will influence whether he is booked after a police contact (Dentler and Monroe, 1961). There is no reason to believe that such biases are not present in this country. The problem is particularly severe with adolescents, as they may be formally cautioned by the police rather than being prosecuted. The police take into account their impression of the home background as well as the seriousness of the offence in making this decision.

A self-report study has several other benefits. It abolishes, for example, the artificial dichotomy between delinquents and non-delinquents by which the latter are presumed entirely "innocent" and allows for the formation of a scale of delinquency on which the involvement of an individual in delinquency may be measured on a continuous scale. It also means that, if a random sample of the population is taken for the administration of self-report methods, there is no problem with adequacy of controls. Most importantly, it allows for the study of the background to the activities of the boy. Official records are notoriously uneven in the information they provide on the background of the boy or on, for example, the background and factors leading up to the commission of delinquent acts (Belson and Hood, 1967). A self-report study allows for supplementary questions to be asked, for example, whether activities were committed in a group or alone and whether they were suggested by the child himself or by others. It also enables a general picture to be built up of the pattern of activities in the area.

Of course, self-report studies have their own methodological problems and difficulties. Here one may separate out those studies investigating attitudes to the home and friends from those looking at specific past activities of the person such as delinquent acts. For the first, the main problems are those of making the questions intelligible, of assuring individual confidentiality and of trying to see that the questions mean the same to the different respondents. In the present studies, this was achieved by preliminary discussions with children in which the idea of the study was explained, and it was stressed that they participated entirely voluntarily and that it would not be possible to identify them in any material that would be made available to outsiders. Considerable pilot work on the wording of the questions was also done.

The second kind of study, of specific past activities, raises more serious problems of reliability and validity. In our studies, the only technique of this type used was the self-report delinquency questionnaire. For both girls and boys, the items used in this were those used in the Cambridge Study of Delinquent Development (West and Farrington, 1973) with minor modifications such as the changing of some of the wording to make it more natural and the removal of some of the items as they would not be intelligible or applicable to such young children (such as obtaining money under false pretences or stealing goods from employers). In all, 27 delinquent items covering most of the criminal activities by children of this age were used in the individual interview given to the boys at ages 11–12, and a further 5 more serious offences added in the retest interview given at the age of 14–15. The girls were given 43 items when tested aged 16. The items

Table 1
Self-reported delinquency admission rates in %

	Boys aged 11/12 N = 54	Boys aged 13/14 N = 52	Boys either age N = 52	All girls N = 105	Remand home girls N = 39	School girls N = 66	Boys West and Farrington (1973); age 16/17 N = 409
I have ridden a bicycle without lights after dark	78.18	96.08	100.00	65.7	61.5	68.2	88.3
I have driven a car or motor bike/scooter under 16	NI	43.14	—	38.0	48.7	31.8	43.5
I have been with a group who go round together making a row and sometimes getting into fights and causing disturbances	63.64	45.10	64.71	36.1	71.8	15.2	31.1
I have played truant from school	34.55	52.94	58.82	80.0	94.9	71.2	82.2
I have travelled on a train or bus without a ticket or deliberately paid the wrong fare	69.09	72.55	80.39	68.5	79.5	62.1	89.5
I have let off fireworks in the street	50.91	60.78	68.63	23.8	33.3	18.2	93.2
I have taken money from home without returning it	27.27	21.57	31.57	44.7	59.0	36.4	17.1
I have taken someone else's car or motorbike for a joy ride and returned it afterwards	NI	13.73	—	12.4	28.2	3.0	18.3
I have broken or smashed things in public places like on the street, in cinemas, dance halls, on trains or buses	29.09	45.10	50.98	19.0	28.2	13.6	25.4
I have insulted people on the street or got them angry and fought with them	58.18	58.82	70.59	31.4	59.0	15.2	35.9

Statement							
I have broken into a big store or garage or warehouse	NI		} —	5.7	12.8	1.5	9.5
I have broken into a little shop even though I may not have taken anything	}	7.84	}	4.8	10.2	1.5	12.7
I have taken something out of a car	7.27	9.80	11.76	12.4	28.2	3.0	14.2
I have taken a weapon (like a knife) out with me in case I needed it in a fight	NI	52.94	—	14.3	25.6	7.6	35.0
I have fought with someone in a public place like in the street or at a dance	45.45	37.25	56.86	35.2	61.5	19.7	32.8
I have broken the window of an empty house	43.64	49.02	60.78	32.4	38.5	28.8	82.2
I have used a weapon in a fight, like a knife or a razor or a broken bottle	NI	NI	—	12.4	28.2	3.0	22.0
I have drunk alcoholic drinks in a pub when I was under 16	21.82	31.37	41.18	81.9	89.7	77.2	79.0
I have been in a pub when I was under 16	61.82	58.82	80.39	91.4	100.0	86.4	80.7
I have taken things from big stores or supermarkets when the shop was open	27.27	33.33	43.14	32.3	66.7	12.1	36.2
I have taken things from little shops when the shop was open	41.82	47.06	62.75	40.9	76.9	19.7	53.3
I have dropped things in the street like litter or broken bottles	56.36	58.82	76.47	84.8	87.2	83.3	38.9
I have bought something cheap or accepted as a present something I knew was stolen	30.91	45.10	52.94	36.2	69.2	16.7	64.6
I have planned well in advance to get into a house to take things	NI	}	} —	6.7	15.4	1.5	7.1
I have got into a house and taken things even though I didn't plan it in advance	}	1.96	}	10.5	23.1	3.0	9.3
I have taken a bicycle belonging to someone else and kept it	9.09	19.61	19.61	1.9	2.6	1.5	14.7

Table 1 continued

I have struggled or fought to get away from a policeman	20.00	23.53	27.45	24.8	46.2	12.1	15.9
I have struggled or fought with a policeman who was trying to arrest someone	*(20.00)*	*(23.53)*	*(27.45)*	7.6	17.9	1.5	5.6
I have stolen school property worth more than about 5p	23.64	62.75	64.71	48.6	84.6	27.2	58.7
I have stolen goods from someone I worked for worth more than about 50p	NI	NI	—	13.3	23.1	7.6	14.2
I have had sex with a boy when I was under 16	NI	NI	—	40.0	82.2	15.2	NI
I have trespassed somewhere I was not supposed to go, like empty houses, railway lines or private gardens	81.82	90.20	96.08	64.8	82.1	54.5	80.9
I have been to an "X" film under age	14.55	19.61	25.49	74.3	84.6	68.2	91.7
I have spent money on gambling under 16	NI	NI	—	31.4	30.8	31.8	22.0
I have smoked cigarettes under 15	49.09	62.75	62.75	72.4	94.9	59.1	47.9
I have had sex with someone for money	NI	NI	—	2.9	7.7	0.0	NI

I have taken money from slot machines or telephones	23.64	39.22	47.06	13.3	23.1	7.6	25.2
I have taken money from someone's clothes hanging up somewhere	7.27	15.69	23.53	12.4	25.6	4.5	8.1
I have got money from someone by pretending to be someone else or lying about why I needed it	NI	NI	—	22.9	43.6	10.6	17.4
I have taken someone's clothes hanging up somewhere	NI	NI	—	3.8	7.7	1.5	NI
I have smoked dope or taken pills (L.S.D., mandies, sleepers)	NI	NI	—	20.0	4.6	4.5	6.1
I have got money/drinks/cigarettes by saying I would have sex with someone even though I didn't	NI	NI	—	6.7	2.6	9.1	NI
I have run away from home	NI	NI	—	37.1	82.1	10.6	NI
I have used any kind of a weapon in a fight (knife, broken bottle, stick, stone)	43.64	37.25	62.75	NI	NI	NI	NI

NI — not included in this questionnaire. Brackets round figures mean that figure includes answers to both questions used are shown in Table 1. Items with neutral or positive connotations and "naughty" items were also included in order to reduce stress at the beginning of the interview and to provide information on other activities of the children. The interview with each child was conducted individually, the items being written on cards which were sorted by the child into boxes corresponding to having done that act (yes box) or never having done it (never box). After discussion of the task, the child was asked about the items placed in the yes box. These questions included whether the items were done in a group or alone, who suggested it and how it came about. General questions as to the peer groups of the child were also asked. A full description of the interview schedules used is given in Shapland (1975) and Campbell (1976b).

The main problems with this kind of measure are whether the answers are reliable and whether they are valid, i.e. whether the children are concealing or exaggerating their delinquent activities. On reliability, the internal consistencies of the questionnaires were very high 0.88 (11-year-old boys), 0.99 (14-year-old boys) and 0.96 (girls). Factor analysis showed a large first component which may be considered as a general factor of delinquency, although the factor analysis of the responses of the boys at the later age gave indications of different patterns of criminal activity by this age. This combination suggests that the boys who perform the more serious acts at the later age and who are becoming more specialized have also, probably at an earlier stage, taken part in the more common, minor group crimes. Delinquency is thus a heterogeneous activity, children doing some of everything such that the more delinquent acts they commit, the more different types of activities they commit. The pattern of activities at the different ages is given below.

On validity, the Cambridge study (West and Farrington, 1973; Knight and West, 1975) has shown that the self-report delinquency score of their boys (the number of different types of offence admitted) is significantly positively related to convictions at that age (14–15 and 16–17) and to future convictions (at ages 16–17 and 20, respectively). Their questionnaire is both concurrently and predictively valid. A preliminary study of the boys in the present study shows that, although they only admitted to 5 convictions and 3 formal cautions by the age of 14, if they were divided into those convicted or formally cautioned, those informally warned and those with no contact with the police, these categories had significantly different self-report delinquency scores in the direction expected. All the other self-report delinquency studies have found similar results on validity. There is, of course, individual concealment or exaggeration of offences (for example, delinquency score is negatively related to scores on questionnaire measures of lying), but it appears that the amount of concealment or exaggeration is relatively homogeneous over the children in the present study such that self-report delinquency score may be taken as a reasonable measure of delinquent acts committed.

Before discussing individual findings of interest to a discussion of child neglect, we give a general picture of the activities of the children in the area, suggesting that it is the interaction of the environmental opportunities for activities with peer groups with neglect by parents that leads to a definition of the child being in need of care and protection.

The Activities of the Children

During the self-report delinquency interview, the question of what groups the child went around with and what kind of things he did out of school was raised for both boys and girls. For boys, it appears that peer group activities vary with age. Most boys belonged to a group between the ages of 10 and 12. Some of these were non-delinquent groups of 5 or 6 friends, the primary activities being fishing, riding bicycles, going to football matches and playing in local youth teams and visiting each other's homes. Others were based on the school or on the street, there being very few facilities for meeting in the evenings and at week-ends. The ones at school were year- and class-based, and there would be rivalry between groups in the playground involving fighting and stealing school property. The street groups, which varied from 3 to 15 boys and were flexible in membership, took their street or area as a territory to be defended. Children of the same age or younger would be challenged and sometimes required to pay small sums in order to come down the road. There were fights between neighbouring streets usually, however, involving at most sticks and stones. The groups would roam the streets at night, playing "knick-knock-nanny" (knocking on a door or ringing the bell and then running away), a game indulged in by both sexes at most ages, and games of catch with milk bottles (which results eventually in someone missing and the milk bottle smashing on the ground). Slot machines would sometimes be tried and adults would be subjected to catcalls and verbals insults, but not physical assaults. Most activities were impulsive in nature such as trespassing on the railways or "scrumping" (stealing fruit from gardens). There were, however, foci of trouble such as after sessions at the community centre or youth club at the school. Stealing would also generally be unplanned and done in smaller groups of 2–3 boys.

By the age of 12–13, most boys no longer belonged to these groups. Several had given up delinquent activity, often after having been caught by a shopkeeper shoplifting and being warned that, if caught again, they would be given over to the police. Others continued to engage in the same kind of delinquent activities but the groups were smaller (between 3 and 7 boys) and groups of friends rather than being street-based. Some continued to steal from shops and stores, usually on their own or with one or two friends, but were much more careful and professional in their activities. Of these a very few expanded their activities into breaking into cash and carry stores, receiving stolen goods and stealing mopeds — one of the main sports of this age group being riding mopeds on a scrambling course near the estate. The more delinquent boys often went around with older boys and adults and stayed out late in the evening.

Two of the boys in the sample said that they belonged to the white gang in the area, which was primarily composed of 16–19 year-old boys. This was a somewhat strange phenomenon as it existed solely for the purpose of fighting other gangs from other estates at prearranged times and places (deserted railway tunnels, lots, etc.). Although weapons (mainly knives) would be carried, the "fighting" involved almost entirely ritual violence. As a result of the reputation of the area for general violence and gangs (mostly undeserved), however, many boys admitted to carrying a weapon whenever they went out after dark, in case they were challenged by any other boy or youth. These boys were very often the non-delinquents, but ran the risk of being picked up by the police for carrying an offensive weapon.

The pattern of activities of the girls was different from that of the boys as it was based more on the home and on clubs, cafés and discos than on the streets. Younger girls (11–13) mainly went round in groups of friends, visiting other girls, sitting in bedrooms and playing records or babysitting (very important financially), although shoplifting from local shops and playing "knick-knock-nanny" were common to both sexes. Both sexes went to the school club once a week at all ages up to 16, although the girls reported that the boys wouldn't dance except at special discos (two per year), so that they had to spend their time on the trampoline and playing table-tennis and the pinball machine. Parties started to include both sexes at about the age of 14, though for the boys up to 16 the "booze" was much more important than the girls. These parties depended on parents being away from the house that night (a very common occurrence in some families).

Older girls (15 and over) tended to spend much more time in the centre of town. Once a week there was a good disco at the local car works which went on until midnight. The town discos (which went on until the small hours) were popular although the lower age limit was officially 18. On Saturday afternoons, they would go to the local town football ground, and on Saturday night go dancing at discos or go to the pubs in town. Weekends were spent shopping (and shoplifting) and hanging around the town meeting friends at the Wimpy, etc. The boys associated with these girls were almost always older and at work as this was considered much more prestigious. Unless an individual had some particular hobby or was good at some sport, or his or her parents were the rare ones that took their children out to do things at week-ends, the general complaint from both sexes was of boredom.

Self-Reported Delinquent Activities

It is perhaps not surprising from this description of the activities of the boys and girls that the majority of self-reported crime in the area is crime committed with a peer group. For the boys, the figure was 60%. Group crime plus solitary crime for boys also accounts for almost all the crime committed so that crime committed with adults or parents is very infrequent. Criminal involvement at this age is hence primarily delinquent involvement, there being very little contact with the adult criminal culture. Each boy was asked for each type of crime, whether he had committed it on his own or in a group, with an adult or with a parent. Answers were weighted so that say shoplifting equally with peers and alone would be scored $\frac{1}{2}$ group $\frac{1}{2}$ solitary; mostly with peers would be scored $\frac{2}{3}$ group $\frac{1}{3}$ solitary. From this it was possible to calculate the percentage involvement in group crime for each type of crime. Again, concurring with the description of the activities above, those offences having a higher percentage involvement were trespassing (85.19%), littering (90.32%), breaking windows of empty property (90.67%) and vandalism of public property (90.32%). These are all minor offences of "street-corner groups". Those having low percentages were stealing money from home (0.00%), drinking alcohol in pubs and going into pubs (16.67%, mostly with adults), stealing school property (31.25%) and receiving stolen property (31.82%). These may be compared with the percentage of boys admitting the various types of crime given in Table 1. Here one may see that although the overall admission of having committed crimes is high, those crimes with the highest frequency of admission are those which are also committed in groups (and the pub questions).

We may conclude for boys that delinquency is very much based on the peer group. It is also true that the more delinquent the boy the more his involvement in group crime (Pearson product-moment correlation 0.30 significant on 2-tailed test at 0.038 level). The types of crimes committed also show the effect of the environment and of the home in that the crimes are mostly street-based. The most important part of the delinquent boy's life appears to be the peer group based on the street, wandering around in the evenings and taking part in impulsive delinquent acts. The more sophisticated criminal involve-

ment of older boys, of breaking and entering and stealing items of
value, comes from the original peer group and is an extension of the
activities of this group to more profitable activities. It is not surprising
that delinquency is found to be heterogeneous, when it is likely that,
although a boy may not be taking part in every kind of criminal activity
at the present, he had probably done so with his group at some time in
the past.

As to girls, Slater *et al.* (1968) in their book "Delinquency in Girls"
state that "the nature of delinquent offences among girls is completely
different to the delinquent offences committed by boys". This position
reflects not only current public opinion but also official criminal
statistics. Statistics indicate that male delinquency is eight times as
common as female delinquency. Powerful differences appear with
respect to acts of violence and vandalism, while the least difference
appears for shoplifting and petty larceny. The general public (and
many textbooks) assume that female delinquency is composed almost
exclusively of either shoplifting or sexual misdemeanours.

It is likely that official statistics are biased for a number of reasons in
favour of the girl delinquent. Police are aware of the relative paucity of
female crime and for this reason ascribe its occurrence to external
situational factors (such as, drink, being "in" with a bad crowd and
neglectful parents) rather than any inherent and enduring "bad
streak" which is often attributed to males. Frequently then, girls escape
with a caution rather than being prosecuted. It is also the case that the
physical attractiveness of the defendant tends to work in her favour.
This has been experimentally demonstrated and applies particularly to
male judges. Third, it may be that females tend to commit less serious
offences and evidence suggests that the likelihood of arrest and
conviction is positively related to the severity of the crime.

Public opinion relating to the prevalence of sexual offences is also
grounded in some fact. In the 1960s, almost 83% of girls put into the
care of the local authority were so placed because they were deemed
to be "in need of care and protection" (Richardson, 1969). These care
orders are used by the juvenile court largely on the advice of social
workers, psychiatrists and psychologists who feel that the girl's social
life is such that she shows a high probability of becoming delinquent
if no intervention takes place. She need not have committed any
offence. The equivalent proportion of care orders among males for
that period was 14%. Social agencies attend strongly to the alleged
sexual behaviour of the girl in making these judgements. Even today, a
doctor's report of the girl's virginity is considered, and one sexual
experience under the age of 16 is sufficient to warrant a care order.

A self-report delinquency study of 106 girls from the research area
quickly dispelled these preconceptions about the nature of female

crime. Compared to an equivalent male group (West and Farrington, 1973) of 16–17 year olds, we find the ratio of males to females overall to be 1.12–1.00. Investigating more closely the types of offences that are committed, girls admit to entering pubs under age, drinking alcohol, using drugs, gambling and smoking as often as do boys. They admit marginally less often to driving vehicles without a licence, truanting from school, fighting in public places, provoking fights on the street and shoplifting. The biggest differences between the sexes occur in bicycle theft and letting off fireworks in the street, items which reflect sex specific interests rather than any degree of seriousness of the act. They actually exceed boys in the frequency with which they admit to taking money from home, littering and fighting to get away from a policeman. A correlation was performed between the frequency of admission of all acts between boys and girls. The resulting value of +0.79 indicates a great deal of similarity. With respect to their sexual behaviour, 40% of the girls admit to having sex under the age of 16, 3% to prostitution and 7% to offering sex in return for money. Similar measures were not obtained for boys, perhaps an indication of the more liberal attitude to male adolescent sexual behaviour.

In conclusion, the main difference between boys and girls in their activities appears to be that girls' activities are based on the home, the club and the centre of town, whereas boys' activities are mainly confined to the streets and neighbourhood in which they live. The specific activities may well reflect the lack of facilities for leisure for adolescents, particularly girls, in the area, making the girls go to the centre of town where they are more likely to meet older men and boys in pubs and discos. The boys do have some opportunities in the area, notably for fishing and for scrambling.

Parental Deprivation

Parental views also contribute to this pattern of activities. Parents are very much more protective of girls so that they do not go out and get pregnant, thereby bringing shame on the family. Often this may be the main concern of the mother, according to the counsellor of the school. Overprotection of this nature by the parents can lead to the girl rebelling and either going down to the centre more often or running away from home, both of which make her more likely to become dependent on an older boy or man by whom she eventually becomes pregnant. Parents are less protective of boys and this, combined with the greater facilities for boys, makes them less likely to suffer from the deprivation by neglect or uncaring overprotection than girls.

It is the view of the counsellor of the school that at least 25% of children in the school are deprived, either by neglect or by abuse. The proportion of those physically abused is very small compared with those neglected. She considers that many parents never know what their children are doing and either do not have standards, such as whether they should be in at night, or do not enforce them. Perhaps even worse is when the standards are enforced sporadically, so that the child is not able to connect what he has done with the punishment he is receiving. There is little difference in these respects between children of one parent families (about 20% in the school) and others. This is consistent with the views of two studies recently published by the National Children's Bureau (Ferri, 1976; Ferri and Robinson, 1976).

Perceived Home Background of the Girls

We have given above a general picture of the activities of the children in the area and how their parents may affect these, based on the responses of the children and staff at the school to open-ended questions in an interview situation. We will also examine this interaction more closely in the case of girls, who seem primarily to suffer from neglect. Detailed questionnaires were given to the girls at the school (Campbell, 1976a) and at the remand home concerning their perceptions of their home life. The answers to these were then linked to the self-report delinquent involvement of the girls.

All previous theories of the effect of the home background on the behaviour of the child suggest that children from disturbed homes should be differentially predisposed to delinquency, but the question of what constitutes a deprived or disturbed home is rarely dealt with. The distinction drawn in this paper is between active physical cruelty and abuse on the part of the parents and neglect or failure to impose systematic sanctions. The question is which of these is most strongly related to subsequent delinquent behaviour?

Before considering our data on the family background of delinquent girls, an aside is necessary concerning an important methodological and social issue. Since the Children and Young Persons Act 1969, juvenile courts have been explicitly instructed to take into consideration, not only offences (if any) committed by the girl, but also factors concerning her general social and psychological adjustment and family situation as assessed by clinicians and professional social workers. This means that girls from deprived family backgrounds are more likely to find themselves in the care of the local authority than are similarly delinquent girls from good family backgrounds. This Act formalizes a policy which has in fact been operating *with respect to girls* for some time. During the 1960s, 75.8% of girls committed to an approved school were on some form of care order, as opposed to a formal charge of law breaking (Richardson, 1969). This is not to suggest that these girls had not broken the law, but only that they were not officially charged with doing so. Conversely, only a very small proportion (5%) of boys in approved schools were on any form of care order. Since girls are committed to approved schools or community schools by virtue of their poor home circumstances, it is not surprising to find that incarcerated, institutionalized adolescent girls show a significantly poorer home life than "normal" school girls.

Many studies of the female delinquent have used an institutionalized and therefore nontypical sample, and failure to employ even the most elementary of control groups has produced a wealth of meaningless pseudo-data. For example, 38% of approved school girls have experienced "psychological" maternal deprivation (Slater *et al.*, 1968). Not only is the measure undefined, but we have no information as to the frequency of this phenomenon in the normal, non-delinquent population.

Previous work suggests that neglect has a stronger effect than cruelty. A substantial proportion of approved-school girls are from single parent families (Slater *et al.*, 1968; Richardson, 1969; Wattenburg and Saunders, 1954; Monohan, 1957) and express a desire to see their parents more frequently (Riege, 1972). Although figures for maternal deprivation in these girls range from 27 to 43% (Slater *et al.*, 1968; Richardson, 1969), the only study to use a control group found no significant difference with respect to this variable.

Many studies report that these girls feel themselves to be rejected by the mother and, less reliably, by the father also. Not only do official agencies describe these girls' home life as being lacking in discipline, but the girls themselves complain of insufficient and slack discipline by the parents (Richardson, 1969; Cockburn and Maclay, 1965; Gilbert, 1972). No data has yet been presented with respect to physical abuse in female delinquency, with the exception of some data on father–daughter incest (3.4%). Under-reporting and absence of a control group make such data unreliable.

Our study used a total of 64 girls drawn from the same school as the boys and from a remand home. The purpose of the study was to learn how the girl herself viewed her home situation, and not to rely, as in previous studies, on the value judgements given by middle-class professional social workers and psychologists.

For each girl, whether from the secondary modern school or the remand home, there was a self-reported delinquency score (the SRD score) as well as data on her *official* delinquency. The home background questionnaire, derived from Hirschi (1969), was composed not of categorical responses (yes/no) but of scaled responses (never/a bit/sometimes/quite often/very often), so that correlations could be computed between the SRD score and each of the 72 items. The items used referred to eight areas of the girl's life at home: parent to child communication, child to parent communication, discipline, supervision, joint activities, emotional attachment, social achievement and decision making. Evidence of neglect was found to appear throughout the answers to the questionnaire.

First, correlations were computed between the SRD score and every one of the 72 items. Twenty eight proved significant beyond the 10% level (Table 2). Many of these indicate parental neglect towards the

Table 2
Significant correlations ($P < 0.10$) between self-reported delinquency score and home-life questionnaire items

Item	r	P
Supervision		
Mother checks on daughter's obedience	−0.16	0.10
Father checks on daughter's obedience	−0.17	0.10
Mother knows daughter's whereabouts when out	−0.28	0.01
Father knows daughter's whereabouts when out	−0.22	0.05
Mother knows daughter's companions when out	−0.32	0.01
Father knows daughter's companions when out	−0.29	0.01
Required home early on school nights	−0.23	0.05
Mother satisfied with daughter's school achievement	−0.42	0.001
Father satisfied with daughter's school achievement	−0.36	0.01
Parents approve of daughter's friends	−0.33	0.01
Mother corrects mispronounced words	−0.22	0.05
Punishment		
Father slaps or hits	+0.23	0.05
Mother withdraws privileges	−0.22	0.05
Father withdraws privileges	−0.17	0.10
Father accuses daughter of hurting his feelings	+0.25	0.10
Father employs abuse and name-calling	+0.27	0.05
Joint activities		
Eat breakfast with mother	−0.26	0.01
Work in garden with mother	−0.19	0.10
Help mother in house	−0.19	0.10
Watch TV with mother	−0.29	0.01
Watch TV with father	−0.19	0.10
Emotional relationship		
Real father present in home	−0.16	0.10
Real mother present in home	−0.43	0.001
Feel wanted by father	−0.37	0.01
Communication		
Mother explains things you don't understand	−0.18	0.10
Father explains why he feels as he does	+0.21	0.10
Decision making		
Daughter influences family decisions	+0.18	0.10
Mother makes unfair rules	−0.16	0.10

child, for example, the negative relationship between knowing where the daughter is and who she is with and delinquency, and the negative association between time required home on school nights and delinquency.

This is combined with a lack of joint activities involving both the parent and child, such as watching TV, helping around the house or in the garden and eating breakfast together. Parental impotency is seen in the fact that, while they feel their daughter is doing poorly at school and they disapprove of her friends, they do not require her to get a good night's sleep or eat breakfast before school, nor do they know who she is with. Their ineffectualness is again shown in their failure to check on their daughter's obedience even when they do issue imperatives.

Discipline items were scored in terms of relative frequency of their use. For instance, the question might be: does your father punish you by hitting you? The answer is: (a) never, (b) sometimes and (c) often. A high correlation for an item indicates that it is a frequent mode of discipline but does not provide an estimate of the frequency with which the girls are punished. The father is characteristically the main disciplinary agent in the home for all girls. Delinquency, though, is primarily associated with the father's use of slapping and hitting, of abusive name calling and accusations of hurting the feelings (emotional blackmail). It is negatively related to the withdrawal of privileges as a sanction. This indicates that punishment *per se* is not damaging but that certain kinds of punishment in certain home contexts are. Privilege withdrawal is a reputedly middle-class technique of discipline. At this point we begin to see the artificiality of the distinction between neglect and abuse. Real damage of abuse may not be the physical pain but the fact that it frequently occurs in a context of neglect and apathy. These two factors obviously exacerbate one another in a complex manner that has not been fully explored.

The full quota of 72 items was unwieldy to work with and so a factor analysis with orthogonal rotation was performed to provide a statistical summary statement of the structures and concepts underlying the girls responses to the questions. Factor I might be termed one of positive caring and communication. It accounted for 12.36% of the variance and was defined by the following items: feeling wanted by both parents, believing her parents would stick by her in trouble, and wanting to be the kind of people her parents are.

Factor II seemed to be a parental discipline factor defined by the following: the presence of a father in the home, the parents not the girl taking decisions about her life, being required home early on school nights, and her father encouraging good scholastic achievement.

Factor III is a parental pressure factor, defined by only a few major items: offering the girl money for good behaviour and good school performance, and being accused of hurting the mother and father's feelings.

Factor IV is clearly a maternal factor being defined by mother items throughout the questionnaire. Interestingly, discipline items have low loadings here as this duty is often performed by the father.

A stepwise regression analysis was performed regressing the SRD scores of each girl onto the first four factors emerging from the factor analysis. The resulting figure gives an equation which best describes the relationship between delinquency and these four home-life factors. Results indicate the strong effect of the maternal factor (−3.87) compared to the much smaller contribution of parental pressure (−0.12) and parental discipline (−0.36). Clearly, a deficient and neglectful attitude by the mother to her daughter is of paramount importance. Correlations do not, or course, show causality. We do not know whether the girl's delinquent behaviour caused, was caused by or interacted with parental neglect. The third possibility seems the most plausible.

Finally, we looked at the 64 subjects for inter-group differences between home and school girls. Since a large proportion of remand-home girls were in care because of their "deprived homes" as judged by outside agencies, we expected a big difference. But out of 72 items only three significantly discriminated the groups (below the 10 significance level), and we would expect three to be significant by chance alone. Effectively, *no differences* in respect of home life could be based on the girl's evaluation of her home and family. This surprising finding suggests that outside agencies hold a very different conception of a good home than does the girl herself.

Conclusions

We began this paper by considering the relationship between the home background and the activities of boys and of girls. Boys, particularly in the 11–13 age group, participate in street and area-based clique activities. Some of those are harmless pursuits, such as fishing; delinquent activities which may occur are predominantly trivial and situational, often starting as games involving throwing milk bottles or ringing doorbells and graduating to shoplifting and vandalism. These activities are often the result of having no approved meeting place where the boys could meet and work off energy. Frustration leads the boys on to the street where boredom often drives them from rowdy games to delinquent activities. Girls by contrast spend leisure time either casually in one another's bedrooms or where money and parental tolerance allow, in the town either at discos or pubs. Their activities are often in the company of older boys who have already left school and are either in relatively unskilled work or unemployed.

The counsellor estimates that some 25% of the schoolchildren have parents whose control and supervision is inadequate and may be neglectful or abusing. Neglect seems more prevalent than abuse but takes different forms between the two sexes. While boys are allowed to roam the streets, the counsellor suggests that girls' parents are more concerned to preserve the family's good name and so are strict about any overt suggestion of either promiscuity or delinquent behaviour. The neglect takes the form of a failure to know where the child is, who he is with and either a lack of regulation over the child's behaviour or a failure to enforce restrictions even if they are nominally verbalized.

This impressionistic view from the school authorities was augmented by data from the girls themselves about their view of the home situation. First, the strongest relationship was found between the degree of the girl's delinquent acts and the paucity of adequate parental supervision over her out-of-home activities. Although parents were seen as disapproving of her friends and feeling that her school work was suffering, they made no attempt to impose sanctions to prevent the situation from becoming worse. There was also a lack of activities involving both parents and children. Although stressing the importance of neglect, we do not deny that abuse also occurs, but neither the questionnaire nor the counsellor's report supports the view that this is substantial. Second, a factor analytic study of the girls' reports indicates the differential roles of mothers and fathers as caretakers and punishing agents, respectively. While the mother legislates over the daughter's behaviour, it is often the father who delivers or fails to deliver sanctions. From the regression analysis, the mother–daughter relationship appears to be critical in female delinquency. A poor relationship not only indicates a lack of appropriate adult models for the girl, but also suggests a failure on the mother's part to supervise the girl's activities and be aware of the kinds of out-of-home activities that she is involved in.

Third, when the sample was dichotomized into remand home and school girls, no significant differences above chance figures appeared with respect to the quality of the home life as perceived by the girl, whose evaluation of the home clearly differs from that of official agencies. The girls themselves do not experience their home lives as deprived even when social workers assess them as inadequate. Unfortunately, we have no equivalent data for boys but the counsellor suggests that there are unlikely to be large qualitative differences between the sexes with respect to their homes.

The second interaction to be considered is that between the children's background as perceived by themselves and as perceived by the social workers and the school. Discrepancies may arise because the girls themselves can compare their homes with their friends' homes in the same community, while social workers, because of the nature of their work, rarely have the opportunity to visit comparable homes which have not produced problem children. The visible differences may be less than they imagine. Another difference may arise through the social workers' concern with the well-being of the family as a whole and not just with the position of the girl.

By contrast, the counsellor and headmaster of the school are primarily concerned with the children themselves. Children come to the attention of the counsellor by a number of routes, referred sometimes by an outside social worker, but frequently the children come spontaneously to discuss problems that they are experiencing at home. Reticent children are often brought by worried friends and school mates. The house tutor may refer him, since neglect can cause the child to demand an unusual amount of attention from some staff member or physical abuse may have been noticed.

Often, abusive or neglectful parents are thought to know one another or to be interrelated by marriage or association. A policy of preventative work is carried out by teachers, supported by the school counsellor, for all children but especially for that 25% who seem to be particularly at risk.

If the situation is of concern but not yet critical, the house tutor is supported in dealing with the child by the participation of the headmaster, the deputy head, the counsellor and other staff. A boy with an alcoholic mother was unofficially exempted from supplying absence notes since his mother's inability to write them herself was only likely to induce the boy to forge them. Any absences were dealt with within the school. Such preventative measures are more valuable than attempts to help a child after he has come to the attention of the police or the juvenile court. Problems at school are brought to the immediate attention of the parents, and this may include home visits by the house tutor. The effectiveness of the whole system depends mainly on the willingness of the child to form sufficiently good bonds with either children or staff, so that his individual problems reach the attention of someone who can help.

The interaction between the school and other agencies is not always as close as it might be. The school counsellor rarely visits the children's homes as she feels that the whole estate is covered by social work agencies and that the parents resent the intrusion of outsiders in their homes. There is not always liaison between social workers working with the family and the school to warn them that the child might be facing difficulties. Follow-up reports are often not sent back to the school by social workers or by institutions. Within the community, the headmaster would like greater contacts between the school and community services, especially old peoples homes and nurseries, as many children show great enthusiasm for old people and young children. This link-up could be not only a valuable learning experience for both sides but a positive step towards integrating a rather fragmented society. The estate grew very rapidly after its opening and attracted predominantly young married couples with children who were mobile and ambitious for a new life. This produced a community with a high proportion of children and young people and a scarcity of aunts, uncles and grandparents to give stability and variety. Social workers themselves express dissatisfaction at the inability to implement the suggestion of the 1969 Children and Young Persons Act, that residential child care should give way to more preventative and integrated activity within the community. They would like to take part in the day to day experiences of the child by visiting parks, playgrounds, discos and community centres.

The study has produced many indications of fragmentation and lack of close communication — between parent and child, between social worker and client, between school and community and between young and old. What has happened and is happening in any social situation can only be discovered by discussion between the participants involved. The stigma of a care order or a finding of guilt in a juvenile court is felt deeply by a child and his parents. This could be avoided through more widespread guidance and counselling in school and home, with liaison between both of these whenever requested by any participant.

Acknowledgements

We are very grateful to the headmaster, staff and pupils of the secondary modern school and the staff and girls of the remand home for the extremely generous help they have given us. We are also indebted to the Oxfordshire Education and Social Services Departments and the Oxford City Housing Department. Both authors were supported by Social Science Research Council Research Studentships at the Department of Experimental Psychology, Oxford University, and the first author is now in receipt of a Home Office Research Fellowship at King's College, London.

References

Belson, W. A. and Hood, R. G. (1967). The research potential of the case records of approved school boys. Parts I and II. London School of Economics, Survey Research Centre.

Campbell, A. C. (1976a). Family background and delinquent involvement in female adolescents (in prep.).

Campbell, A. C. (1976b). The role of the peer group in female delinquency. Unpublished D. Phil. thesis, Oxford University.

Cockburn, J. and Maclay, I. (1965). Sex differentials in juvenile delinquency, *Brit. J. Crim.* 5, 289–308.

Dentler, R. A. and Monroe, L. J. (1961). Social correlates of early adolescent theft, *Amer. Sociol. Rev.* 26, 733–743.

Ferri, E. (1976). "Growing Up in a One-Parent Family". N.F.E.R.

Ferri, E. and Robinson, H. (1976). "Coping Alone". N.F.E.R.

Gilbert, J. (1972). Delinquent (approved school) and non-delinquent (secondary modern school) girls, *Brit. J. Crim.* 12, 325–356.

Hirschi, T. (1969). "Causes of Delinquency". University of California Press, Berkeley.

Knight, B. J. and West, D. J. (1975). Temporary and continuing delinquency, *Brit. J. Crim.* 15, 42–50.

Monohan, T. P. (1957). Family status and the delinquent child: a reappraisal and some new findings, *Social Forces* 35, 250–258.

Piliavin, I. and Briar, S. (1964). Police encounters with juveniles, *Amer. J. Sociol.* 70, 206–214.

Richardson, H. (1969). "Adolescent Girls in Approved Schools". Routledge and Kegan Paul, London.

Riege, M. (1972). Parental affection and juvenile delinquency in girls. *Brit. J. Crim.* 12, 55–73.

Shapland, J. M. (1975). Behaviour and personality in delinquent children. Unpublished D. Phil. Thesis, Oxford University.

Slater, J., Cowie, V. and Slater, E. (1968). "Delinquency in Girls". Heinemann, London.

Wattenberg, W. and Saunders, F. (1954). Sex differences among juvenile offenders, *Sociol. Soc. Res.* 39, 24–31.

West, D. J. and Farrington, D. P. (1973). "Who Becomes Delinquent?" Heinemann, London.

For Discussion see p 157.

11. Alternative Families

Jane Rowe

The dictionary defines "alternative" as a "choice between two courses either of which may be chosen but not both", i.e. one must be given up. Thinking about alternative families means considering choices, first between natural and substitute families and then between types of substitute. It must also involve some consideration of the role of the family.

I propose, however, to touch only lightly on the first and third of these tasks and then go on to devote most attention to the subject I know most about, fostering and adoption as alternatives to the biological family. This is partly because I lack specialized knowledge on the management of child abuse cases and the taking of decisions to separate in these situations. But in any case, the points I wish to make are valid whether the proportion of seriously abused or neglected children needing alternative families is 5, 25 or 50%.

The choices which have to be made in all cases of family breakdown involve decisions which are painful as well as difficult. Temporary separation is relatively easy to manage successfully and not too painful to contemplate, so decisions about this are taken quite readily. Permanent separation, however, is so drastic a step that those involved instinctively recoil from it, try to put off the decision as long as possible and tend to seek unrealistically for solutions which will avoid final choices and achieve the best of both worlds; but, too often, the result is that the child gets the worst of all worlds. If we wait too long hoping for improvement in his home situation, he may be too damaged or too old to adjust to a substitute family. If placed in care on an indefinite basis in order to keep the options open, he may have a series of short-term placements or become a yo-yo child with periods of care alternating with periods at his own home. Sometimes indeed, we seem to confuse the words alternative and alternate and use the expression "alternative families" as though a succession of families were acceptable and final choice could be successfully avoided. Unfortunately, avoiding and postponing final decisions about separation may make life easier for professionals, but only at the expense of the child's lack of security and continuity.

In reviewing the literature on child abuse, I am struck by the almost complete absence of any discussion of the psychological and practical issues involved in providing alternative families for these children. Most research studies and authoritative texts on child abuse merely refer to the decision to place the child in care voluntarily or by court order. There is seldom any discussion about the type of home that may be most suitable, whether it is likely to be available, the support services needed or the prognosis for successful placement.

Lack of consideration of these matters is serious in view of what seem to be increasingly gloomy reports on the effectiveness of rehabilitation services and in terms of securing a reasonably adequate home environment for abused children. It is evident that, even if further physical injury is prevented, emotional neglect and/or rejection often continue. Thus the Battered Child Research Team of the N.S.P.C.C. in their recent report "At Risk" states that "we wish to emphasize that even if there is evidence to suggest that the risk of physical injury has diminished, there still remains the question of whether the home is conducive to the child's emotional development". Looking back over their cases, this team evidently feels that at first they had a tendency to be over-optimistic about the long-term outcome.

Martin and Beezley's follow-up study of 50 abused children (1976) speaks of "the pervasive psychic injury that continues", and indeed a high proportion of the children in their study who remained with their parents were still receiving excessive physical punishment or suffering neglect or rejection. It seems clear that until preventive services have improved, there are going to be a considerable number of neglected and battered children who require temporary or permanent substitute family care.

The Role of the Family

An ordinary family gives the child nurture and protection, intimate continuing affectionate relationships, social training and education in the culture of the community. Parents take responsibility for their child, they make decisions about him, they provide role and behaviour models for the child to imitate and a secure base from which he can grow to independence. Parents seldom carry out all these tasks themselves. They are shared with members of the wider family circle, with school, neighbours and community groups. However, when a child comes into care, the parental role is divided in a much more drastic way and most of the rights and duties are given over to the court and/or the care authority which, in turn, delegates many of them to residential staff or to foster parents. The consequences of such a division of role are profound but, as yet, little studied and poorly understood.

When a child comes into care, the aspects of family life which are most difficult to reproduce for him are commitment, individualization, continuity, perspective and reciprocity in relationships. All these are regularly provided by even inadequate families. They are essential ingredients with which the child can build a sense of personal identity, a capacity to take responsibility for himself and for others and an ability to form lasting and affectionate relationships. It may be well to consider each of these aspects briefly because all are important to any consideration of the pros and cons of fostering and adoption.

Commitment is the bedrock of security. A rather sensible 9 year old described it very well when he said "I don't know exactly what a family is, but I know one thing. Your friends can go off and say they don't want to be your friend any more, but people just can't go off and say they don't want to be your family any more".

To be treated as an individual is essential to one's self esteem and to the development of identity. The extent to which ordinary families cater to young children's whims has been strikingly documented by the Newsons in their study of young children in Nottingham. When dealing with a group of children, i.e. in a children's home, the best one can do is to treat them all equally; but families do not treat each child the same.

The problems of providing continuity and perspective for children in care have been referred to in many studies which have disclosed the number of moves and the number of social workers which these children frequently experience (Rowe and Lambert, 1973; Shaw, 1976; Walton and Heywood, 1971). This means that all too often the child in care loses his past. Newson (1971) writes the following.

He has no single person who shares his own most basic and important memories, no one to confirm whether these memories are in fact correct or figments of his imagination, no-one to polish up a fading memory before it is too late. Such a deprivation seems so damaging that I am not at all sure that we can ever fully make up for it artificially.

What is probably even worse is that the child in care has no predictable future. Bryce and Ehlert (1971) write of the psychological damage this causes.

It is our conviction that no child can grow emotionally while in limbo, never really belonging to anyone except in a minimal way (just enough to survive), if tomorrow the relationship may be severed ... To grow, the child needs at least the promise of permanency in relationships and some continuity of environment.

At a more mundane level, to assess the importance of continuity for a child, we only have to think of the number of occasions in an ordinary family when parents and children reminisce or anticipate future developments, of the popularity of photograph albums, the frequent discussion of children's future careers and, for the younger child, the endless questions such as "where was I when so-and-so was born?" or "who was Uncle Jim's mother?" Only in a permanent family can such queries be readily answered and a child given a true sense of his place in the scheme of things.

Finally, reciprocity in relationships has to be reproduced. To feel oneself a responsible and important member of a family group is a necessary preparation for wider responsibilities. A child must grow up knowing that affection and dependency are reciprocal. For him to value himself as a person, he must know that not only is some adult important and vital to him, but that he is important and vital to some adult (Watson, 1968). The heaviest psychological burden of many children in care is perhaps the realization that, however kindly they are treated, it does not matter very much to anyone whether they come or go. This is also the essential difference between a caretaker and a parent. Almost all parents are deeply emotionally involved with their children and, for a variety of reasons, the children are important to them.

It is clearly difficult to reproduce for the child in care these essential elements of family life. There have been almost no follow-up studies of children who have grown up in care, but it is evident from what is known about children's experiences while in care that, even with the enormous expenditures of effort, skill and money that have been poured into them in recent decades, children's services still leave a great deal to be desired. The decision to separate a child from his family and place him in long-term care cannot be taken lightly because there is no guarantee of a successful outcome for this form of treatment. It has also become clear that group care will seldom or never be able to meet the needs of the young child whose own family has broken down to the extent that his parents will not be able to fulfil the essentials of the parental role in the reasonably near future. The choice then will lie between a long-term foster home, which, in theory at least, will allow continued contact with the natural family and will retain the possibility of eventual return home, and the more drastic step of placing the child for adoption.

Foster Care, Theory and Outcome

One of the main problems in discussing foster care is that we tend to speak of it as an entity when, in reality, it encompasses a wide range of situations. Fostering may last for a few days or weeks, or for an indefinite period, or until the child reaches adulthood. Foster parents may fill the role of caretaker, therapist or substitute parent, or an uneasy mixture of all three. Often they are unclear about which role they are supposed to undertake or the role may change as time goes on. Such change may be desirable and part of an evolving plan, or it may result from lack of well-defined objectives on the part of the placing agency. Only too often, what starts out as a short-term placement becomes long-term by default. Since the tasks of short-term and long-term foster parents are essentially quite different, this can have serious repercussions.

Short-term fostering may be for assessment, for therapy or for caretaking, but it is never substitute parenting in the full sense. Questions of commitment, continuity and reciprocity do not arise and individualization is quite easy providing foster parents are given adequate information about the child's likes and dislikes.

Many short-term foster parents are truly professional in their skills and their outlook. Whether or not they are given the title or look on themselves as professionals, they offer their family life in the service of children. They usually specialize, either taking a particular kind of child, such as disturbed adolescent or a handicapped child, or they offer a particular kind of service, e.g. pre-adoption care for babies or assessment of children on admission.

Long-term fostering presents very much greater difficulties because the parental role is divided between natural parents, agency and foster parents, with all the inevitable possibilities of confusion, overlap and gaps. These undoubtedly help to account for the high rate of fostering breakdown. In Britain, as in many other countries, failure rates are high. Up to 50% placements fail within 5 years. Most breakdowns occur within the first 12 months, but significant numbers fail after several years have passed (Trasler, 1960; Parker, 1966; George, 1970).

Natural parents frequently find the fostering situation a painful one. They feel guilty, anxious and acutely aware of their own shortcomings in the face of the foster parents' competence. Social work text books have laid great stress on the importance of parental contact but little success has been achieved as far as foster children are concerned. In my study "Children who Wait", only 10% of foster children saw even one parent as often as once a month and similar situations emerge from other studies. Whether natural parents are absent by choice or default or are excluded by agency policy or foster parent hostility, their absence means that foster patents almost inevitably take on the role and duties of parents although they have none of the rights of parents.

A few foster parents can cope with a truly open-ended situation. They are prepared to care for a child for as long or as short a period as needed. Others really cannot share the child at all and go into fostering as a route to adoption or at least quasi adoption. However, most long-term foster parents probably start out with the idea that the child will remain only for a limited period, will keep in touch with his parents and later return to them. However, as time goes on, they may find it increasingly difficult to share the child with his parents. This is particularly the case when the foster child comes to them very young. Babies and toddlers arouse protective, possessive and parental attitudes in their caretakers and professional detachment soon evaporates.

Yet shared care and limited commitment are essential elements in foster care. To some extent at least, foster parents must share the child with the natural parents and with the agency. The balance of power depends a good deal on whether the parents place the child voluntarily, whether a care order has been made by a court or whether the local authority has assumed parental rights. But in none of these situations do the foster parents acquire any parental rights and they must defer to the agency for all major decisions about the child.

Several studies have demonstrated an alarming lack of agreement between foster parents and social workers, with the foster parents seeing themselves as truly substitute parents and the social workers urging a more professional approach in which foster parents help the child and natural parents towards rehabilitation (Adamson, 1973; George, 1970; Shaw, 1976).

In theory, foster parents should receive continued advice and support from the agency, but in practice this may be illusory because of changing or inexperienced social workers. This division of the parental role is bound to lessen the sense of parental authority. I wonder how many foster home breakdowns in adolescence are due to this splitting and subsequent lack of control. Does shared care sometimes weaken rather than strengthen? Foster parents have no right to keep the child, but they have no obligation to do so either. If there is a family crisis, it may be that the bedroom is needed for another member of the family, or if the child's behaviour is unacceptable, foster parents can ask for the child's removal.

All this leads to a pervasive sense of insecurity and many foster children are understandably disturbed and confused. Thorpe's interviews with foster children provide vivid examples of their anxieties. Derek, aged 12, said "I think you are only out in a certain place for a certain length of time, say 2 or 3 years, and then you're supposed to be moved. I don't know why — perhaps people get fed up with you." And Judy, aged 9, said "Well I don't know really. It's a matter of being good or naughty you see. It's hard to understand to be good and that, isn't it? You go and do the wrong thing, perhaps you forget sometimes. If I'm naughty I might have to go away."

Some psychologists and social workers have paid considerable attention to the effect on the child's development of being in what Malone (1960) has called "an in-between world". Foster children's problems of mixed and uncertain identification, excessive fantasy and insecurity have been theoretically described by Weinstein (1960) and Krugman (1964) and in more practical terms by Hagan (1969). Hagan says "if parents can't talk about the future in terms of 'when you get bigger' or 'next year you can have a bike', the child tends to feel cared for on a day to day basis and his self-concept develops accordingly." A 12 year-old foster boy interviewed by Thorpe put his situation succinctly: "The rest of the children belong to my mum and dad, but I'm just brought up as another member of the family. I don't actually join it, I just fitted into it."

Without denying the effectiveness of many "professional" foster homes, or disputing the need to develop more of them, we may question whether it is often possible, or indeed desirable, to maintain an "open-ended" type of fostering indefinitely. If natural parents remain in touch and effectively retain at least some aspects of the parental role, mutual commitment of child and foster parents is neither necessary nor appropriate. But when natural parents are not actively involved, the advantages of open-endedness have to be balanced against the possibility of permanent insecurity and the risk of emotional malnutrition in the child through shallow relationships and lack, of what Barnes (1967) calls, a "parental force".

Back in 1955, Anna Freud said that foster care is inherently unlikely to be able to fulfil the child's need for continuity.

There may be affection, there may be stimulation, there may be mutuality for a while, but there is not the tie between the foster parents and the child that guarantees his continuity. It does not seem reasonable to expect full parental involvement without guaranteeing them full parental possession.

Adoption, Theory and Outcome

Adoption does, of course give possession by transferring full parental rights to the new parents. It offers an alternative family in the full sense and not just "an experience of family life", though it cannot be considered an easy option. Adoption arouses strong emotions, and among those in the caring professions opinion on adoption has become polarized. This is probably because few people are in a position to see it "in the round". Adoption workers, who are involved in the early stages, tend perhaps to be complacent about the outcome since they only see the adopters when they are in the first flush of enthusiasm and pleasure about the new member of the family. Child guidance clinic staff and residential workers, on the other hand, see almost nothing of successful adoptions but find themselves faced with a number of children where the adoption has been a failure. Surveying the literature, Hersov (1973) concludes that adopted children do appear to be over-represented in clinical populations attending child psychiatric clinics with more boys than girls presenting with conduct disorders. However the reasons for the over-representation are not yet entirely clear.

A number of follow-up studies present a more encouraging picture. Kadushin (1970) surveyed fourteen follow-up studies and reports an average success rate of 74%. The definition of success is inevitably difficult because usually there was no comparison with children in their own homes. Two studies have been able to provide this. The National Child Development Study has made it possible to compare a number of sub-groups of children with the general population, and in 1972 Seglow *et al.* reported their findings in "Growing Up Adopted". Their conclusions were that adopted children at the age of 7 years were doing as well or better than the rest of the cohort, although adopted boys from middle-class homes had more problems than their non-adopted counterparts. The illegitimate children remaining with their natural mothers had many more problems than those in adoption homes in which they were offered a much more advantageous environment.

Bohman (1970, 1973) has also compared adopted children with those who remained with a single natural parent and he also compared them with children placed in foster homes. He, too, found that the adopted children were doing well. Since the children were 15 years old in his second survey, his findings are particularly encouraging for those who see adoption as a potentially helpful solution to the problems of certain groups of children.

In both the Seglow and Bohman studies, most of the children had been placed for adoption in infancy and relatively few of them had physical or mental handicaps, although they had frequently had a rather poor start in life with little pre-natal care and sometimes a number of changes during the early weeks or months after birth. Franklin and Massarik (1969) followed up a group of children with medical conditions who had been placed for adoption by the Children's Home Society of California. The medical conditions were found not to be of major significance in the adoption outcome. A follow up study by Jaffee and Fanshel (1970) disclosed the surprising finding that children who were adopted beyond infancy (though mostly under 2 or 3 years old) had a better social adjustment than those adopted as young babies. This runs counter to most adoption findings which have shown a higher proportion of problems in late adoption placements. Tizard's findings on older child adoptions are also encouraging (1975).

As far as adoption for abused children is concerned, much the most important study is that of Kadushin (1970). He focused specifically on the adoption of school-age children, many of whom had come from seriously rejecting and depriving home backgrounds. His study "Adopting Older Children", included 91 children who were all between 5 and 11 years of age at the time of adoption placement. They were white, healthy and of normal intelligence. (Children who were adopted by their foster parents were excluded.) All the 91 children had been committed to the agency by the courts because of neglect or ill treatment. Most came from disorganized multi-problem families where the parents just could not cope. Thirty-one percent of the mothers and 21% of the fathers were considered as definitely unstable emotionally. Twenty percent of the mothers and 40% of the fathers were alcoholic. Almost all the marital situations were unsatisfactory and 69% were described as "parents living together with considerable discord, arguing and fighting constantly. Marriage characterized by instability — pattern of brief separations and/or desertions, extra-marital affairs". The children's records were said to present "a depressing, monotonously repetitive litany of inadequate care, with the parents too busy, too inept, too unhappy and too frustrated to give the children the care that they need". The average age at which children had been separated from their parents was $3\frac{1}{2}$ years and the average at adoption placement was 7 years 2 months. In the interim, they had experienced an average of 2.3 foster placements, and Kadushin describes this period for the children as having been "psychologically in limbo, belonging fully neither to his 'own' nor to the foster family; a period during which the child probably faced a problem of confused identification".

At the time of the follow up, the children's average age was 13 years 9 months. The principal criterion employed to ascertain the "success" of the placements was the level of satisfaction in the experience expressed by the parents. Some rather elaborate evaluation procedures were involved and, according to the methods used, the percentage of successful placements ranged from 73 to 82% successful, with 13–18% unsuccessful and 9% intermediate. Only two children had been removed from the home after the adoption. This would appear to be a remarkably high success rate, particularly when compared with the failure rate of 78% of children aged 5 years and over in foster homes (George, 1970).

The vital ingredient for success in these adoptions seems to have been mutual commitment of parent and child, though Kadushin offers a sociological explanation. He points out that, as they moved into adoption homes, the children made two changes. They left behind a home which offered little in the way of affection, support and encouragement and gained families where these were supplied. They also moved from problem families into families in which they had some status in the community. Thus their self concept was built up, not only by the acceptance and support of their new parents, but also by the messages they unconsciously received from the community.

A major question must be whether genuine emotional bonding can take place when children are placed for adoption well past infancy, and when conscious and unconscious memories and feelings about the child's original family have to be handled. Kadushin deals with this subject at some length but not altogether satisfactorily.

Adoptive parents coped with the problem of memories by being receptive to the child's desire to discuss this material, by permitting contact with past family members as an aid in helping the child adjust to the transition, and by a patient confidence that the child would ultimately lift the emotional anchor from the former family and place it in the adoptive family. Children resolved the problem by ventilating feelings regarding past ties, by conscious suppression and "forgetting" and by repression; in a lesser number of instances children seemed not to have resolved affectional ties to the past, and in 14 of these cases the failure to resolve the problem occasioned conflict for the adoptive parent and child.

Other reports of older-child adoptions (Donley, 1975; Edwards, 1975) emphasize the crucial importance of helping the child to understand and settle his feelings about the past before moving on to a new family, but they, too, demonstrate the remarkable ability of many children to overcome trauma and make good use of a healthy restorative environment.

Implications for Practice

For children needing permanent substitute parents, the adoption picture is considerably more encouraging than the fostering one. Adoption does offer full acceptance, commitment, continuity and reciprocity of relationships, but it has its own inherent hazards as well as its proportion of outright failures. It seems probable (though unproved) that most children, adolescents and adults who have been adopted have rather more than the usual difficulty in achieving a comfortable sense of their own identity, particularly if basic facts about their origins remain shrouded in secrecy. Curiosity and fears about biological parents, feelings of worthlessness connected with having been "given away", and anxiety about hereditary factors all occur regularly to some degree and can become emotionally crippling.

Nor can we yet confidently offer adoption as an available resource for any unwanted or abused child; there are both practical and legal complications. In the first place, homes for older children are in short supply. There is no difficulty in finding adoptive families for pre-school children, even if they have quite serious physical handicaps, provided they are not mentally impaired or severely maladjusted. Adoption prospects are less certain for children over the age of 6 or 7 years with particular difficulty for sibling groups and for coloured, school-age boys, especially when their school performance is poor. In May 1976, the Adoption Resource Exchange had 136 children on its lists and these are only the tip of the iceberg of unplaced children. What seems to be happening is that some social workers at least are becoming more willing to consider adoption as a possiblity for children permanently separated from their natural families, but homefinding skills have not kept pace with the need.

It is also increasingly obvious that, on the basis of the child's age alone, delays in coming to final decisions about separation seriously impede the chances of securing a suitable alternative family. Many of the children on the Resource Exchange list have been in care for years but the adoption decision was relatively recent and perhaps too late. Reasons for delay are multiple. They include the very real difficulties of diagnosis and prognosis. Professional uncertainty leads to arrange-ments which keep options open. There is a pervasive tendency to identify with adults who are usually seen as the primary clients even when lip service is given to the needs of the child, and, finally, we have a deep rooted and basically sound belief in the importance of family ties.

Social work training has included heavy doses of poorly digested theories on maternal deprivation. An essentially correct emphasis on keeping children out of care and returning them to their natural parents can result in too little attention being paid to ensuring either adequate physical and emotional nourishment or reasonable continuity and security during childhood. Fostering has been preferred to adop-tion because it does not necessitate such painful, irrevocable decisions on the legal severing of family ties. Long-term foster homes are, however, in even shorter supply than adoption homes and there are many situations in which marginally acceptable short-term foster homes, which have been used in an emergency, drift into becoming less than adequate long-term homes.

The law is a great upholder of family ties, anything which is thought to undermine family life being seen as a threat to the social fabric. Parents' rights often take precedence over children's needs, not out of any deliberate wish to inflict hardship on children, but because of the delicate balance between the concerns of the state and the freedom of the individual. The Children Act 1975 takes some significant steps towards putting children on an equal footing with adults before the law and to making parental rights dependent on fulfilling parental duties. When fully implemented it will (a) make it possible for agencies to bring children before the court to request that they be "freed for adoption", the parents' consent being dispensed with on one of the statutory grounds; and (b) make one of these grounds serious ill-treatment if, in addition, rehabilitation of the home is considered unlikely. Under the Act, courts are required to give first consideration to the welfare of the child throughout his childhood, but it remains to be seen how judges and magistrates will interpret these clauses. Only the other day, a judge refusing a local authority application for a care order, declared that a father had a right to beat his child, and courts are notoriously reluctant to dispense with consent to adoption even if evidence of genuine parental affection and responsibility is conspicuously lacking.

If earlier final decisions are going to be achieved, continuous efforts by the legal, medical and social work professions will be essential.

References

Adamson, G. (1973). "The Care-Takers". Bookstall Publications.
Baher, E. (1976). "At Risk: N.S.P.C.C. report". Routledge and Kegan Paul, London.
Barnes, M. (1967). The concept of "parental force". *Child Welfare* 46, No. 2.
Bohman (1970). "Adopted Children and their Families". Propeus, Stockholm.
Bohman (1972). Unwanted children — in prognostic study. *Child Adoption*, No 72.
Bryce, M. and Ehlert, R. (1971). 144 foster children. *Child Welfare* 50, No. 9.
Donley, K. (1975). "Opening New Doors". Association of British Adoption Agencies.
Edwards, M. (1975). Adoption for the older child. *Child Adoption*, No. 84.
Jaffee, B. and Fanshel, D. (1970). "How They Fared in Adoption". Columbia University Press, Carolina.
Franklin, D. and Massarik, F. (1969). "Adoption of Children With Medical Conditions". Children's Home Society of California.
Freud, A. (1955). "Safeguarding the Emotional Health of Our Children". Child Welfare League of America.
George, V. (1970). "Foster Care: theory and practice". Routledge and Kegan Paul, London.
Hagan, C. (1969). Permanent planning for children. (Unpublished).
Hersov, L. (1973). The psychiatrist and modern adoption practice. *Child Adoption*, No. 71.
Kadushin, A. (1970). "Adopting Older Children". Columbia University Press, Carolina.
Krugman, D. (1964). Reality in adoption. *Child Welfare* 43, No. 7.
Malone, B. (1960). Help for the child in an in-between world. *In* "Social Work in Foster Care". Ed. Tod. Longmans, London.
Martin, H. and Beezley, P. (1976). The emotional development of abused children. *Develops. Med. Child Neurol.* (in press).

Newson, E. (1971). "The Parental Role". National Children's Bureau Conference Report.

Parker, R. A. (1966). "Decision in Child Care". Allen and Unwin, London.

Rowe, J. and Lambert, L. (1973). "Children Who Wait". Association of British Adoption Agencies.

Seglow, J., Pringle, M. and Wedge, P. (1972). "Growing Up Adopted". N.F.E.R.

Shaw, M. (1976). Children between families. *Child Adoption*, No. 84.

Thorpe, R. (1974). The foster child. *Concern*, No. 14. National Children's Bureau.

Tizard, B. (1975). The adoption of children from institutions after infancy. *Child Adoption*, No. 79.

Trasler, G. (1960). "In Place of Parents". Routledge and Kegan Paul, London.

Walton, R. and Heywood, M. (1971). The Forgotten Children. A Study of Children in Care. University of Manchester.

Watson, K. (1968). Long-term foster care: default or design. *Child Welfare* **47**, No. 6.

Weinstein, E. (1960). "The Self-Image of the Foster Child". Russell Sage Foundation.

Discussion

(Chapters 7–11)

When a child and especially a young baby was removed from parental care, some assurance was needed that family functions could be discharged in the alternative setting which had the responsibility for performing the same roles as the biological family and which could as easily fail. The practical alternatives were a nursery or a children's home, fostering and adoption.

In nurseries or other institutions standards varied greatly and might be difficult to maintain, not least because of high staff turnover. To satisfy the child's emotional needs, basic requirements were nurturance and support followed by gradual failure of such support to encourage self-reliance and independence. Children needed "boundaries" within which to function as children in relation to parents, who provide the right degree of stimulation and set standards of behaviour in the process of the child's socialization and the building of his self-esteem. Importance is attached to family tradition, anecdote, the fun and the sadness peculiar to the family, all of which provide reference points for the child's own development towards maturity. Was group life really suitable for the baby and the young child? More use might be made of loyalty, the kind of allegiance felt for example by the "Barnardo boy" which had no counterpart among those brought up in local authority homes. Perhaps "institutional" babies might be able to make better use of group life later on, though this was doubted and we agreed that it was an important subject about which we did not know enough.

Foster parents could provide better for these needs, but did not always succeed. Failure could be due to inadequate preparation and lack of the support which used to be given by the old child care officers. Was there a gap in social worker training over the subject of preparation and support for foster families? Even if no gap existed, a high proportion of social workers was untrained. With greater financial rewards, fostering could compete with such careers for women as work in factories. A fostering profession, trained and instructed, could follow. One difficulty, the expectation of responsibility without the granting of rights, might be removed by the Children Act 1975. This should give security and freedom from the fear that the loved foster child might be returned to the damaging environment from which it had been rescued.

The question of professionalism as an obstacle to good communication was raised. Would it be good or harmful to professionalize fostering or indeed nurseries or day nurseries or any other caring places? Did we reallly know how best to run such places? The answers clearly depended on the goal of professional education. The fashionable belief was put forward that the true aim of the professional was to assist the client in problem-solving. Unfortunately, technical education tended to produce authoritarian workers who felt the compulsion to impose the solutions which they had learned. Nurses, health visitors and social workers could, like doctors, become "opinionated". Taught techniques, they were unprepared to face emotional demands and not all had insight. On the other hand, we needed a "knowledge base" from which to function. To help to solve the complex problems of child-rearing within the family, love and common sense were not enough. Again, more well-controlled studies are required.

More is known about adoption based on past research. Perhaps the detailed inquisition that precedes it has a continuing harmful effect on relationships. If the decision was to remove a baby at birth, the baby's interests demanded a rapid and secure placement such as only adoption could provide. But would the need for permanent separation be foreseen with sufficient certainty at the time of birth? Even the incompetent mother, unable to cope with a family, needed someone to love. If a baby was required as the object, was her love for it good or bad? It was likely to be selfish in part at least. We lack a vocabulary from which to define love.

Perhaps not enough was being done to help a family to keep the child. If ultimate rehabilitation of the family remained a practical aim, could it be effectively carried out while the child was separated? Day nursery care and other ways existed for extending the family out into the community and could encourage peer group interaction for the children. More should be done to humanize maternity ward care so as to minimize stress on young mothers. Given accurate prediction of vulnerable families, early intervention could alter parents' perception of infants and improve their competence as parents. Self-help groups among parents should be encouraged, although the tendency towards isolation among abusing parents was recognized.

Underlying all the discussion was the question of whether the abusing environment was necessarily more damaging to the child than the alternative actually provided. Continuity of care was of prime importance to development and a succession of foster-parents or residential nurseries cannot be a correct solution for the child. Deprivation and its effects on bodily growth were clearly described by Dr MacCarthy. There was some discussion about the apportionment of blame for failure of intellectual development on deprivation of food, of love and of adequate social conditions.

The need was accepted for more studies, such as those of Carolyn Jones, about the fate of abused children under the varying conditions of their lives, and bearing in mind that intervention itself, with parents under observation, whether helpful or not, produced its own effect. The assumption also is dangerous that any studies of children in a particular area could be used as controls for children in another area where cultural habits and social conditions differed. Several kinds of help and of helpers were needed. Links between nurseries and foster-parents or between child-care centres and cookery and homemaking classes at school should help to disseminate knowledge and good practice. However damaged children might be by their earlier experiences, hope had been engendered by the success in Kent of fostering difficult adolescents.

Joanna Shapland and Anne Campbell, in their report, brought the discussion back to the children themselves and how assessments and judgements by the adults in charge struck them. What did they themselves think about themselves and about what was happening to them? There were recognizable differences between boys and girls. The girls were inclined to show off if returned to the original school, nevertheless, given effective professional help, they benefited from a return to their old friends. Their basic reaction was to look on being "put away" in a remand home as punitive and to ask "what is wrong with me?" Boys by contrast say "it's a fair cop". The reaction of both sexes is influenced both by class and by cultural expectations. The temptation is to live up to the label. The middle-class child can be very disturbed, while in families in which police, courts and prison loom large, the incident is a kind of initiation and may even be a status symbol rather than a stigma. In the background, while for many the caretaker is not the biological parent or there is only one parent, more importance attached to quarrelsome and chaotic families than the presence or absence of one or other parent.

The general conclusion was that while we can identify what goes wrong, what helps to overcome the difficulties is still largely unknown.

Too many decisions had to be made against a background of uncertain and unvalidated criteria. Those making court orders had little opportunity to learn the sequel. The best solutions could only be reached after careful follow-up studies. In the gathering of data, agreement was essential about methods of assessment and scales by which to measure success and failure.

12. The Nature of Aggression

A. Hyatt Williams

Aggression consists of the use of force to express feelings and to achieve aims. It is used to intimidate, to impress, to manipulate and sometimes to subjugate other people and the environment and the various things contained in it. In former times, the vanquished, whether other human beings or animals, were not necessarily killed but were enslaved so that they became subordinate factors and aids to achieve the further aims of the victor. Aggression is used for purposes of self preservation and very much in the service of species preservation. It is used at times altruistically to save, rescue and defend. These functions contrast markedly with the opposite functions mentioned above, namely, to dominate, to annihilate or simply to seize and use. Aggression thus has a positive developmental function as well as a predatory function exercised for egotistic purposes, usually to the detriment of other people.

Pathological Aggression

These two aspects of aggression might be termed its normal parameters, but in addition to these there is a kind of aggression which, from the first, is essentially pathological. In this type of aggression, which may be characteristic for the particular individuals who use it as the habitual currency of their inter-personal relationships, there is violence and destructiveness beyond the need of the task in hand. Some of these people smoulder sullenly for long periods of time only to burst out into flagrant aggressiveness in an episodic way for adequate or sometimes for totally inadequate reasons. The important point is that the severity of the explosion into aggressiveness greatly exceeds the provocation which triggered it off. This suggests that there exists something inside the individual of an aggressive kind rather like a time bomb which is so situated or anchored within the psyche that certain kinds of provocation can detonate it. Sometimes the detonating agent to us seems minimal and totally inadequate. What is this something? It is insufficient an explanation to say that some people simply have a chip on their shoulders which makes them trigger happy without enquiring into the way in which this state of affairs came about in the first place. It is particularly with those people whose aggressiveness is excessive, odd or in one way or another inappropriate, that we wish to concern ourselves. I refer especially to those in whom aggressive action appears to be built into their way of life so that aggression is an invariable extension of diplomacy and for them a usual substitute for verbal negotiation. As far as words are concerned there seems to be no give and take in these people. In relationship to their method of physical confrontation what usually occurs is a bipolar situation in which they either boss other people about if they can subjugate them or kotow to stronger individuals (or groups). The underlying principle is based upon the maxim that might is right. The other features of the syndrome are that there is usually neither tolerance of differences nor espousal of a democratic interaction with the aim of achieving a negotiated solution acceptable to both sides. Control or be controlled by somebody else is the order of the day. These people are authoritarian but not necessarily perverse. As far as child abuse is concerned, what is often encountered is an excess of punitive zeal in quelling turbulence so that, with an unruly or disturbed child who does not find it possible to conform to rules, there is a resort to cruelty amounting eventually to gross abuse. This occurs when the child resists the conditioning of the authority, and one of the difficulties is the way in which the parental or other authority retains an attitude of moral righteousness and a belief that dreadful punishments are being inflicted only for the child's good. Sometimes, mounting aggressiveness is found to be exciting to both the authority and to the defiant, provocative child. This excitement can be quite sexualized, the one side practising brinkmanship and the other pursuing a cat-and-mouse game which gets more dangerous even to the point of life-risking as the excitement mounts.

The Provocation of Aggression

The various provocations which trigger-off such an escalation of violence may be due to disobedience, defiance of moral codes of behaviour or persistent acquisitiveness such as stealing. Sometimes the child is greedy and the demands upon the parent(s) or their substitute(s) go beyond the need of the subject and beyond the capacity or willingless of the objects. Sometimes the demands for food, toys, money, privileges or love are from one specific individual, the mother, and sometimes greed is diffused into all relationships, including particularly those with siblings. Demands may be made aggressively and, when unsuccessful, the aggression may mount into quite frightening violence. To cope with this, the parents or other authorities may find themselves responding by violent retributive actions in an attempt to get the greedy child back again within its boundaries so that he is not felt to be a threat.

Sometimes it is the need of the parents or school teachers which expresses itself greedily and a perfectly ordinary child receives punishment for not fulfilling the ambitions of parents or other authorities. In the case of the child who was being trained by her father to be a swimming champion who collapsed and died through being forced to do strenuous swimming at a time when she was physically ill, the ambitious greed of the father made his daughter into an infantile prodigy at swimming and obscured his capacity to think of the child's needs, rights and the limitations of her capacity. Greed may be expressed in the implementation of sibling rivalry, in which case aggressiveness and cruelty tend to mount. Greed directed against parents felt to be depriving by the child can result in violence either way so that the child threatens the depriving parent who in turn feels threatened by the child. Violence breaks out and in an escalation of this kind the killing of the weaker is not unknown.

Envy is much more dangerous than greed. Although the greedy person makes quite outrageous demands upon his or her object — parents, their substitutes or their latter-day derivatives — at least it is based upon a kind of love, and the need for more and more does indicate a presupposition that something good exists. This contrasts with envy which, as Chaucer said in the fourteenth century, is the deadliest of all the deadly sins because it attacks all the virtues and destroys all goodness. The envious person attacks the good object because that object is good and has something to give. The envious individual bites the hand that feeds it and sets to nought all the best endeavours of the most giving and generous people in the social environment.

Being punished for badness, default or dissimulation is what the average child expects and is usually quite willing to tolerate, as long as the punishment is regarded as full atonement to be followed by forgiveness and rapprochement. If, after the punishment, there is a continual harping back in the form of nagging, reproach or even reminding the young person of his or her wrongdoing, a secondary rebellion may flare up and eventually result in a further delinquent act. Sometimes authorities, including parents, are envious in such a way that they exploit the contrition of the young person and penalize the kind of constructive remorse which, if fostered, could have a very good outcome in relationship to future personal growth and development and also in its psycho-social repercussions. The worsening cycle of malevolence, in which an envious adult often pillories an envious child or vice versa, may end in a surge of destructive aggression.

This may be initiated by the child or by the parent but, in either case, escalation of the violence can and does lead to a beating, a battering, a maiming or even a killing, usually of the smaller and weaker person. Most often there is a constant interchange of violent projections. Projective identification, a term suggested by Melanie Klein, is used a great deal. Projective identification consists of a splitting off and projection of parts of the self and the forcing of them upon another person who may then be attacked for containing those parts. This is a pathological use of the unconscious psychic mechanism and method of communication which we might call normal projective identification. Sometimes the recipient of the projective identification feels taken possession of and may shout out such phrases as "stop it, you'll drive me mad". Such outbursts are no meaningless expressions of intolerance. Sometimes aggression is unconsciously designed to put madness into somebody else, i.e. drive them mad in the hope and expectation that the subject may remain sane.

Disburdening the self of feelings that are regarded as being unbearable is what every baby does to his or her mother or the person acting in the role of mother during the earliest period of the life of the infant. To lesser degrees, the father and after him more peripheral family members and people outside the home, come in for this kind of treatment. The mother or her substitute may make that which is communicated to her by projective identification somewhat better, and then relay it back to the infant in such a form that the latter is able to accept it and work with it. This course of interchange you will have recognized as the desirable and healthy one. It leads to emotional growth and development. There are other possibilities, however. For example, the mother or her substitute may block the communication or even make it worse, and feed back to the infant a worsened version of it. Blocked communications are very provocative as far as a flare-up of aggression is concerned. Just as parents can block the communciations of children, children can frustrate parents. This may be intentionally, unconsciously or coincidentally, in which case it is likely to consist of a spill over of their own disturbance in the capacity to communicate. For example, sometimes a pain is so frightening and persecutory to the child that he or she cannot talk about it clearly but conveys to the parent a misleading story. Some even go so far as to locate the pain in some part of the body far away from that which is actually hurting. This seems to be a spill-over and spread of the wish to deny the existence of the pain at all. I have known parents to be drawn into this kind of displacement and denial for some time in the course of which there has been a dangerous delay in the calling in of appropriate professional help.

Aggression and the Victim

We can take it that we all have an aggressive component. The question is, how is it linked with other parts of the self and how does it function or cause a person to function in relationship with other people, i.e. in a small group or a larger social setting? Within the self the aggressive component may be stronger or weaker. It may be directed towards the perservation of good internal object images and by externalization of their outward representations in the form of good people or worthy causes. On the other hand, the aggressive component may be used to defend or to perpetrate externally bad, undesirable parts of the self, including cruel, aggressive, greedy or destructive external projects. More complicated still is the situation in which bad methods are used in attempts to further good aims. These people are very difficult to deal with because they feel self-righteous, and it is hard to show them what they are doing in the course of their activities. When conducted in a solitary way by an aggressive "loner" using destructive methods often of a kind which can be life-risking to other people, the individual who perpetrates the acts of destructiveness tends to become increasingly, personally unstable. This is shown in several ways. There is sometimes an escalation of violence. Sometimes, there is an increasing paranoia which would be manifested as self-reproach if the feelings were allowed to operate on the self and not projected on other people. However, because they are repeatedly projected into the outer world, members of which are then attacked, thus the actual hostility of society or the police is increasingly aroused so that the individual does tend to bring upon himself a concretely expressed persecution. To match this, there is even more persecution from internalized figures in the fantasy life of the aggressor and a constant reinforcement of external and internal forces and vice versa. This process could be termed "the brutalization of the solitary aggressor".

When the various depredations are carried out by a group (or gang) the situation develops somewhat differently. The presence of like-minded people with a common aim tends to give to the group a coherence of its own in isolation from the rest of society. This coherence consists of an ascription of all good things to the in-group, who are the group members, while the bad characteristics are projected or ascribed to outer-society. Thus the aggressive group can carry on for a lot longer than the loner. Nevertheless, when disruptions occur within the group, the fact that general brutalization has taken place is shown in the cruel and violent measures which are used to maintain group solidarity and pull back potential deviants into the group on the basis of "conform to the group's standards or else be rejected absolutely" (not infrequently by execution).

In child abuse, a parent or parental surrogate may behave like the loner described above or a family or institution may operate like a gang or criminal group. In this case, the leader is likely to be the illest member of the group, family or institution. Families can behave like gangs in certain circumstances and then a scapegoat victim is usually selected, often quite unconsciously. This individual, who is often the baby or the most overtly weak member of the family, becomes the target for all the projections of the family group.

One such instance was a violent family with shared delusional ideas about their aristocratic status and origins who made their elder daughter the receptacle of most of the family mental instability. At first, she developed a state in which she behaved as though she were mentally subnormal. There were marked learning difficulties, so that she was unable to read or write until she went away for some months to an adolescent in-patient unit, where she suddenly found that she could learn to read. The family consisted of an intensely variable, warm and loving, but violent, father, a mother who was cold, distant, critical and dignified, an elder brother, a younger brother and a younger sister. It became clear that the individual psychotherapy which eventually was given to this young woman had little or no possibility of succeeding. With hindsight, it was evident that the family, largely unconsciously, set about the task of dismantling everything favourable that was happening in the therapy of this girl, so that she was constantly and repeatedly reinstated as the family scapegoat. Quite often the mother would ask to see the therapist and complain about the lack of improvement in her daughter. She would enquire when the treatment was going to work as if complete health and recovery would occur when the therapist found the magic word with the open sesame effect. Eventually, when some small amount of ground had been gained from the furious family inundation, the therapist was confronted with a catastrophic relapse in the patient who seemed to be back at or even beyond square one. On enquiry, it was found that the father had picked up his daughter's very special pet cat which promptly scratched him, whereupon the father seized the cat by its hind legs and bashed out its brains against the wall of the daughter's room in front of her. Each subsequent improvement was set to nought by an over-determined contrived catastrophic event, ranging from a serious head injury, sustained by the sister in a strange fall from a hitherto docile horse, to the damaging car crash of the elder brother who had passed his advanced driving certificate.

Without going into further details, the lesson to be learned from this therapeutically unsuccessful and frustrating experience is that the whole family must be seen and treated together when it is found that one family member is carrying the crippling and disturbing burden of all the family projections. When it is the baby, perhaps the baby who was unwanted in the first place, who is subjected to the process of scapegoating, there is considerable risk to its mental health and even to its physical survival in a disturbed family setting. In child abuse, the cruel parent and his or her relationship with the young victim is often only the visible part of the iceberg. The invisible part is situated in the unconscious mind of one member of the family or is shared between members of the family. It may be focalized in one parent, and that parent enacts concretely the fantasies shared by the other family members.

In some cases, a disturbed child, with an unconscious sense of guilt stemming from secret fantasies or actions, evokes cruel punishment from a parent or sibling in order to assuage and mitigate the uncomfortable feelings of guilt. Often there is an interaction between the fantasies and impulses of the aggressor and the needs of the victim. The interaction may remain in a low key, muted as it were, for long periods of time, so that violence and cruelty may erupt episodically. Alternatively, there may be a tendency to over-control with eventual eruptions of violence which may or may not escalate.

The question arises "what makes some cases of violence appear to be self limiting and, on the other hand, what makes for escalation in some cases?" In the former category, the aggression seems to be expressed, but once it had broken, it is like a wave breaking harmlessly upon a sandy beach and thereafter receding. In the latter category, the characteristics are of a tidal wave, mounting in successive stages until finally it overwhelms everything in a terrifyingly destructive catastrophe.

When some cruelty has been perpetrated and the aggressor sees the damage that he or she has done, damage to a child for instance, healthy feelings of guilt and remorse are usually able to make themselves felt and so limit the wave of cruelty which then recedes as the anger and rage die down. Most cases are like this, but in a minority of cases, a very dangerous minority, something different happens. There is a tendency for the sight or even the thought of harm done to the victim to result in further attacks being made upon that self-same victim. The intrapsychic processes in the aggressor seem to be as follows: the sight of the damage done to the victim shocks and dismays the aggressor and remorse begins to make itself felt in a painful manner, but the very pain of the experience is quickly felt to be unbearable and causes the psychic state of the aggressor to slide down from the more advanced and civilized feelings of depression and sadness over the harm done to the victim into one of mounting persecution. It is then that the eyes of the victim are felt to be boring into the aggressor with accusation and reproach. To end this situation and in a state of mind which is essentially paranoid, the aggressor attacks the victim further. This process can and often does go on and on until the victim is killed. Sometimes it goes further so that the identity of the victim is masked and obscured by defacement or even more completely obliterated. In the play by Peter Shaffer, "Equus", this situation is shown very clearly in relationship to the horses blinded by the emotionally disturbed young man who loved them and practised a perverse sexuality with them. When he fell for and had sexual relations with a young woman in the stables and the horses stamped their feet, he felt that he had been unfaithful to them and that they were looking at him with tremendous disapproval and reproach. He could not bear it and therefore attacked and blinded them.

We have not dealt with aggression which is primarily sadistic, in which the aim is for the subject to derive pleasure from the infliction of pain upon the object, the satisfaction being enhanced by the obvious signs of pain and distress which can be seen in the victim. In some families, one or other parent may behave in a sadistic manner towards one or more of their children. Some school masters derive pleasure from the infliction of pain upon young boys. In sadism, it is important to recognize the sexualization of the pleasure in the cruel transaction. It is largely the sexual excitement which causes sadistic behaviour to be repetitive. The role of the victim of ill treatment or more serious injury is complicated and, of course, many victims are masochistic. The masochist derives pleasure, ultimately of a sexual kind, from the infliction of pain upon him or her. There is a male/female sex-linkage with the pair of opposites just described; there are more male sadists and more female masochists. The study of aggressor/victim relationships, called victimology, is still in its early stages and needs much more investigation. Let it suffice to state that the pairing of aggressor and victim is rarely a matter of pure chance. They tend to select one another mutually for definite though usually unconscious reasons and purposes.

Reparation and reparative aims and activities are undertaken to put right, as far as possible, the injuries and depredations committed by the aggressor against his victim or victims. Reparation can proceed only if the pain of guilt and remorse about harm done can be borne and sustained sufficiently for significantly long periods of time. If the self-reproaches and remorse are switched unconsciously and automatically into persecutory feelings, the result tends to consist of further attacks upon the victim rather than further reparation. It is easy to see how serious the consequences of aggressive damage done can be when we are dealing with that kind of person. It is to be emphasized that some of the further damage may be due to the mental image or representation of the victim within the mind of the aggressor. The acting out with further damage to the actual victim may be immediate or delayed, delayed sometimes by many years.

Working Through the Depressive Position

How do people become so different in their attitudes and actions, so that at one end of the scale intrapsychically something is built in which limits aggression whatever the provocation, and at the other end a very much less favourable situation prevails? In the people at this other end of the scale, aggression tends to escalate. Although there are no clear-cut boundaries in nature over this issue, there does seem to exist something like a watershed. The question is, can this be related to any situation or phase in infantile or childhood development which, if dealt with satisfactorily, leads to a capacity to limit aggression and, if left unnegotiated in an unsatisfactory state, leaves such people with no such capacity? These are the people who tend to be goaded by the sight and realization of damage inflicted upon a victim. It is necessary to explain the development of the depressive position and of the partial substitution of the more primitive, persecutory form of anxiety by the more integrated and "civilized" depressive anxiety in the human being.

In the first few months of life, the infant who has at that stage relatively undeveloped perceptual powers and only very limited capacities to conceptualize, mother or the person who looks after the infant is perceived not as a whole person, but as parts. These parts, e.g. eyes, breasts and hands, are apparently relatively unrelated to each other. At this stage also, a feature of normal development is the sorting out of experiences and objects (experienced, of course, as part-objects) into gratifying pleasurable experiences stemming from good, even idealized, sources (the good part-objects) and, at the opposite end of the scale, into painful, depriving and frustrating experiences, supposedly derived from bad, denigrated, part-objects. Without going into greater detail, the frustration and deprivation due to the absence of a good part-object are often experienced as being caused by the presence of a bad part-object.

At some time just before the middle of the first year of life, the neurophysiological and the psychological development of the infant have developed sufficiently so that it becomes possible to recognize mother or her surrogate as a person, i.e. as a whole object. The realisation that here is the whole-object mother results in the untenability of the polarization into good and bad part-objects. The infant's own hostile feelings towards and fantasies about the bad depriving part-object (e.g. breast) are felt to have harmed, even destroyed, the good, gratifying, loved breast. As a result of relating these two opposite attitudes, namely love and hatred towards the same whole person, mother, the infant experiences a different feeling. This new feeling amounts to depression, sadness and concern for the mother, lest his hostile feelings should predominate over his loving ones. To this stage, Melanie Klein gave the name Depressive Position. Some holding on to the painful anxieties at this phase by the young infant, i.e. some negotiation of the Depressive Position, is important for future growth and maturation. Without such negotiation, the infant remains dominated by the more primitive kind of anxiety called Persecutory Anxiety, which is based upon a feeling of being got at, threatened, and is productive of an abiding sense of grievance. With some success in dealing with the Depressive Position, Depressive Anxiety, which is to do with anxiety over harm done by the self predominantly to one's good object, is able to be felt and sustained. This kind of anxiety leads on to feelings of responsibility and hence to attempts at reparation for harm done, to sublimation and to every form of creativity.

The working through of the Depressive Position in the middle of the first year of life is never complete. Re-negotiation of the anxieties and relationships to do with the Depressive Position is necessary again and again, particularly at times of personal crisis and developmental change such as adolescence, the menopause, the mid-life crisis in the thirties described by Jaques. Successful re-negotiation of the Depressive Position is followed by a further efflorescence of integration of the self and therefore of favourable psycho-social repercussions.

Although the Depressive Position and its negotiation does indeed constitute a watershed in emotional development, it must be stressed that the situation is not entirely an all or nothing one but one of degree. If this were not so, it would stultify the very numerous and complicated efforts on the part of many people who work in the caring and remedial services. Not only can there be some improvement, even in the most disturbed people, if there can be some secondary negotiation of the Depressive Position, but also disturbed individuals, including those who are most violent, can be helped to contain their violent feelings and impulses without immediately seeking to enact them in full in action upon another person or upon other people. Several kinds of mitigation may take place. One is the expression of violence against things instead of people. The man who smashes the telephone or breaks a glass rather than beating up his young child with whom he is annoyed has made a considerable step forward. Further steps lead to an increasing ability to contain violent impulses without acting them out at all. These impulses are often expressed in conscious fantasies or in dreams and, although it is recognized that some fantasies may be the precursors of action, I am referring to the extremely important use of fantasy as a substitute for action: Mr Pugh in "Under Milkwood", who said that he was taking his wife a nice cup of arsenic and weed-killer biscuits, actually took her a nice cup of tea and wholesome biscuits each morning. Harmless substitutes for violent and aggressive actions may be sustained in the absence of a containing environment or they may be able to stop at a fantasy level only in such an environment. Violence tends to occur when too much happens either too quickly or when hostile feelings accumulate in those people and in those situations where psychic digestion is impaired or when a sudden rush of violent experiences exceeds the capacity of the individual who is subjected to them as far as psychic digestion is concerned. Often it is at this point that urgent intervention of a professional kind is required and can have most influence.

The way in which there can be a drift from fantasy to action is usually by means of the following series of steps.
1. There is a loosening of the grip on depressive anxiety which is gradually replaced by persecutory anxiety as shown in the following diagram:

$$D \rightleftharpoons P/s$$

D = Depressive anxiety and P/s = Paranoid-schizoid or persecutory anxiety.
2. Then follows the designation of the potential victim as a persecutor. He or she, whether child or adult, becomes singled out as the enemy.
3. Gradually, the potentially violent individual suffers from an increasing distortion of his perception of the persecutor. For example, in one case a disturbed adolescent girl experienced her stepfather as a large bear-like animal who gradually became regarded as a bear with all the implied threat of sitting at breakfast with a grizzly bear.
4. There is then a breakdown into part-object perceptions, so that the persecutor in the case of the step-father as seen by the adolescent girl changed. Finally, all that she could see was a knife and a fork threatening to stab her and carve her up.
5. There is a gradual breakdown in the capacity for and use of symbolization, so that what would stand for something else becomes experienced as that thing in itself. For example, the phallus of the rapist is regarded as being a sword or a dagger. In retaliation or in the interests of self-preservation, an actual knife may be picked up and used against the threatening persecutor. Another example of a breakdown in symbolization is when burning feelings become con-

cretized into an impulse to set something on fire which is then indulged and a fire started with incalculable results.

6. What has been said demonstrates how action, which is dynamized by persecutory anxiety, is likely to be of a violent, destructive kind.

7. After the violent episode has run out of power and drive, a precariously held equilibrium is gradually restored.

The restoration of equilibrium may be hastened by appropriate action on the part of the social agencies. Far better, of course, is the recognition in advance of the mounting danger of violence. When the violent escalation has not gone too far, social agencies, and particularly knowledgeable, caring and understanding individuals working for the social agencies, can be significantly successful in helping to restore equilibrium without the violent acting out taking place at all. The following diagram (Fig. 5) may help to illustrate these processes. Not everyone, of course; has violence which is dangerously situated within the psyche.

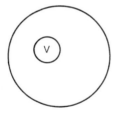

Represents the split-off encapsulated violent enclave (V) within the person

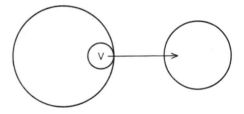

Violence surfacing and being expressed upon a victim

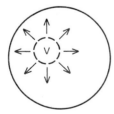

Violence breaking-loose within an individual who then devotes *all* his energy in perpetrating violence upon a victim

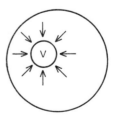

Violence again well-encapsulated

Fig. 5

Discussion

A theory is desirable and Dr Hyatt Williams had described one. According to the container analogy, the therapist's task was to act as the container. The situation might deteriorate during treatment but the cycle had to be broken. Was the baby safe while the mother was battling with persecutory anxiety? The feeling was expressed that account should be taken of theories other than the Kleinian one. It was difficult to see how it could explain eye contact or the baby's need to relate to other people than the mother, for example father or grandparents, although the relation to mother was closer and occupied more time. There was some danger in trying to force the world into one category.

13. Social Work Intervention in Cases of Child Abuse

Jack Chapman

Except in certain cases of clearly diagnosed mental illness or sexual perversion, ill-treatment of children almost always originates in the breakdown of relationships between their parents. Though such a definite statement cannot as yet be supported by any authoritative research, those who work within the field of marital breakdown, divorce and separation, are well aware of the severe repercussions on the well-being of the children involved. A fact more clearly attested is that much delinquency among children stems from unstable or broken home backgrounds. In addition, many young parents who injure their children are now seen to have come from such homes themselves.

In view of this, it is perhaps surprising that such a small proportion of the total social work effort goes directly into the twin activities of marriage conciliation and mending the effects on children of separations and divorces. To say this is not to minimize the amount of time and work spent in this way by social workers, probation officers and marriage guidance counsellors. It is rather to draw attention to the fact that, in the main, the concern is with indirect effects rather than on the dire consequences to children of faulty and sometimes hostile interaction between their parents. Where the marriage guidance councils are involved the emphasis is, quite rightly, on the possibility of reconciliation between husbands and wives and the responsibility is not *primarily* for the children who may be involved. The people who are often best placed to discover when children are at risk through marital disharmony are the professional workers who have the authority, and in some cases the obligation, to visit homes and investigate or supervise in that setting.

In this paper, child abuse is taken to include parental attitudes which cause suffering or psychological damage to children, as well as actual physical cruelty or parental neglect. As these comments are concerned mainly with reports prepared for the courts (though including some other kinds, e.g. for the parole board), they deal with all children for whom the courts have responsibility, which are those up to 16 years of age, or up to 18 if they are still at school or college.

Parental Discord

What are the particular dangers to which children with warring parents are exposed? In the experience of those who deal with matrimonial, wardship and guardianship cases in the courts, the most serious factor, fundamentally, is the emotional stress caused by the children's divided loyalties, especially where this inner conflict is sharpened deliberately by parents who are contesting the child's custody and not scrupling to use the child as a tool in their battle for possession. This frequently involves allegations of neglect or cruelty by the other partner, and, although these may turn out to be baseless, they nevertheless need to be examined and sifted most carefully because often they contain a grain of truth. There are, for instance, cases where the alleged cruelty is not by the other spouse but by a step-parent or cohabitee.

Many of the most distressing situations occur in family units where the parents or step-parents are not legally married, although to the neighbours they may appear to be. In Britain to-day, increasing numbers of couples, even with divorce made easier by recent legislation, either prefer not to get married or cannot do so. This may be because of the religious scruples of a previous partner. On the other hand, one of the couple with parental responsibilities may be using the relationship for his or her convenience and has no durable ties with the home or with the children of the family, and this makes ill-treatment of children more likely.

However, among those who observe these situations at close quarters, the only certainty is that there is no uniform or easily recognizable pattern. The looseness and fragmentation of our current social culture have reached the stage when there are no longer any prescribed rules of conduct and morality, either within or outside marriage; reliance has to be placed on the simple, instinctive feeling that it is wrong to harm children. Unfortunately, for a variety of reasons, this inborn inhibition, if not reinforced by strong social conventions, tends to break down when parents or substitute parents come under severe private stress. Natural parents are often as culpable as step-parents. In fact, a child's only protector against its own father or mother may be the partner with whom its parent is, or has been, living.

In the experience of welfare officers dealing with marriages which have broken down, the children concerned come to be ill-treated through the following process. Initially, the wear and tear resulting from severe friction between the spouses causes one or other of them to turn to their children for reassurance, perhaps to ease their sense of inadequacy in solving the crisis. This plea for support may take the form of enveloping the children in an over-protective and unnaturally emotional relationship; or it may result in insisting that the children conform to that parent's ideas over religion or discipline. Whichever way it goes, the other parent whose battle up till then has been with the partner, feels that he or she is being outmanoeuvred and makes a bid to capture the allegiance of the children. This is the danger point, whether or not the parents have actually separated.

In their state of agitation, each of the parents may sincerely believe that the regime they wish their children to adopt, and their particular way of dealing with them, is entirely conducive to the children's happiness. But, if the strains within the marriage have brought out hitherto latent differences between the spouses over the best way of bringing up their children and if the children are then exposed to two conflicting sets of demands on them by their own overwrought parents, it is evident that from the child's point of view the situation can literally be a menacing one. This is particularly so if one or other of the parents has a sadistic streak or is a firm disciplinarian. On the one hand, there may be indulgence and deliberate spoiling; on the other, there may be punishment, including corporal punishment, for infringement or an arbitrary code of conduct.

Collecting Information

The majority of those who have accumulated extensive experience of child abuse are specialists in a particular discipline and their attention appears to have been concentrated largely on non-accidental injury to children under 2 years of age. Probation officers (who are also known as court welfare officers) and local authority social workers, on the other hand, operate as multi-purpose practitioners. They have to deal with an immense variety of human problems among which child abuse, although it must be accorded the highest priority, is only one. Yet it is from among the ranks of such relatively non-specialized workers that the courts must normally look for the vital information they need concerning home conditions and relationships within the home setting. Few other people except G.P.s and health visitors have the opportunities of observing these at first hand.

For this reason, probation officers and social workers although they cannot be described as experts in the strict sense, have a clearly defined function in the area being studied, and are an essential link in the chain of responsibility for reducing child abuse and preventing non-accidental injury to children.

Reference has been made to the importance of first hand observation in the home. It is a strange fact, which was originally highlighted in the official report on the Maria Colwell case, that if parents are determined to prevent entry to a home where it is suspected that child abuse is occurring, there are few people who have a statutory right to pass the doorstep. The health visitor, despite her duty to visit, is not among them.* It was for this reason, among others, that Maria's supervising social worker was deterred from visiting more regularly. A non-lawyer must tread warily in stating the position: but if it is as substantial as just described, it would seem to follow that changes in the law are necessary, even at the cost of some invasion of the privacy of the home, in order to ensure that, when there are reasonable grounds for anxiety, someone has the authority to enter a dwelling to find out what is happening within.

We come here to the heart of the problem facing the courts in dealing appropriately with cruelty to children or, in civil cases, making the best possible dispositions for their future welfare. Judges and magistrates must have before them, in addition to expert evidence, information concerning the home which has been gathered on the spot by someone who is an unbiased, trained observer and can describe accurately what has been seen and heard in the course of his visit. If supervision of some kind is already being exercised, this should be a relatively simple task; but in the great majority of cases, where the home has not been seen previously, this means that the necessary data for a full and adequate report have to be gathered in the course of one or two visits lasting perhaps no more than 2 hours each.

On learning this, many people are inclined to say: how can this result in anything more than a superficial and probably misleading account of the situation? In High Court cases, a good deal of background information is available to the welfare officer in affidavit form before he visits. But, because of the plausibility or entrenched defensiveness of nearly all battering or damaging parents (even including some who are asking for the custody of children), there is a high risk of the probation officer or social worker being "conned". Because of this High Court judges have vetoed "split reports" in disputed custody or access cases; if the same reporting officer sees both parents, however far apart they live, it at least helps him to assess the truth of what they are each saying to him. It may also give him the

---

* The position of the health visitor in relation to visiting families in their own homes is often misunderstood. The area health authority has a statutory duty to provide a health visitor service. This is the limit of any statutory obligation. The health visitor employed by that authority has a duty to visit all her families with children under the age of 5 years. She is expected to do the best that she can, but no sanctions can be applied against her or the family if they never see each other. Her visit is a matter of accepted practice and no more.

opportunity of seeing the children with each of the parents. The experienced social worker is aware of the pitfalls of interviewing in "fraught" situations and his ability to penetrate people's defences is a measure of his particular expertise. Though it is not easy, when being alternatively cajoled, threatened or flattered, to retain objectivity and establish the real facts, the attempt has to be made in order to provide one piece in the jigsaw, without which the court cannot complete its picture of the situation, and come to the best decision in each case.

So, visits have to be short because of the limitations of resources and manpower; from the moment he arrives outside the home, the good probation officer or social worker will be on the *qui vive,* taking in facts and impressions of a hundred and one different kinds, all of which may be grist to the mill of his report to the court. He must, of course, note the state of the home both inside and out (though untidiness within limits may be a virtue rather than a fault: it is the atmosphere that counts). He must observe and note the attitudes and stability of the parents. He must be capable of drawing some reliable conclusions from their interaction with their children. He must see the parents on their own (or with their new partner if they have remarried). Above all, unless the children are very young, he must talk to them on their own, and to each separately if there is more than one. Through all this, the social worker must have his antennae at full stretch, while outwardly doing all he can to gain the confidence and trust of both adults and children. It is a difficult part to play while at one and the same time acting as a sharp-eyed detective and showing genuine sympathy and understanding. But it must be done successfully if the reporter is to act effectively as the eyes and ears of the court in the one place where perhaps no one else can go.

During the home visit, the attention of the social worker will be focused on two vitally important matters, the adequacy and stability of the parent or parents, and the mental and physical condition of the children. Have the parents the capacity to show real, loving warmth, or are they locked in the world of their own self-centred needs? Is the mother able to function as a reasonably competent housekeeper? Does she show signs of bizarre behaviour or other evidence of mental illness? Are the children unnaturally withdrawn? Do they suffer from psychosomatic ailments, such as asthma or skin rashes? Are they plainly frightened? Do they show any evidences of unexplained injury? Do the things the children say tally with what the parents have told the social worker? These are the kinds of questions which will be constantly in the mind of the home investigator.

Who Requires Reports?

The legislastion in the field of child abuse is bewilderingly varied and complex, and embraces many successive Acts of Parliament over the past 30 years. The court situations in which social reports may be requested or directed are correspondingly numerous, the following being the main ones:

1. Care proceedings in juvenile courts.
2. Matrimonial proceedings in domestic courts.
3. Criminal proceedings against adults in magistrates courts.
4. Wardship proceedings in the High Court and
5. Divorce proceedings in the High Court or county courts.

The approach adopted in (3) will clearly differ to some extent from that in the other types of case, since in criminal proceedings the main object of the social enquiry report is to assist the judge or magistrate in deciding on the most appropriate sentence. However, in the majority of cases where an adult is convicted of an offence against a child, there will be parallel proceedings in some other court where a fuller social report is certain to be requested, and where the child's welfare will be the focus of concern.

In the criminal courts, there are wide variations of attitude towards offences against children, but in general, and for lesser offences, sentences tend to be shorter than for offences of violence in the community. This may be because social reports in some cases show clearly that the acts took place in moments of extreme stress, or because psychiatric reports point to the likelihood of mental disturbance. However, short prison sentences for comparatively grave assaults on children can, paradoxically, bring their own problems. If the sentence is for 2 years or more, or for life, a full report on the home conditions is automatically called for before release, and if it is considered timely, the person is then released under the supervision of a probation officer. But if the sentence is for under 2 years, there is no report and no statutory supervision although the offender may be returning to the very same home conditions which precipitated the offence. Voluntary after-care can be given by the probation service but if the offender does not choose to avail himself of it, no kind of surveillance can be exercised.

Sexual Offences

One type of child abuse familiar to every probation officer seems largely to be ignored in the literature; this is the sexual offence, incest or indecent assault. In divorce and wardship cases, allegations of sexual irregularities are common, some of which may lack foundation but others, when true, lead to criminal proceedings. The real truth is notoriously difficult to obtain for a reporting welfare officer, but special regard should always be paid to sleeping arrangements, especially where it is discovered that a parent is sharing a bed with an older child. This again emphasizes the importance of on-the-spot investigation and observation.

Preparation of Reports

Turning to civil (i.e. non-criminal) matters, probation officers or social workers are required to prepare reports in almost all contested custody or access cases. They may also be called upon for reports in divorce cases where, for some reason, the judge feels unable to express satisfaction with the arrangements made for the children, as he is required to do by the Acts.

It should be regarded as axiomatic that, during the preparation of reports on children, contact should be made with any relatives or others who have been involved in the situation recently, such as grandparents, uncles, aunts, neighbours or friends. In addition, the reporting officer should communicate with all those in any official position who may be presumed to have knowledge of the children, e.g. teachers, general practitioners, psychiatrists, ministers of religion, health visitors and other social workers. In particular, school reports should be obtained on all children attending school or nursery school and, if necessary, interviews sought with staff. Where a child of any age has been under treatment, the psychiatrist should be asked to send a report, though in some cases problems of confidentiality may arise.

Although another paper deals with psychiatric reports to the court, it may not be out of place to comment on these from a probation officer's point of view, since this will bring out one important principle which, ideally, should apply to all professional reports to the court. This is that all such reports should be clearly seen as essentially impartial documents and not used as evidence on behalf of one or other party. To emphasize this, a court welfare officer in the High Court is not normally required to take the oath and should only be questioned on matters of fact in his report. Any attempt to cross-examine the welfare officer as if he were a witness is sternly frowned upon by the judge. The same protection should apply to doctors, psychiatrists or teachers, whose reports should be regarded as neutral assessments based solely on their professional knowledge.

Custody and Care and Control

In contested custody cases, the task of the welfare officer is to provide the background material which will assist the judge or magistrates to weigh up the merits of two or more alternative homes. In wardship proceedings, the legal custody of the child remains with the court until such time as the child is "de-warded"; in other cases, custody may be given to one or other parent or guardian, or there may be a joint custody order. However, care and control must be always granted to the parent with whom the child is going to live and who will be responsible for its day-to-day upbringing.

Welfare officers are often asked if they make recommendations in these contested cases. The answer is that, in the High Court, the judges prefer them not to, if this can be avoided, for the simple reason that an enemy does not want to be made out of either party, and the facts, if fairly set out, often speak for themselves. However, in the lower courts recommendations are often expected and asked for.

Access

Some of the most highly contentious matters dealt with in court reports are those involving disputes over access to children. Considering that, after every divorce or separation in which children are concerned, there remain two households whose week-end and holiday arrangements are governed strictly by access provisions, this is a problem which now has to be faced in a very large number of homes in Britain. No doubt, in the majority of these situations it is accepted as a fact of life, and the necessary careful planning of family activities goes fairly smoothly and without serious harm to the children. But in a minority of such cases where there is continuing bitterness and outright hostility between the parents, the children concerned can be caught up in a "double-bind" situation and suffer almost unbearable stress and conflict of loyalties. Such clinical symptoms as bed-wetting, tantrums, aggressiveness and lack of concentration at school are common effects of these inner anxieties. In the worst cases, children may be literally terrified of visiting a parent who has either abused them at an earlier period or been violent in their presence. In other cases, children may be totally confused by being subjected to an entirely different regime when visiting. In yet other cases, they may suffer religious indoctrination or be the victims of insistent cross-examination about their home life. The occasional possibility of sexual interference has already been mentioned.

Supervision

Social work reports in all the categories mentioned may result in supervision orders under the appropriate Acts. Supervision in such cases is nowadays usually undertaken by local authority social workers, but probation officers can be, and sometimes are, nominated as supervisors. At some courts, the judge or magistrates may call for periodical reports by the supervising officer. Whether this is done or not, the welfare officer or social worker has the power and the responsibility to bring the matter back before the court at once if a crisis arises which demands action and may necessitate a variation of the order (e.g. the making of a care order). This calls not only for a written report, but for the ability to open the case and give a verbal explanation of the reasons for seeking the court's fresh guidance. This power can only be exercised, as the law stands, under a matrimonial or wardship order: juvenile court orders do *not* give the same discretion to the supervising officer.

Separate Representation of Children in Court Proceedings

When Sections 64 and 103 of the Children Act 1975 come into operation, it will become possible to appoint a social worker or probation officer to act for a child, in the same way that the official solicitor does in the High Court. This will apply only in certain juvenile court proceedings similar to those that preceded the Maria Colwell tragedy. The person appointed will be referred to as a guardian *ad litem* (not to be confused with guardian *ad litem* in adoption proceedings), and his function will be to safeguard the interests of the child when there is a possibility that these may be overlooked or ignored by all the other parties involved. The guardian *ad litem* will not simply be producing a social report; he will have to put an independent view himself, either orally or by obtaining legal representation for the child.

If this first step towards protecting specially vulnerable children can later be extended to further categories of cases, it may prove to be a landmark in helping to prevent child abuse. But it will require exceptional ability and "toughness" on the part of the social worker involved.

It follows from this, and perhaps from all that has been said, that proper training in court work relating to children at risk is vital. This applies particularly to the preparation of social reports since these need to be unusually thorough, and the results, in terms of court decisions, often have far-reaching consequences for the children.

For Discussion see p 216.

14. Punishment, Retribution and Rehabilitation

A view from the probation service

Jill Tibbits

Among all the other subjects for this symposium, the title of this particular paper at first appeared an out-dated and rather negative concept. It seemed so much less focused on the problem of understanding, and then dealing with, child abuse which presents so many strains on all concerned. It seemed like the sort of thing a probation officer would be deemed to have expertise about, and apart from feeling singularly inexpert amongst an almost byzantine "field of flowers" of experts, I found I was reluctant to acknowledge this specialization in "punishment, retribution and rehabilitation".

Inevitably over a period of 25 years in the service, the old penological arguments for training have been the ground base of much dialectic. Evidence, first to that abortive marathon, the Royal Commission on the Penal System, has taken up much time and thought. Recently, my riper or more elderly attitudes have found themselves much more in sympathy with Leon Radzinowicz's cross-examination of a witness to the Royal Commission.

Is it really necessary to agree specifically what the purposes of punishment have to be in order to introduce important changes in our penal system? Can we not really introduce a great number of changes without putting them down on paper in a form which must always necessarily be irritating and which must produce conflicts?

Is what he wrote in 1964 still true in 1976?

I wonder sometimes how far ... we should pursue arguments about first principles of punishment.... It is not, at least nowadays, arguments about first principles that influence the strength or direction of public opinion or waken public response to the need to cope with crime and criminals. What does appeal to the imagination, and move public feeling, is the successful salvage operation....

In the light of some of the response of the media to recent happenings, it seems not wholly applicable. Successful salvage operations do not create the interest which accrues to the failure. Desire for retribution seems a concept which if buried is certainly not laid to rest, even though it may now be as much focused on those who unsuccessfully and "negligently" spend and earn the ratepayers' money as on the offender. In any sheaf of newspaper cuttings on child abuse cases, phrases like " the public will demand" and "the community has a right to expect" feature continuously. The indignation is correct but it is an uneasy bedfellow with failure to produce home aids or spend money on what might be called "respite" centres when family crises threaten.

Although for those of us in the probation service, the rehabilitation and de-labelling of the community service idea seems like a breath of fresh air, its immediate and favoured growth may well have depended on a happy ability to look like retribution and rehabilitation at the same time. If so, then any treatment programme in which an "offence" is concerned has to take account of such concepts in its planning.

Somehow the law has grown up in an uneasy balance of the three. The law focuses on an offender and a victim. To some, this seems an over simplistic answer to such a multi-faceted problem as child abuse. To others the right to be responsible for one's own acts is inalienable. At times, legal powers in the multi-disciplined and effective treatment of child abuse seem irrelevant, yet they have to be there as a framework for the protection of the child. Without a willingness to accept this aspect from all the experts concerned and real public interest, danger can spring from legislation by newspaper reporters. In some respects the last Children Act, although it contained some very good things, is an example of piecemeal legislation "by reaction", in which careful thinking through could sometimes have produced a different result.

It is possible that the desire for retribution is not dead and that some aspects of modern living contribute to its continued existence. Without the old rigid limitations, life is so much more complicated and it might well be very helpful to have an unpardonable sin for which retribution is justifiable. Ideally, of course, this is not what we are all about. We might feel that we came much nearer to John Stuart Mill's "The only purpose for which power can rightfully be exercised over any member of a civilized community, against his will, is to prevent harm to others".

The above admirable sentiment seems foolproof until consideration is given to some of the violent, destructive people who have been under supervision and for whom it would not be possible to say that power was exercised "against their will". Many people often want, and seek, protection from doing the wrong of which they are capable. Many baby batterers do not think what they do is right and long for people not to talk about them but "to do something". To some it may be questionable whether the law is always the best way to "prevent harm to others". There are many experts on child abuse who would not agree with this, but others feel that only the law affords ultimate sanction to protect the child.

Judge James Delaney (1972) talks of the criminal process in these terms:

The criminal prosecution of an abusive parent merits critical examination. First, we need to look at the methods by which the law exacts its toll, and the effect on those most directly concerned, the parent and the child. Second, we must assess the results obtained in terms of lasting benefits and detriments to these same parents and children.

A criminal proceeding, once set in motion, is formidable, impersonal and unrelenting. It is supposedly the public conscience censoring a fellow member; its aim is primarily punitive rather than therapeutic.

However, he goes on to note;

These comments are meant to explore and discuss the ways in which the juvenile and family courts can be an effective resource in treating, even preventing, child abuse. The true aim of the law should be to give us a better way of life. If we use courts only to arbitrate commercial disputes and punish public offences, we restrict one of our most effective resources. The true goal of a good legal system should be to make the law work for the people it serves.

In the view of some courts, punishment of certain acts gives them "a value-crystallizing function". Some of us will feel that values expressed negatively are a poor substitute for purposeful aims and positive principles, but it could be argued that the realities of life make the negative method most effective.

Punishment and the difficulties it presents, seem to be at the very hub of the problem in cases of battered children. It is what it is all about. Judicial punishment ideally should be considered, appropriate and measured, but the punishment meted out by the child abuser is generally subjective, unreasoned and disproportionate. The aims of judicial punishment are to set limits on behaviour for the offender and for others; to exercise control; to produce better behaviour; to perpetuate the idea that certain behaviour is wrong because it is punishable and to give legitimate relief to the feelings of those in immediate contact or, more generally, in the outside community.

How relevant is it to punish the core type of child batterer? Most have been excessively punished in childhood and have a very low self-value. They do not appear immediately promising material for further punishment even though they may seek it and sometimes want it. There is certainly some evidence that the fear of punishment leads to delay of requests for help. A healthy fear may well be extremely useful amongst the so called normal society, but the fear in such families is not healthy. In any case, how healthy is society itself in matters of punishment and violence? Whether it is the I.R.A. or the Special Force in Ireland or some educational bodies, physical violence is quite clearly seen as a means of control and getting what one wants. Punishment as a deterrent is again most effective where those to be deterred are fairly stable. It is not easy to deter where offences spring from "a deep and spontaneous inner impulse".

In the period of my own social work life, there would seem to have been three phases as far as our present subject is concerned. One might be called the "pre-Kempe" when foremost in the mind was the need to protect the child and to keep balance between revulsion against violence and understanding of the causes. This was underlaid with a fundamental distrust of punishment in such cases, but a feeling that sometimes courts were the way in which conflicts came out into the open, could be recognized and dealt with. The second stage, "post-Kempe", was a period in which it seemed that there could be real progress; theory was evolved and simply stated from apparently appropriate research, and treatment appeared to show results. At a symposium 10 years ago, a tentative remark from me about the use of courts was firmly condemned by a member of Doctor Kempe's team. The third phase for all of us must be the "post-Maria Colwell" period. Overstretched social work departments of all types are now battling with what seems like an increasing, even if only increasingly identified, problem. Defensive barriers have gone up against criticism; registers, two in the case of our service, one for ourselves and the Home Office and one for the child abuse authorities, have attempted to monitor the problem. But we are still left with what to do about it, and we are still left with the question whether punishment is a necessary moral condemnation and the only way to deal justly with such cases.

There is the even greater problem of identifying what rehabilitation means. Does the abusing parent who has a newborn child removed from her care, because she has harmed another, see that as rehabilitation? Indeed, as social workers, are we at the moment more involved in safeguarding our own image or safeguarding the delicate balance between accepting a risk or denying a chance for a more healthy family tie in a new unit. Nils Christie (1975) believes, "in my opinion, on the whole, the best protection is afforded to the weakest party in a system employing compulsory measures if these measures are given their harshest names". Perhaps we sometimes talk about rehabilitation without examining what that may mean.

It would seem important when considering this aspect of child abuse to look more carefully at that umbrella term. Is there not a difference between those who offend against those nearest to them, spouse or child, because they are inadequately prepared to deal with the stress of close personal living, and those who offend against this group of people because in the home there is the least chance of being reported and it is possible to disgorge badness privately while keeping up every appearance of respectability in public? Do not some abusing parents have a multi-problem situation, emotional and material, showing features of inadequacy, addiction, criminality? It is difficult to make a stereotype of the abusing parent. If indeed, as I believe, there is a child abuse syndrome, may this not be present in different forms which sometimes require different treatment. One of the difficulties about labelling is the fact that it prevents an open mind. Methods take on a religious aspect long after, in fact, movement has been made in some other direction.

Some cases come to mind from the past. The first, many years ago, concerned a marriage between two very young people. The wife's mother had resisted growing up and had always taken a sibling role with her daughter, trying to dress inappropriately and to move her life in parallel with her daughter's development. So much so that in her mid-forties she became pregnant at the same time as her daughter, now married, conceived. What is more, she produced a "successful baby" whereas her daughter produced a child with an intestinal difficulty so that it had to remain in hospital after birth for two and a half months at a distance of 50 miles from her home.

The husband was an intelligent, lonely, depressed young man, over-possessed by his mother. They longed for the child's return but it was already eclipsed by the other baby and in 3 months it had suffered the usual impossible accidents. It was taken into care, returned, as it transpired too early, and was returned to hospital a few months later close to death. On the second occasion the parents were charged and a probation order was made. This was the·first time that the parents' problems were really tackled, a long and partially successful task.

An adoption case still leaves me with anxiety. The young, middle-class wife had already had a number of miscarriages. Her husband was an absentee, having a professional job in one of the services. There was no real history to support enough anxiety to refuse, but the joy of adoption as far as this young wife was concerned was expressed entirely in terms of her husband's pleasure and it was only with great difficulty that his presence was ever obtained. The potentials for abuse were probably present.

A young unmarried mum who had spent most of her life, up to teen-age, in a hospital for mentally defectives, had met a married man of a good deal of instability and who offered her excitement and self-value, in contrast to a fairly hum-drum life living in a hostel and working in a laundry. When they set up home together, the new baby proved not to be a doll and there was no extended family on which to fall back. Nor were their own personal resources good, a very limited maturity of emotional reaction. The baby suffered permanent brain damage and the girl was charged. A probation order saw her through the end of this affair and the marriage to a father figure with a resultant further birth. Tremendous support enabled her to cope fairly satisfactorily until a genuine cot death occurred. This was heavily investigated and there was no evidence of any damage, only great threat to the mother. A third birth followed and again with a great deal of support of a daily sort, the child has grown up.

In another case, a child was killed by her mother in the midst of great tensions of a material and emotional kind because the father of the child was not free to marry. A probation order was made, and in spite of advice another pregnancy occurred. All concerned were presented with a very grave decision and the child was brought before the court on birth to be placed back with the mother under supervision. She reached the age of 18 months before an injury occurred, when once more, inner and outside tensions mounted. The child is now in care in spite of many efforts to prevent this last injury.

All of these cases have their differences as well as their likenesses, and how alike are any of them to the killing by William Keppel? It does seem that flexibility of approach, both as far as legal action and treatment are concerned, is more important than some may have felt in the stereotype pattern. Once again it might be necessary to look at the danger as well as the value of a label.

This is probably equally important in relation to the term "rehabilitation" which implies a return to a previous good and blessed state of happy parentship. This seems to deny both the inherent difficulties in living in close contact with dependent or demanding family relationships and the lack of previous example in the childhood of many "abusers". Rather we seem to be talking about dealing with a potential situation, very threatening to the parents (and possibly a dangerous one to the child), in such a way as so to overcome the old sense of failure as a child that tolerance can be achieved to the stress of apparent lack of success as a parent, or at any rate the average tolerance of most parents.

How real are the possibilities of rehabilitation under present circumstances anyway? We have not achieved a personal social service in the way that most of us hoped. In some ways the probation service has been able to keep more professionally trained contact with the people with whom it is statutorily involved, but sometimes that contact is pitifully small. Voluntary workers attached to the service can often be enormously helpful. Lack of staff in the social services may lead to a greater number of removals into care where there is a risk of repetition (and when is there not?), because there are too few professionally trained workers at the contact level. More removals will require more foster homes. There is a limit, possibly, to the number of foster homes obtainable and this would lead to an increasing number of children with an institutional background. In any case, this is a choice of method for the wrong reasons, if it is made only on this basis of lack of supervisory staff.

It is self-evident that high risk cases are a category requiring special treatment and their supervisors need special support and organizational backing. The difficult question is whether social work priorities should be placed with such cases or with those with a more positive prognosis where the maximum effectiveness can be assured. In some areas such a decision has to be made. It might be affirmed that dealing with a very few such high risk cases successfully, because of the damage they can do, has a greater effect than dealing with a larger number of more moderate problems. Or that the less professionally trained should take more of the burden of the vast area of non-risk work.

My own service has to face an increasing "burden" of after-care cases with a high risk from overcrowded borstals and life sentence discharges, as well as high risk families. Clearly, the emphasis of our service must be on rehabilitation. It might be worthwhile looking at some of the requirements over and above normal casework supervision which appertain to high risk child abuse cases.

First, there is a need for the recognition of what is a very special situation with the client. Even if no court appearance or warning has preceded supervision, the client must always have some fear of removal of the child. It is difficult to see how this can do anything but "heat up" an already sensitive situation. No trust between worker and client can be real unless this problem is faced between them, preferably perhaps with all the other interests involved. The client is generally the absentee at case conferences. It is open to question whether their presence would be helpful or too threatening to them or the conference. If there is a shared stress between client, helper, N.S.P.C.C. and police, would it help the client to have this honestly discussed? It is arguable whether this would be supportive or whether it would add a further stress, but it might make discussion rather more reality-based as the client sees it.

Mrs Jones in Jean Renvoize's "Mother's Story" exclaims, "Once you're on their books! They keep having conferences about our family: it's wrong! They call them without your knowing, they hold them behind your back and so many outsiders go to them". One of my own cases asked me with obvious suspicion and anxiety, "What do you talk about at all these meetings?".

Second, the workers have to recognize their own feelings, as supervisors, about the revulsion from the original act. Probation officers often supervise after a death or a very severe battering as well as dealing with families where there are the early signs of risk. It is important to be aware of denying the revulsion because it implies denying the act. So in the following supervision, there is a danger of belittling the problem, of defending the client against all other less perceptive agencies, failing to see whether things are going less well, demanding success where total success is not possible for the client, and so making real breakdown inevitable because partial breakdown would be letting the worker down. This is not to say that liking the client as a total person is not enormously important in such cases, if it is the real person that is liked and not an idealized version.

Third, it is important to keep a balance between seeing the family in the light of the child abuse label and the known theory, whilst at the same time being alive to its own individual interaction and needs, so that the label is an *aide memoire* but not a stereotype.

Fourth, experience has shown that what is important is parenting the abusing parent and not the child. It is so easy for anxiety about the child, even pride in its thriving under the family care, to reduce the parent once more to being the child's sibling.

Fifth, sharing the responsibility is all important. The abusing parent is often possessive as well as battering. Supervisors can be collusive in possessiveness, but they cannot carry all the burden of such cases. What is needed is a really shared responsibility and that it should be considered normal for such cases and facilitated by the management of the agency. Consultation is vital, but it is not automatically the same thing as genuine acceptance of joint responsibility.

Rehabilitation may have involved the fact that a child will have to be removed permanently from the abusing parent. Just as physical rehabilitation sometimes means teaching the disabled to cope with an irremedial situation, so rehabilitation will have to go on with the parents even though it may remain a childless family. Sometimes this would seem to be a real gap in programming. It is probably the most painful piece of supervision, but if this piece of work is omitted it is not impossible for the situation to repeat itself because names are changed and area moved in the wild hope of starting again. One thing that has become clear from 12 months of the child abuse register is the fact that there is a high rate of mobility amongst the abusing families.

This paper has really only tried to raise questions, and perhaps with all high risk cases, the need to keep alert and to continually look for new ways of helping is the all important thing. Olive Stevenson in a letter to *The Times* said the following:

Many factors increase the stress which precipitates violence against children If we concentrate upon environmental problems such as poverty or housing, we create sympathy, but at a price. The price is that we are less sympathetic to those who injure their children out of inner desperation and misery. Thus we may neglect the middle class "battering" parent who urgently needs help, and we may insult the poor by assuming their problems may be solely environmental.

Much research is still needed about effective methods of intervention; some of these would involve the sort of philosophical concepts of my title, others might include the more practical aspects of the problem such as the effect of the sort of jet lag produced by many days of nights being turned into days by sleepless children.

References

Christie, N. (1975). Utility and social values in court decisions on punishment. *In* "Crime, Criminology and Public Policy". Ed. R. Hood. Heinemann, London.

Delaney, J. (1972). The battered child and the law. *In* "Helping the Battered Child and his Family". Ed. C. H. Kempe and R. E. Helfer. Lippincott, Philadelphia.

Radzinowicz, L. (1967). The cross-examination of Hugh Clare. "The Minutes of Evidence Taken before The Royal Commission on the Penal System". H.M.S.O., London.

For Discussion see p 216.

15. Court Problems in the Management of the Family

Margaret Booth

The family problems with which the court has to deal are diverse and in so far as they relate to children the courts' powers to deal with them, with one exception, are derived from statute. As the law relating to children has developed so this has resulted in a multiplicity of statutes conferring powers and duties not only upon the High Court of Justice but also upon county courts and magistrates' courts. In relation to children alone the statutory output has been such that few lawyers can profess to have a working knowledge of all the relevant legislation that includes the Children Acts of 1948 and 1958, the Children and Young Persons Acts of 1933, 1963 and 1969, the Adoption Acts of 1958, 1960, 1964 and 1968, the Guardianship of Minors Acts 1971 and 1973, portions of the Matrimonial Proceedings (Magistrates' Courts) Act 1960, the Family Law Reform Act 1969 and the Matrimonial Causes Act 1973 and the most recent major enactment, the Children Act 1975. This is far from being a comprehensive list. It omits, for example, any reference to the powers and duties of the court under the social legislation such as the Education Act 1944 and the Mental Health Act 1959. It omits also any reference to the numerous statutory rules, orders and instruments which govern the procedures introduced by many of the enactments. But that list, incomplete as it is, illustrates the first problem with which the court must deal in its jurisdiction relating to children: i.e. the need to master the sheer bulk of legislation that is now on the statute book.

Although the title of this paper speaks of the "court", there is in this country no one family court with exclusive jurisdiction to deal with the problems of the family. Instead, the magistrates' court, which includes the domestic proceedings court and the juvenile court, the county court and the High Court all exercise jurisdiction with regard to the family depending upon what aspect of family life and what statutory enactments are involved. In some instances as, for example, in adoption and in guardianship cases, jurisdiction lies in the magistrates' court, the county court or in the Family Division of the High Court, so that the parties may select their tribunal according to the complexity of the matter or their convenience. In other cases jurisdiction is exclusive to one court, examples being the care proceedings under the Children and Young Persons Act, which are dealt with in the juvenile court, and affiliation proceedings which may only be heard at first instance by a magistrates' court sitting as a domestic proceedings court. Equally diverse are the appellate courts which include the Divisional Court of the Family Division of the High Court, the Crown Court and the Court of Appeal.

The multiplicity of statutes and diversity of courts produces obvious problems common to most aspects of the law relating to children. But this symposium deals with "child abuse", so that it is pertinent to consider those problems at present experienced by the court more particularly in relation to this.

The Juvenile Court

The court in the context of child abuse cases is, more often than not, the juvenile court exercising its jurisdiction in respect of care orders under the Children and Young Persons Act 1969. A juvenile court is a specially constituted court of justices, having a legally qualified clerk but otherwise generally composed of lay men and women with varying degrees of experience in this type of work. It is regrettable but true that for the most part the experience of the advocates who appear before it is limited. While such a court undoubtedly provides an easily accessible tribunal well able to deal with those cases of child abuse in which the evidence is clear and the remedy unquestionable, it is not well equipped to cope with the more complex cases requiring a lengthy forensic investigation. Unlike the Matrimonial Proceedings (Magistrates' Courts) Act 1960 and the Guardianship of Minors Act 1971, the 1969 Act makes no provision for a case of complexity to be transferred from the justices for hearing by a High Court judge.

In any contested matter the juvenile court has been, and continues to be, severely handicapped by its inability to secure proper separate representation for the child whose future is the subject of the dispute, a situation which is only partially remedied by the provisions of the Children Act 1975 which comes into force in November 1976. Legal aid for the purposes of proceedings under the 1969 Act has been available for the child, but not for his parents. In effect, however, it was granted to his guardians who for the most part would be the parents or persons with whom the child makes his home and whose interests in so many cases would be in direct conflict with those of the child whom they allegedly represented. It was inevitable that in such circumstances a direct confrontation developed between the parents or guardians on the one side and the social workers or local authority on the other, with no independent voice speaking on behalf of the child.

Some relief from the manifold disadvantages of such a situation will be provided by the 1975 Act which specifically empowers the court, where a conflict of interest exists between the parent and child, to appoint a guardian *ad litem* to represent the child. As a corollary, legal aid will in future be available not only for the child but also to enable the parent or guardian to take part in the proceedings and advance his or her own case.

The Offical Solicitor

The extent to which these statutory provisions can resolve the present dilemma has yet to be ascertained. Unfortunately, there are not, and will not be, available in the juvenile court (or indeed in any magistrates' court or county court) the services of the Official Solicitor or any equivalent court official who through his own department can undertake the entirely independent legal representation of the children. A juvenile court, in common with any other court exercising jurisdiction over children, may require a welfare officer to enquire into and report as to the welfare of those children. But while such a report will include facts and matters relating to the children of which the court should be aware before coming to its decision, it is not the function of the welfare officer to represent the child or to make specific recommendations on his behalf, although he may express his views and assessments based upon what he has seen and heard. In this the functions of the welfare officer differ from those of the Official Solicitor to the Supreme Court who holds office under the provisions of the Supreme Court Judicature (Consolidation) Act 1925. Among his other duties the Official Solicitor may be appointed by the High Court, subject to his consent, to act as guardian *ad litem* of a child in any High Court proceedings in which that child's interests may be affected. In so acting, the Official Solicitor will prepare and place evidence before the court and where necessary will be represented by counsel to argue the case on behalf of the child. The Official Solicitor is not a welfare officer nor does he stand *in loco parentis* but acts for the child only during the course of and for the purpose of the legal proceedings in respect of which he was appointed. Nevertheless his intervention ensures an independent investigation of the facts, an independent assessment of what is believed to be in the child's best interests and an independent argument addressed to the court on behalf of the child. In many cases the intervention of the Official Solicitor can eliminate much personal bitterness which is likely to arise when there is a direct confrontation between parents on the one hand and social workers on the other. Being a creature of statute and confined in his work to the High Court and in certain circumstances the county court, the Official Solicitor is unable to accept an appointment from any inferior court regardless of the nature of the case concerned and the need for a child to be legally represented.

Wardship

Doubt must, therefore, be cast upon the competence of the juvenile court as a tribunal to hear and determine the more complex of the child abuse cases. For this reason it is of benefit to consider the use in this context of the one High Court jurisdiction in relation to children which does not stem from statute, that of its inherent jurisdiction in wardship. In the words of Mrs Justice Heilbron:

Wardship is a very special and ancient jurisdiction. Its origin was the sovereign's feudal obligation as *parens patriae* to protect the person and property of his subjects, and particularly those unable to look after themselves, including infants. This obligation, delegated to the Chancellor, passed to the Chancery Court, and in 1970 to [the Family Division of] the High Court (*In re D.*(1976) Fam. 185, 192).

The powers of the High Court to protect its wards are not limited, as is illustrated by the recent example of the refusal by the court to allow an 11 year-old girl to undergo a sterilization operation despite the wishes of the mother, the only guardian, that she should do so (*In re D.* supra). Section 1 of the Guardianship of Minors Act 1971 enacts that where in any proceedings before any court the custody or up-bringing of a minor is in question the court shall regard the welfare of the minor as the first and paramount consideration. This is the criterion upon which the court will make its decision, but while it may, in theory at any rate, have an unrestricted jurisdiction to do whatever is considered necessary for the welfare of the ward, that welfare is not the sole consideration. The jurisdiction of the court will be exercised with due consideration for the rights of others, so that, for example, the court has refused to restrain the publication of a book containing material relating to a ward's deceased father which would un-doubtedly endanger the ward were he to come to know of it [see *In re X (a minor) (Wardship: Jurisdiction)* (1975) Fam. 47]. On the wholly exceptional facts of that case, the freedom of publication was held to prevail over the interests of the ward. But such cases are few and far between, while in the great majority the court will take the welfare of the child as being its first and ultimately prevailing consideration.

Wardship proceedings are far from being cumbersome and slow as is so commonly believed and the court will act to protect a child as quickly as the parties before it will allow it to do so. Indeed the speed with which the court will act in the interests of its wards is still relatively little appreciated. Any person having an interest in a child may, by a simple procedure of issuing a summons, make the child a ward of court. Thereupon the court is forthwith empowered to make orders to protect the welfare of that child. If satisfied that it is in the child's interests to do so it may, for example, immediately order his removal from an unsuitable home or, on the other hand, may restrain any person from removing the child from the care and control of another or from the jurisdiction of the court. Where it is necessary for the protection of the child, the court can order a parent or any other person to leave the property in which the child is living and thereafter not return. Injunctions may be made restraining persons from assaulting, molesting or otherwise interfering with the ward. Immediate relief can be given to alleviate any harmful situation in which the child is currently placed. In cases of extreme urgency such orders may be made before the summons is issued and before the child in question is technically a ward of court, although this is rarely necessary as the procedure by which the wardship proceedings are commenced is in itself so simple and speedy a process. But in all instances the court, before it makes orders, must be satisfied on the evidence that the relief sought is necessary for the welfare and protection of the child, particularly where the rights and interests of other people are involved.

Wardship jurisdiction may be invoked in respect of any British child or any alien child who is at present in the country (other than one whose parents have diplomatic immunity) and the summons may be issued not only by a parent or guardian, but by any person who has a genuine interest in the child's welfare as, for example, the educational psychologist who took that initial step in the sterilization case. Once seized of the matter, the court may make orders giving any necessary immediate relief and further has wide powers to ensure that it is properly informed of all matters relating to the child's welfare. In addition to any necessary orders to alleviate an immediate harmful situation in which a child is placed, the court may act to ensure that it has all necessary information relating to the ward for example by compelling the attendance of witnesses to disclose the whereabouts of a missing child or to give evidence at the hearing. It would undoubtedly act to ensure that a child was visited by a social worker or other authorized person where the facts gave rise to a reasonable apprehension that the child's welfare was endangered and access to him was being denied. The local police might be enlisted to assist in gaining access. In addition the court will, where appropriate, appoint the Official Solicitor, subject to his consent, to act for the child.

A Wardship Case

A recently reported case illustrates clearly the advantages of the wardship procedure in a complex child abuse case. In *In re Cullimore (a
minor)*, *The Times*, 24th March 1976, the issue before the court in wardship proceedings was whether the several fractures suffered by a baby
girl of 16 months had been caused by non-accidental injury or by
reason of the fact that she suffered from osteogenesis imperfecta. The
medical evidence was conflicting, but the child was already the subject
of a place of safety order and both parents had previously been
criminally prosecuted on charges of grievous bodily harm of which
they had been acquitted. There was unfortunately considerable anti-
pathy between the parents and the social workers. Sir George Baker,
the President of the Family Division of the High Court, before whom
the wardship proceedings were heard, is reported to have summarized
the position in these words:

Many doctors had seen the child and gave different diagnoses. At least one
paediatrician had changed sides, bowing, it seemed, to the greater knowledge and experience of a senior. Social workers and others were apt to see
the matter in black and white, and some could make no allowance in their
own minds for the possibility that the parents were not at fault. The dilemma
was that if the injuries were wrongly held to be non-accidental, the parents,
who were both 25, could suffer unjustly and be held in hatred, odium and
contempt and pilloried in public while the child would be deprived of the
loving care of parents and spend its formative years in an institution. If a
diagnosis of "brittle bones" was made and that was wrong, the child was
gravely at risk if allowed to continue living with brutal parents.

The hearing lasted for 5 days at the end of which the President held
that on the balance of probabilities the child was suffering from brittle
bones. He accordingly discharged the place of safety order and granted
her care and control to the parents directing that she should remain a
ward of court and that the Official Solicitor should thereafter act for her
as guardian *ad litem* in any further proceedings.

Undoubtedly that case required the consideration of the High Court
but, had not the father of the child made her a ward, in all probability
the matter would have been determined by the juvenile court under
Section 1 of the Children and Young Persons Act 1969. That court
itself has no power to order the transfer of such a case before it for
hearing in the High Court and it is a fact that in the past there has been
a reluctance on the part of local authority officials to invoke the aid of
the High Court. It is well established that the prerogative jurisdiction
of the High Court is ousted in respect of a child over whom a local
authority has already assumed parental care under Section 2 of the
Children Act 1948 and in respect of a child in care under Section 1 of

that Act, the court will exercise its jurisdiction only in exceptional cases and then to supplement the local authority's powers. Save also in exceptional cases, a court will not intervene in the exercise of the discretion of a local authority in whose care a child has already been committed under Section 1 of the 1969 Act. The demarcation of the separate jurisdictions of the court and of the local authority has now been so clearly drawn that there is, perhaps, a failure to appreciate how closely the two can work together to provide what is best for a child. Unless officials of a local authority can feel free to invoke the aid of the High Court where appropriate, that court will not be able to realise the full extent of its powers in the protection of children in need. In a recent case concerning a ward of court who was also subject to a care order under Section 1 of the 1969 Act, Mrs Justice Lane said:

Further, as a matter of general application, it seems to me that there may be various circumstances in which a local authority would be grateful for the assistance of a court exercising wardship jurisdiction. Local authorities are sometimes faced with difficult and onerous decisions concerning children in their charge; responsible officers of their welfare departments may be subject to various pressures from within or from outside the authority itself. I consider that there would be no abandonment of, or derogation from, the statutory powers and duties were they to seek the guidance and assistance of the High Court in matters of difficulty, as distinct from the day to day arrangements with which, as the authorities show, the court will not interfere" [*In re B. (Wardship: Child in Care)* (1975) Fam. 36. 44].

The same view was expressed in another case by Lord Justice Ormrod who referred generally to the situation when a ward of court was already in the care of a local authority and said:

In such circumstances there is a potential conflict of jurisdiction between the statutory powers of local authorities and the ancient prerogative powers of the court exercising, in theory, the powers of the Queen as *parens patriae*. It is a conflict which both sides recognize, have always recognized, and as far as I am aware, have always done their utmost to avoid. There is no necessity whatever, in my judgment, for these two parallel powers over children to lead to difficulties if both sides act with reasonable discretion and understanding of the other parties, powers and interests in the matter. No court wants to embarrass a local authority, and I am certain that no authority wants to oust the court, even if it does not always agree with the court's view in a particular case.... I feel bound to say that I think that local authorities might find, if they look into it, other situations in which it would be positively to their advantage to invoke the wardship jurisdiction themselves. It would sometimes avoid them having to take unpleasant, awkward decisions themselves which sometimes cause great pain and anguish [*In re Y. (a Minor) (Child in Care; Access)* (1976), Fam. 125, 137].

Conclusion

The function of any court is to hear and determine cases. It is dependent to a large extent upon the litigants before it as to what procedure is followed and what evidence is placed before it. It is, therefore, essential that all professional persons who have the responsibility for caring for the welfare of children, be they doctors, social workers, welfare officers or lawyers, appreciate the function of the court and know how best to enable it to make orders that are not only for the welfare of a child but also that do justice between parties in dispute.

For Discussion see p 216.

16. Is Child Abuse a Crime?

Jan Carter

Child abuse has surfaced to public attention through a scientific rather than a legal route (Carter, 1975a). For this reason the question of the professional domain into which child abuse "fits" is still uncertain. Perhaps the most disputable issue is the way in which child abuse connects with the current legal structure. It is beyond the scope of this paper to deal with this problem in detail although it is a fundamental issue behind the question "is child abuse a crime?".

First, for the purposes of this paper the legal apparatus which deals with child abuse is treated as a single structure, although in fact there are two systems of justice (adult courts and juvenile courts) which both deal with child abuse cases. The enormous variation and discretion operating within the legal system is in no sense denied, but a macro-sociological perspective can often show areas to which more detailed attention can be paid later.

Second, to explore the question "is child abuse a crime?" does not in any way answer the very different evaluative question "should child abuse be a crime?". To chart a kind of taxonomy of the first question could, however, help to make sense of the second.

Law, Science and Morality

The question "is child abuse a crime?" raises some very awkward issues. Are we talking about law, science or morality? It is clear that child abuse is a crime in the legal sense: "if any adult who has the custody charge or care of a child wilfully assaults, illtreats, neglects, abandons or exposes him he is said to be guilty of an offence" (Children and Young Persons Act 1933). However in actual practice, assault, illtreatment, neglect, abandonment or exposure are not always easy to define and definition has to take account of the age of the child and the norms of the subculture and the community in which the offence takes place (Gil, 1970).

For others the answer to the question "is child abuse a crime?" has been modified by science. In applying the methods of positivism to the study of offenders, scientists are less concerned with crime than the characteristics of the criminal. The scientist, taking the legal answer to the question for granted, interests himself in the descriptive characteristics of the offender (Smith *et al.,* 1973).

For yet others, the question "is child abuse a crime?" impinges more on the area of morality. What has been called traditional morality would want to emphasize the free will of the offender and the importance of justice. It would attempt to deal with child abuse within the framework of the formal legal code. However, what has been called situational morality would stress the moral importance of compassion rather than justice and seek to modify (or at times even circumvent) the application of the formal legal code in favour of treatment for rehabilitation. All these statements are important issues which will be returned to later in the paper.

Discussion of child abuse within the context of crime raises some extremely painful dilemmas, the first being the nature of justice itself. The second is the conflict within the legal apparatus, which claims to provide for such parents both punishment and rehabiliation simultaneously, something that complicates sentencing in both criminal and juvenile courts as well as the recommendations of individual social workers. Third comes the question of the morality and the effectiveness of sentencing people to receive help compulsorily. The issue of involuntary rehabilitation has barely surfaced in the child-abuse literature. Fourth, there is the problem of whether child abuse is appropriately dealt with in the area of operation of the criminal law. The conventional criminal law reform viewpoint holds that private morality is no concern of the criminal law (Morris and Hawkins, 1969), when no harm results to another human being. This is not the case with child-abuse. Pragmatically however, it could be argued that all offences involving familial or domestic relationships might be better dealt with within a special legal structure (for instance a family court) outside the system of criminal courts.

The possible logical responses to the question "is child abuse a crime?" are as follows.
1. Yes, it is always a crime.
2. Yes, it is sometimes a crime.
3. Yes, it is rarely a crime.
4. No, it is never a crime.
5. It's an irrelevant question.
6. It depends what you mean by crime.

The answer given by individuals will largely depend on their basic beliefs or ideologies* about the nature of child abuse. These beliefs or ideologies have been outlined elsewhere (Carter, 1974, 1975b). Child abuse is or is not a crime according to the ideology of the onlooker.

Legal View

Within the framework of the legal code, child abuse is a crime if the court says it is; i.e. if the act of child abuse can be proved to have taken place. As the legal code assumes that the majority of people agree about the values it upholds it can be said to hold an absolutist view. It is based on the assumption that a rational man before committing an offence (of child abuse) weighs up the advantages against the penalties. Penalties can be applied until the disadvantages become too great and at that point deterrence is achieved. The strong legal emphasis on individual responsibility has been diluted by the introduction of later theories which are largely based on scientific determinism. These theories must influence the answer to the question under discussion quite markedly, since the philosophical view of the free will of the abuser is clearly fundamental to the legal position.

Medical View

Those adhering to the various scientific views would answer the question in various ways. Probably doctors confining attention to physical pathology, i.e. to the child's injury alone, would argue that the question was outside their professional boundaries of interest. Many adult psychiatrists working in the forensic field are prepared to work to the provisions of the criminal law and to get on with their task of identifying and diagnosing disease processes in the individual offender. The degree of the psychiatrist's optimism about rehabilitation depends on the particular medical ideology espoused. Some psychiatrists, who adopt an organic view of disease processes, tend to see their diagnoses as assisting the courts or the formal legal apparatus rather than maintaining a primary commitment to the patient. Another group, psychiatrists with research interests, adopts the thinking of the public health model, and sees child abuse as a social analogue of an infectious disease such as tuberculosis. It should be possible to isolate the (single) bacillus or virus and bring the "disease"

---

* A justification for the use of the term ideology has been made elsewhere (Carter, 1975a). Following Armor and Kleerman (1968), a professional ideology is a coherent system of both existential and evaluative ideas. Such ideas should explain what is ("existential") and what "ought" (evaluative), and should be linked together in a functional way. These ideas, according to Armor, should be strong enough to form a part of the identity of the practitioner.

under control in the same way as infectious disease.* This assumes that social phenomena can be described and classified in the same manner as the physical sciences; an assumption whose correctness is now strongly disputed by many social scientists.

Rehabilitation View

The rehabilitation view follows assumptions of psychodynamic theory, and its supporters would argue quite strongly that to ask the question "is child abuse a crime?" is really irrelevant. The aim being to change the personality of parents, the question of individual motivation is most important. A number of groups employ the rehabilitation perspective, for which one of the main claims is that it reflects humanitarian philosophy. However, Bean (1976) suggests that this exclusiveness is not logically necessary. It is only because the other points of view lack concern for the individual that humanitarianism is considered to be restricted to the rehabilitationist. Basically, according to the rehabilitation view, offenders need and require understanding and will receive insights as a result of a relationship with a therapist which will alter their attitudes. This will deter them from committing further offences.

A number of the difficulties, which arise from operating the rehabilitation view within the legal framework, have been discussed by Bean. He suggests first, that the rehabilitation view has made the sentencing of individuals in (criminal) courts unpredictable and second, that the rehabilitation view is a thinly disguised form of social control. He argues that help offered to offenders in child abuse under compulsion is control and not truly help at all. The expert, whether psychiatrist, social worker or probation officer, in making decisions and recommendations to a court and in taking on a function as part of a sentencing procedure, is acting as an agent of the state rather than of the patient. "If the professions assume what are essentially corrective rather than therapeutic functions it is surely important that they should be done openly and not by any specious pretence..." (Wootton, 1963).

In Britain over the past few years there have been strong organizational and professional pressures for connecting child abuse with formal legal procedures. Psychiatrists, social workers and probation officers are under pressure to take their cases to courts, either adult or juvenile. Whether or not this provides an effective deterrent in

---

* This is a new approach to child abuse. The difficulty is that it has never been proven that control of infections has been achieved by specific medical intervention. Some would argue that general social changes directed to the population at large, specifically sanitation and diet, are more important controls than specific medical interventions (Renaud, 1975).

the management of child-abuse offenders remains an open question, but it certainly conflicts with some rehabilitationists' claims. Rehabilitationists therefore could be divided up on the basis of their attitude to providing "help" under compulsion.

Radical Social View

As yet the radical social view has made little impact on child abuse thinking. Briefly it argues in favour of a diversity of values in sub-cultures of our society and is critical of the guardians of the established order (Taylor *et al.*, 1975). Police, correctional officers and the judiciary are seen in the same light as social workers and doctors. All are regarded as the agents of social control and both as real and symbolic custodians of the status quo. On this view the claims to superior status and knowledge of the three ideologies described earlier would be disputed and their scientific and individualistic emphasis criticized. Compulsory intervention by professionals would be strongly disapproved and the movement towards de-professionalization as strongly supported. To explain child abuse as a crime without reference to the society within which it takes place would be regarded as wrong. The community is seen as pluralistic, comprising many sets of values which are perpetually in conflict. All people are potentially deviant and most have deviant impulses which are not confined to those who abuse their children. Deviance is the quality bestowed on child abuse by the dominant social order which also can ignore censure or even collude with child abuse. In this sense, taken-for-granted behaviour is transformed by public definition into deviant behaviour: such has been the recent history of child abuse. This social reaction is said not only to maintain but also to increase the individual's problem. Being publicly labelled can lead to intensifying and amplifying the stigma and to repetitions of the act. The selection by official agencies of scapegoats (i.e. those child abusers brought to justice) is often arbitrary and tends to discriminate against the more powerless groups of the society. The probable aim would be changes in the wider society which would be expected to lead to the total prevention of child abuse.

Conclusion

Is child abuse a crime? Any answer to this question is bound by the pre-suppositions and assumptions of the questioner. This may shock some and offend others but supports the case of those social theorists who claim that our social order is not arbitrarily given, but is a series of symbolic worlds, negotiated around the purposes of different groups.

The attempt to show how variable is the response to the question *"is child abuse a crime?"* may pave the way to discussion of the ensuing issue *"should* child abuse be a crime?"

References

Armor, D. J. and Kleerman, G. L. (1968). Psychiatric treatment orientations and professional treatment ideology. *J. Hlth Soc. Behav.* 9, 243–255.

Bean, P. (1976). "Rehabilitation and Deviance". Routledge and Kegan Paul, London.

Carter, J. (1974). Problems of professional belief. *In* "The Maltreated Child". Ed. J. Carter. Priory Press, London.

Carter, J. (1975a). Community involvement and responsibility for child abuse. Proc. First Austral. Nat. Conf. on the Battered Child, Perth, W. Australia, Aug. 25–28, 1975.

Carter, J. (1975b). Co-ordination between health and welfare services and professional ideologies. Loc. cit.

Gil, D. (1970). "Violence Against Children". Harvard University Press, Cambridge, Mass.

Morris, N. and Hawkins, G. (1969). "The Honest Politician's Guide to Crime Control". University of Chicago Press, Chicago.

Renaud, M. (1975). On the structural constraints to state intervention in health. *Internat. J. Hlth Services* 5, 559–71.

Smith, S., Hanson, R. and Noble, S. (1973). Parents of battered babies: a controlled study. *Brit. Med. J.* 4, 338–91.

Taylor, I., Walton, P. and Young J. (1975). (Ed.) "Critical Criminology", Routledge and Kegan Paul, London.

Wootton, Baroness (1963). The law, the doctor, and the deviant. *Brit. Med. J.* 2, 197–202.

For Discussion see p 216.

17. Society's Obligation to the Family

Andrew Mann

It is at the most 20 years since society has been aware of the problem of the excessive use of violence on children and, in particular, the use of violence on children in the private home.

Violence is nothing new; it plays an integral part in the machinery of many of the world's societies today and some would say it is an integral part of human nature. Certainly, among the best-selling books in recent years have been studies of animal behaviour that show, it is claimed, that the human species shares many of the supposed violent attributes of other non-human species. To many, violence is human nature after all. But what is new is the definition of this particular form of violence as a problem of the utmost urgency that involves all of us and requires immediate massive social intervention. Not that excessive violence on children is in any way a recent phenomenon, nor is there any evidence to show that there has been a significant increase in the rate of violence on children. But what is sure is that the problem of child abuse is a rapidly growing subject of specialist concern and of academic industry.

Even if this symposium were not justified by the need of practitioners to share experiences, it would certainly be necessary to call it simply to digest the mass of literature on the subject of child abuse now pouring out from all sides. What makes this symposium more than just a sifting of specialist argument, or a shuffling of papers, is the knowledge that violence on children is a subject of general *public* concern, often heated and certainly very deeply felt.

I am very conscious of not being a practitioner, of not being involved at the coal face or even at the grass roots of non-accidental injury and, of course, of not being a professional with a specific function in the developing network of agencies involved in child abuse.

I have no direct experience of what is unhappily called non-accidental injury, but it is as a parent and an occasional surrogate mother, and as a family man with everyday experience of what I would call child abuse, that I feel I do have something to contribute to the debate. Further, as a member of a campaigning neighbourhood group, The Children's Rights Workshop, I will try to speak for other parents and other families, who make up many of the clients, the customers, the patients, the consumers, and the occasional victims of the welfare state, and, more pertinently, who provide the clay, the cause and effect of the professional blood-letting, occasioned by the Maria Colwell tragedy. The professional and public response to that tragedy generated much of the energy behind the many current initiatives on child abuse today. The link between this symposium and the historically significant Maria Colwell report may contribute to a significant change in the well-being of society's children, families and neighbourhoods.

The debate on child abuse should be opened up to the general public as well. My outsider's browsing through the literature on child abuse leads me immediately to the main purpose of my contribution, which is to attempt to place child abuse in the context of society as a whole, a society racked by contradiction and conflicting forces. Indeed, the two admired publications making up my latest reading, both from the N.S.P.C.C., the At Risk Report of the Battered Child Research Team and the recent pamphlet, Registers of Suspected Non-Accidental Injury, genuinely demonstrate the acute social pressures of everyday life that create stress in the individual family. They also reflect the traditional rehabilitatory casework approach conducted on a one-to-one basis and consisting in the assessment of individual I.Qs, the building-up of individual case histories and the compiling of registers of individual cases and incidents. Not that any of this work is not urgently needed or worthless. But, unless accompanied by the rigorous reference to socio-economic and other environmental factors that can no longer be ignored as crucial determinants in child abuse, these therapy-cum-research programmes relentlessly reinforce the definition of child abuse as a special phenomenon with unique features arising from distinct social and psychological factors in the individual batterer or abuser. Understandable as this preoccupation is with individual assessment and treatment, particularly if we take the history of the recent awareness of the problem into account — after all, lives do have to be saved or protected at the very least, and people do need help now — nevertheless, there is an urgent need to put equal energies and resources into a systematic assessment of the total environment of child abuse. Without the development of theoretical models that try to encompass all the factors, all the variables, and all the contradictions and references to social stress, even to class, however genuine, will be mere statements of belief. At worst, they will clear the way for the development of specialist provision on the basis of incomplete and even biased assessment and partial commitments.

To include all the variables, all the factors and all the theoretical models, is a daunting task which requires thorough and ongoing inter-disciplinary co-operation as well as in-depth surveys of patterns of be-haviour at all the different levels of social interaction, from the individual one-to-one or within the family to class aspirations and cultural norms and values. The work already being done on, for example, child–parent interaction, on ante- and neo-natal experience and on the effect of particular forms of therapeutic intervention will provide the essential starting-point for the development of a more comprehensive model and assessment of treatment.

It is precisely because research and treatment have reached their present stage and precisely because they are asking the questions that they are now asking that we need to widen the criteria and extend the terms of reference. No longer can we be satisfied with pragmatic response to individual need, or the empirical collection of cases, numbers and sizes of bruises. Our clients live in a world that is often wider, deeper and more complex than that experienced by the agency workers who are trying the help them. To be truly effective, the workers themselves need wider frames of reference and more rigorous criteria.

As a parent involved in daily child care, with two small children, I recognize in myself and my neighbours the extremes of despair and frustration and genuine impatience in trying to respond positively and adequately to all the demands of my immediate environment, which include the obvious obligation to earn a living, to fulfil the adult commitments to the neighbourhood and to colleagues and friends, to share in housework and, last but not least, but often at the bottom of the list of priorities in fact, to share in child care. I also recognize in me the need to explode and to lash out, whether in sound or in gesture. How many parents at work in child care can honestly deny the same pressures? Additionally, how much worse it is for those parents who live with the same pressures, but more intensely and in more con-centrated form, as well as suffering from other pressures including iso-lation and cramped living quarters.

The Stresses of Family Life

It needs to be stated, unequivocally, that pregnancy and child care in modern society, especially child care in the early years of a child's life, are far removed from the ideal world which women have been taught to expect. The pregnant woman rarely escapes patronization and special attentions, and yet is expected to withdraw from ordinary social life. The parent kept at home by the needs of child care is not only less mobile, but is suddenly inexplicably deserted by friends of old. In our society, a woman surrounded by children is less interesting, not really a woman, something different deserving sympathy. This loss of identity affecting women from all backgrounds can lead to unbearable pressures. Similarly, the parent cooped up at home with the sharply expressed need of children is an explosive mixture at the best of times. It helps little if other adults are available at the beginning or end of the day, usually adding their own needs to the mixture, and usually unmindful of the agonies that have been developing throughout the day.

How much do we know about these pressures, these stress factors, these automatic features which are family life today, and which need stringent efforts to alleviate them? As to the emotional and undoubtedly physical explosions that do occur so easily in the home situation, how do we classify them? By the number of the bruises? The number of times voices are raised or tears flow? It is now recognized that the extent of the injuries is primarily due to chance. What do we do with that? Do we ignore violent outbursts that leave no marks? It would be hardly surprising if the practitioners found enough to keep them well exercised without adding to their problems by looking at these questions, without attempting to build models that can encompass the whole spectrum of family life.

We have an unprecedented opportunity to share public concern and at last to shine the light of enquiry on the way our society lives and treats itself in that most private and embattled place, the family home. But we must ensure that such enquiry is part of an agreed overall programme of social intervention, involving the whole population and looking into all the factors at all levels of daily life. We must not allow such investigations to be conducted merely to clarify or justify particular arguments or policies. One of the most telling experiences of the Second World War for many of the officer class is said to have been to learn for the first time the reality of the living standards and culture of the working people called to serve under them, and the other ranks had a good look at the officers. Surely we do not need another World War, with all its horrors and waste, before we get to grips with the pressures and deficiencies of everyday life today. Is it too much to hope that Maria Colwell's death might provide the impetus for all our people to unite towards understanding and change?

Workers now specialized in ongoing investigation and treatment of child abuse will perhaps not themselves feel willing or particularly able to undertake the onerous task of building new, expanded theoretical models of social enquiry or of establishing criteria that cover all the contexts and all levels, at the same time encouraging society at large to look at itself at such close quarters. Perhaps this is the primary function of inter-disciplinary meetings such as this symposium. Child abuse is at the tip of the iceberg of family life in modern society. The question is surely, can we expand our scratching at the visible parts above the surface to a systematic attack on the treacherous mass of out-of-sight, beneath-the-surface, behind-closed-doors reality?

Whether or not the proposed expanded theoretical framework is tackled in the near future, three tasks need urgent attention to clear the theoretical air that both workers and clients are currently breathing. First, we must consolidate the tendency to consider baby-battering or non-accidental injury as part of a continuum that stretches from mental cruelty at one end, to severe neglect, such as the starving of food in the Stephen Meurs case, at the other. "Abuse" is to my mind the most appropriate and precise word or concept to cover all the manifestations with which we are concerned. Second, a research task that is urgently needed is a blanket survey of an area in which cases of child abuse have been identified, so as to ascertain to what extent the cases identified are typical or atypical of that area and, if atypical, to identify those processes, maybe stress or pressure, that are atypically at play. If the cases of child abuse are typical, how do those members of the population of that area, who do not abuse their children and who are in the minority, escape from the factors that so influence the majority?

Third, the rapidly changing patterns of family life must begin to impinge on our concepts of the ideal family and the ideal child-care situation. For example, the family can no longer be assumed to need, at very least, a stable, heterosexual couple among its members. There have been too many variants on this model for it to hold sway any longer, and hopefully we can look forward to the day when a variety of home situations will be available to fostering and adoption agencies. In my opinion, no viable household should be excluded from the possibility of caring for children or, indeed, from enlarging its membership from any other age group.

An important corollary of a flexible and dynamic model of the family would be to remove the pejorative light in which one-parent families are now viewed. For it is surely not the number of adults legally responsible in a family that matters, but rather the stability of that family unit and the access mechanisms available to it to enable regular contact with other children and other adults. Like the individual, the family is not an isolated unit; individuals thrive in society, families do have neighbours. Certainly, single parenthood should not be seen as automatically stressful.

A preliminary conclusion might be that society's first obligation to the family is to become aware of it, of what it actually is and does, and how it functions and, in the light of child abuse, to investigate what is actually happening to the members of the family, particularly those members who were never asked whether they wanted to join in the first place, in other words, the children.

Responsibility within Society

It is appropriate now to attempt to describe the society whose obligations to the family we are discussing. Earlier, I have referred to "society as a whole" "racked by contradiction and conflicting forces". In fact, society is constantly undergoing change, not necessarily in any one direction or at any one particular pace, but invariably in response to the dictates of a central contradiction which, I believe with Marxists to be class-based. Unlike Marxists, I see the fundamental contradiction of modern society not as between the owners of the productive forces on the one side and their workers on the other. The conflict is between the mass of the population on one side and on the other the "class" of decision-makers. Ownership is one, but only one, form of control of decision-making.

A thumb-nail sketch of British society reveals a class-based society in which the vast majority of significant decisions affecting people's lives are made by a powerful minority, an elite of decision-makers, of managers, while the mass of people themselves are mostly on the receiving end of these decisions, excluded from the effective control and planning of their lives. Because power, and by power I mean the power to make significant decisions, is a very scarce resource, British society, like society in most developed countries of the world today, is highly competitive, hierarchical and secretive.

Information and ideas are commodities very well controlled by a well-watered consensus, but not unusually by energetic applications of the privacy–confidentiality principle and by a systematic, if unconscious, censorship by various agents of the managing elite. Competition has to be believed in and this is well-sustained by the excessive emphasis on the potential of the individual member of society, as distinct from the group, the family or neighbourhood, to achieve success, progress or growth; all concepts now under some criticism. Success itself breeds failure and British society is peopled by an alienated majority who accept the labels given them and have little or no say in the content of their lives or environment. It is also peopled by those who increasingly see themselves as being branded as failures and deemed unable to achieve a meaningful place in life, let alone success.

Some see this last category of people as created by "the cycle of deprivation". Certainly it would appear that it is among this last group that most cases of child abuse are detected, which would seem logical in the scheme of things, for those who believe least in themselves feel the most threatened by the demands and expectations made upon them, whether by authority or by dependents or by life itself. I myself do not find the concept of the cycle of deprivation particularly useful in the understanding of child abuse. For one thing, it presupposes that the primary causes of violence on children lie in earlier influences not necessarily present at the time and place of the abuse. Second, it presupposes that life inevitably repeats itself. Third, it presupposes that our behaviour is determined by forces outside ourselves which are not significantly influenced by the choices or decisions that we make.

The upwards social mobility of individuals disproves that one of course, but it is important to stress that people are able, and have been shown to be able, however "deprived" or lacking in self-confidence, to organize themselves into purposeful and responsible groups which can both protect themselves as well as enact change. There are formidable obstacles, of course, some of which I have already touched on. One such obstacle, professionalism, I will discuss later.

Before the ingredients that people require to pick themselves up and contribute to the meaning of their lives are described, Dr Mia Kellmer Pringle's summary of children's four basic needs in her book "The Needs of Children" should be considered. Without them children are deemed deprived. The first is the need for love and security, without which, it is now clear from all the research, no child will thrive, let alone grow. The only debate concerns what kind of person or what kind of consistency is required at that early age. The second is the need for new experiences, the need to play, to discover oneself and to experience a variety of influences and contacts. Then there is the basic need for praise and recognition, shared by most adults. Finally comes the need for responsibility. Most of us would agree with these four basic needs. They make a good summary of the debate so far.

About the last need, for responsibility, we are quick, are we not, to regret that such and such a person does not show any responsibility for what he or she has done or for putting it right. We are apt to refer to particular groups of people as "irresponsible". But it is well nigh impossible to show, let alone take, responsibility, when a person is denied any real opportunity to exercise that responsibility. Responsibility doesn't grow on trees, nor are we necessarily born with it. Responsibility has to be experienced to be understood, by children as well as by adults. Above all, responsibility needs to be exercised to have any meaning, and to be needed, but responsibility cannot be exercised without the power to choose between real options. It is power that is lacking among the majority, and particularly among the deprived the power to make decisions and to make choices for themselves. For children and for adults, responsibility must be worth exercising, and it is only through access to real choice between real options that power is exercised; the genuine power to assume responsibility for our life and for our neighbourhood. So I propose that choice is an indispensable ingredient of a healthy life, whether of an individual or of a society, and it is precisely this ingredient of choice, that is either denied or seriously hidden from the majority of the population in modern society. Little wonder that the powerless are driven to the extremes of rejection and destruction that we recognize in child abuse.

Those who manage society do not necessarily doubt that ordinary men and women can assume responsibility and effectively run their lives; what they do is actively to obstruct access to real choice and thus to responsibility. As an example, it is the professionals who form the most consistent and energetic obstacle to people taking responsibility.

The Professionals

What are the fundamental aspects of "the professional" or the professional practice? Two quite distinct parts are worth considering. The first comprises the genuine knowledge, the skills and expertise, which provide the professional's basic, valuable contribution in any one context. Equally important, and unfortunately often of more importance to the professional him or herself, is the status accompanying the knowledge, skills and expertise. Not only do professionals invariably sit comfortably within a hierarchy, but they can only achieve and sustain their status in that hierarchy through constant competition with others both inside and outside the profession. I have already referred to hierarchy and competitiveness as basic features of modern society; these features are now recognized in other people's professions if not in one's own. For those outside the hierarchy, for those at the receiving end, all professions are the same. Now we must make ourselves clear about this, for not all professionals are power-mad aggressors, "red in tooth and claw". But professionals do draw the line between themselves and everybody else, who are thereby excluded from and yet totally dependent on professionals' knowledge and decisions. Teachers, doctors and social workers will recognize this phenomenon, for only they can teach, only they can heal, only they can support. This obvious absurdity is however what we now have. It is the professional's obsession with hierarchy and rigid role definition that is the most serious obstacle to the sharing of information, skills and experience. It is a moot point whether it is the professional or the client pupil or patient who need each other more. As for responsibility, that's for the professionals alone.

It would be foolish and naive to deny that knowledge, skills and expertise are needed by every community and by every person in our society. Professional people with those skills are needed and asked for at every level of group activity in our society. The need for a professional person or for a role to be fulfilled by people with special skills, knowledge and confidence, will sooner or later be clearly expressed in the growing voluntary movement in neighbourhoods, particularly in urban areas were groups of mothers organize together to run play schemes, adventure playgrounds, self-help groups, food co-operatives and so on. The collective experience of these groups is that they need support and help.

Help can either be got from other groups that have had the same experiences, or have resources they can share, or particular knowledge or ideas that can be built on. But equally often, what is being sought is people who have the time, the confidence as well as the experience to step in and take on a job, who can solve a particular problem, or who can provide informed advice and support. Very often, it is the professional or professional experience that is being sought, not status nor hierarchy, but skills, knowledge, experience and ability to cope. In this way, the experienced and successful darts player ("he's a real pro' ") is as welcome and needed as the experienced G.P. or the hardened maths teacher. The local group's need of such professionalism is not a shirking of responsibility, but rather an example of informed and responsible decision making.

One of the basic ingredients for growth of responsibility in a neighbourhood is the availability of professionals, prepared to open up, not standing on their status and privilege, but offering their skills, space in the institutions where they work and their time, making themselves available on demand, or, at least, fitting in with the demands of the neighbourhood. It is these people who are crucial today in the active social growth in our neighbourhoods. Unfortunately, it is mainly the professionals who are obstructing, who are not making themselves available; and yet, it is professionals, in the last instance, who are the most able to help. They are linked to today's choices and power.

Some of our discussions have shown that professionals do not know the way out; they are lacking support in their work and ideas, and in confidence on the way to go ahead. It is of course hardly surprising that the doubts and concerns of the professional practitioners should be voiced at this symposium. Neither will it come as a surprise to anyone reading the evidence of the Maria Colwell report, which spells out a relentless account of professional confusion, presumption and rank inadequacy. After such a catalogue of professional malfunction, who can feel any confidence about the future for professional intervention? What is perhaps most surprising in the tragic Colwell case is not so much the malfunctioning of the welfare agencies but the vast numbers of professional people who were supposed to be responsible for Maria's welfare right up to her end. Indeed, the most compelling image is provided by the fact that the home in which Maria was quietly being destroyed was surrounded by a galaxy of professionals buzzing around and filling their files. Meanwhile, the articulate, vociferous and many-sided concern of Maria's family's neighbours went unheard or was mistrusted.

Neighbours

In the light of such failure would it not be reasonable to turn back to the very people who are excluded from professional practice: the neighbours and the local neighbourhood groups, and offer them our professional skills and resources and decide with them how best these should be developed and served? Such decisions can no longer be left to the professionals alone. The one positive ray of hope that I think we can concentrate on this week is that the turning back to the neighbourhood is happening more and more in our society. Schemes for legal rights, health, support and education are cropping up in many of our populated areas in community centres and, as local resources, providing a framework for the elaboration of comprehensive policies for whole neighbourhoods and providing the facilities and opportunities for all the age groups within those areas. Instead of exclusive reliance on the professionals of the welfare state, people are beginning to see that the only reliable way to plan and protect their lives and that of their environment is to rely on the strengths, skills and solidarity of the people living in the immediate neighbourhood. The most exciting future can be guaranteed to those people who are prepared to untangle and revitalize the untapped and forgotten resources of our environment and of the people who live in it. We have seen that professionals will have an important part to play in this rediscovery of local skills and responsibility. Many professionals are already showing the way through their commitment and example.

Linking this reliance on local resources and people, that we commend, to the acute problem of child abuse, we can enumerate: the development of a variety of play facilities; the growth of local self-help groups, of long term support schemes, of day fostering, of neighbourhood schemes providing home visiting. All of these, together or singly, can go a long way to relieving some of the pressures that lead to child abuse in the home; all the more so if such provision is local and seen to be such by the people it serves. Joint practices and health clinics are, in some cases, showing a concern to respond to the needs of a whole neighbourhood, in conjunction with local residents, and are anxious

to move beyond the traditional approach based on the individual complaint. Clinics, like community centres, are still places where people
meet and relate, and they increasingly provide genuine focal points for
the expression of need, distress or concern. The development of
umbrella-type local centres, whether incorporating traditional professional practice or not, is now common enough, and successful
enough, for such centres to be considered the most viable framework
in which to pour resources and support, and in which to develop
programmes based on local responsibility and initiative. The way
ahead is thus growing clear for professional workers at present striving
against formidable odds to make their practice relevant, let alone useful. To encourage open debate within the agencies and within the
locality about one's practice, aims and assumptions — that is the first
step. This will surely lead to increased co-ordination and co-operation
between agencies, whether statutory or voluntary, above all in response
to an awareness of the realities prevalent in that particular area and in
consultation with those who live and work there.

Conclusion

We have not met here this week to discuss the shape of things to come,
or how to dismantle the old order. But I hope I have shown that the
old order is on its way out, and that important experiments are now
under way that do show a way ahead. The professionals of today need
not fear, there will always be a place for skill and experience provided
they are deployed free of the inhibiting factors of status and hierarchy.
Responsibility for professional intervention must lie in the neighbourhood, and in the people who live there. Responsibility needs to be released by the professionals who now assume it. In conclusion, society's
obligation to the families that live in it is to provide genuine choice and
the power of responsibility.

Discussion

(Chapters 13–17)

Society could discharge its obligations to the family in many ways, the
most practical and obvious being through neighbourhood groups.
Children in vulnerable families could be supervised by older women
with experience, sympathy, love and time to spare. The need for supervision either of the families or of key people who helped them, by
professionals was not always accepted, e.g. in connection with battered
wives. On the whole, the group did favour professional supervision,
partly because the neighbourhood helpers might not realize, beneath

the perceived need, what was the real need. Neither battered wives, some of whom were themselves violent, nor battering parents form a homogeneous group.

The disadvantages of professionals stemmed from the difficulties in communication between those possessing and those without knowledge and skill. They also have to perform two distinct roles, "mothering" the client and at the same time enabling maturation. The art of motherhood is to achieve a balance between the two roles, the providing of love and security for the child and the withholding of support which, under suitable conditions, is the necessary stimulus for maturing towards independence. Difficult as it is for a mother, it is even more difficult for the professional social worker; and the professional social worker found it hard to share decision-making with the client.

The discussion in this way approached Andrew Mann's thesis about power and real power-sharing. Not only the working class but also the professionals today were claimed to be without power. Mann observed that the doctor's position was ambivalent. He had lost control of many things in his professional life, but his skill and his knowledge did give him power in relation to his patient, and this should be used in a sharing way so that the client could choose and play a part in the making of decisions. What the professional had to learn was less techniques than how to cope with feelings, and this came only through experience and through working things out the hard way.

Society's obligation to the family also involved its attitude to the structure of the family and its enlargement of the normal. The following questions were asked: "Who decides what is normal? Is there a general community acceptance of what is normal?" Some support was given to experimental families including the single-parent family and the suggestion was made that all resources and energy should be spent on pressing for the implementation of the proposals in the Finer Report, even at the expense of any more work on child abuse. Nevertheless, much more research was essential despite the real problems of funding for family studies, and the methods to be used required closer examination if results were to be comparable. For example Smith's Birmingham questionnaire depended on precoded answers and rating scales, while Kempe and the N.S.P.C.C. used participant observation and knowledge of the families. The former was preoccupied with reliability, the latter with validity. Were the results comparable?

Another difficulty is the absence of any typology of families. We can now learn about individuals but not about families. Out of the thousands of possible observations, we do not know which are important. We do not know how to define the family. If society's altered view of the family includes "experimental" and single parent families, do we know whether such families can provide the love that the child needs? As to security for the child, this must call for stability. Is stability possible in a family which insists at the same time on flexibility and on a "dynamic relationship around the couple"? Again, are such flexible, experimental families in these days any less stable than the old-fashioned nuclear family? Certainly the nuclear family can be dangerous for the child. On the other hand the "arranged" marriage can be very stable.

Whatever the family pattern, the questions of morals and discipline were ignored while free choice and flexibility held the stage. In so far as insistence on these last represents a degree of immaturity, the research worker should try to avoid such labels. The worker's label is the client's stigma, and a stigma is resented. It seemed from the discussion as if the structure of the family was a matter of personal choice, that society had an obligation to accept such choice, and that no norm existed to conform to which the family had the slightest obligation.

This loose sounding arrangement of society was echoed by Jan Carter who described sub-cultures within society with diverse values and exhibiting behaviour stigmatized as deviant because they refused to accept the standards of the dominant social order.

18. The Moral Strengthening of the Individual

Ronald W. Hepburn

I have been asked to write some remarks that can precede Dom Benedict Webb's paper, and to raise some of the same questions that he will raise but from a religiously uncommitted viewpoint. This means that I shall be chiefly concerned with the problems of how to give a non-doctrinal basis to some parts of morality, and how a non-believing person may find strength to live the moral life.*

It seems clear that in some cases of child abuse, moral and religious issues are not immediately and directly relevant. For instance, a parent may be psychotic, and his illness an incapacitating one that takes away his moral responsibility through delusions or compulsions. He cannot work effectively with moral concepts until his mental health improves. But in many other cases in the literature, the problems have an undeniably moral component. A parent, say, lacks an adequate sense of moral responsibility and moral concern for a child as an individual, a new centre of awareness; and although such a parent may be immature, confused and disorganized, he or she may not be beyond the reach of moral persuasion and reason. A mother, it may be, sees her infant as the instrument of her own comfort and the means by which she may come to feel loved and needed. But if her child is not efficient in meeting these desires, then it will be disliked and rejected. A father, jealous of his child's close relation with its mother, fails to see his jealousy as bad and destructive, and as blocking the way to a better set of family-relations. These are paradigm-cases of moral problems; and to cope with them appropriately does involve raising questions about

---

* (a) I describe my viewpoint as "religiously uncommitted" rather than as "humanist". Although I have written for Humanist publications, I do not identify myself closely with it as an organized movement. (b) This paper is presented in the most tentative way. Although I have read some of the recent literature on child abuse, I have no specialist knowledge of the subject.

the " grounding" and the "authority" of moral principles, about the sources of motivation for the morally good life, and the question whether only certain religious beliefs can provide the foundation morality may be thought to need.

A relevant comment was made very recently:

It is not true that men cannot organize a world without God. But what is true is that a world without God can end only in being a world hostile to men. . . . Since men have ceased to know God, they have more and more to be defended against one another (Cardinal Suenens, Archbishop of Malines Brussels, *The Times*, April 14, 1976).

Religiously Uncommitted Morality

It is often claimed by religious people that a non-theoligical ethic can be a shoddy affair at best, able to appeal only to egoism, to the prospect of the agent's gratification. It may appeal, at its most refined perhaps, to what the agent "really" or "in the long run" wants, but never simply to what he *ought* (irrespective of his own desires) to do or to what other people need from him. But I require no theological premise to infer from my experience that pain, unlovedness and many other sorts of misery are bad, and that they are bad not simply and solely *for me*, but bad as such, in their nature and bad for anybody; and that they provide me with a reason to act so as to mitigate them, when they are suffered by someone within my sphere of action (Nagel, 1970). I do need to make a leap, a shift of standpoint, from the egocentric to the interpersonal. So too does the religious person who moves from a concern with his own salvation (and with the doing of good as only a means to that) to a real concern for the good and the salvation of others. To think oneself into such a moral viewpoint is to see oneself not as the centre of the world, but as one sentient being among others. It makes possible the giving of primacy to the attitudes of respect, love of one's neighbour and justice in one's dealings with others.

If we acclaim the love manifested in the New Testament picture of Jesus Christ as the single morally most important fact about Christian teaching, then we do so by virtue of our independent (autonomous) moral capacity to *recognize* love as supremely good: and the religiously uncommitted can do that as well as the believer.

It is true, however, that the cosmic context in which traditional Christianity sees love operating is very different indeed from that in which the twentieth-century agnostic sees himself; and the question may properly be raised, Can the cosmic background, against which the agnostic sees human life as being lived, possibly facilitate and sustain a moral life of love and justice? Or can only the Christian picture of the world do that? The unbeliever cannot claim that there is any ultimate providential redressing of evils and rewarding of self-sacrificing goodness. He cannot deny that love may be repudiated, misinterpreted and squandered with no good outcome, or that love, ultimately, lasts only so long as the planet tolerates human life. He cannot claim that a person's efforts to love and be just are backed up by supernatural aid. Yet it does not at all follow that he should on that account withdraw his love, lower his sights to self-concern and gratification of immediate impulse. Even against that far more austere and chilling background, a universe governed by impersonal laws, human beings can be seen in a light that evokes a sense of astonished wonderment that they should exist at all, intricate, sensitive, aware; and a deep compassion for the precariousness of their wellbeing.

The very indifference to value of the cosmic setting and the vulnerability and brevity of the individual human life certainly furnish a powerful motive to any person to take responsibility for, and to cherish so far as he can, human life; indeed the more vulnerable, the greater the responsibility. Without God, the nurturing and fostering have to be done by men and women alone; and what they spoil and destroy cannot be rectified in a hereafter.

Viewed in such a light, I am saying, men's situation is one that gives ample grounding and motivation for a morality of neighbour-love, compassion and justice, and for the devising of working rules and moral institutions by which to regulate moral life. What must be added in all candidness is that there certainly are some ways in which the moral life is more difficult to live for the unbeliever. He cannot, in crisis, draw resources from a sense of the presence of God nor be fortified by such New Testament claims as that of Philippians 4.13: "I can do all things through Christ who strengthens me".

What I have been arguing so far carries very obvious practical implications for the moral education of young people. Without at all wishing them to be argued out of Christian belief, I do want to urge the importance of a moral education that makes clear the logical independence of moral judgment from religious doctrine. If a person believes or half-believes that the two stand or fall together, then should his religious belief at some point wane or come to be rejected, he is bound to feel that his moral convictions are weakened or undermined along with the religious: that his actions do not have the value, good or evil, that he once had reason to think they had. Doubt and uncertainty at the religious level will bring loss of seriousness at the moral level; and if I am right this is both sad and gratuitous.

It is one thing to argue that a secular ethic is possible, but quite another to say that such an ethic is well-understood or is in a thriving state in our present society, insofar as that society is secular. It is totally untrue that "if God does not exist, everything is permitted"; and yet some have seen an anarchic permissiveness as the only alternative to a religious structuring of life. That would follow only if the moral life were in its nature no more than a passive obeying of commands from without. For then, lacking a commander, the "commandments" would lapse. But a mature morality is altogether different from that : its rules and principles are endorsed by autonomous moral agents who are capable of seeing the *point* of the moral regulation of life, and are aware of what morality seeks to safeguard and foster.

Several threats to a thriving secular ethic might be discussed; I shall mention only two. For various reasons, we are very much more aware today than ever before of social trends and tendencies, movements of public opinion, the expectations that go with membership of a section or class of society and of what conduct is acceptable or unacceptable, well- or ill-adjusted to a particular social group. It is easy to allow such social and sociological concepts to oust the more distinctively moral notions, and to screen ourselves from distinctively moral appraisal of the ways of social life themselves. A *social determinism* is tempting also, according to which social factors mould the individual, and he cannot be other than he is. Against that, however, we need to reaffirm a doctrine of human moral freedom: the freedom to deny that any set of social roles exhausts anyone's humanity, the freedom to criticize and to reject if need be the roles society seeks to thrust upon us.

Second, therapeutic attitudes are tending to displace, in many situations, attitudes of moral appraisal. Where this results from the recognizing of forms of illness that destroy responsibility and make a person quite unresponsive to persuasion, then the replacement is fully justified while the illness lasts. It is justified also as a temporary expedient in the counselling of less drastically disturbed people, who can be helped towards self-understanding and to some mastery of their problems only if the counsellor abstains from all moral censure and advice. The ultimate aim here is that the disturbed person will come sooner or later to manage his own decisions, including moral decisions, autonomously, coming to see himself as a self-directed member of the moral community and not as a victim for ever passive under psychological forces beyond his control. (However far a person may be from that at any stage, it is in that direction that his counsellors should be incessantly guiding him.) Suppose, on the other hand, that the therapeutic and counselling attitudes are generalized and extended far beyond the sphere of mental illness, then again the distinctively moral dimension will fail to be acknowledged, and our image of man may suffer a drastic and gratuitous impoverishment. Human beings then become essentially and irremediably the playthings of largely unconscious urges and impulses. There is nothing about the therapeutic attitude that *compels* such an overextension. The therapist and counsellor, as I understand them, seek to guide a person to gain insight into (and hence to gain ascendancy over) his patterns of feelings, thought and action. The underlying assumption is that he can be helped towards fuller rationality and moral freedom. The counsellor must presuppose that in his own counselling work he is himself no plaything of irrational drives, but is free and reason-directed. In a word, the very practice of counselling and psychotherapy confutes any generalized psychological determinism. And the therapist cannot attribute less power of rational self-determination to humanity-at-large than his own practice requires him to possess.

To speak of men and women as at least potentially free, autonomous and rational moral agents prompts many religious moralists to say, here is a typically over-optimistic "humanist" view of man. Secular morality has believed that man "can achieve the good life unaided", and that his "progress may...be unlimited" (Bull, 1969) and Utopia attainable by social engineering. Christianity has known better. It knows that man is sinful, that selfishness and moral weakness can insinuate themselves even into the thoughts and acts of those who engage in the most morally worthwhile projects, and that wishful thinking and self-deception constantly cloud reason and restrict freedom. Christianity, I want to say, is right: so long as the point is not exaggerated to become a total denial that moral action is possible. There is nothing in the nature of a secular ethic that prevents it learning that lesson and reckoning fully with human fallibility and moral weakness. Utopias may well be unattainable and man not at all perfectible. There may be no final escape from motives and aims that are only very imperfectly moral. Yet *partial* escape and modest bettering of human affairs do not, on that account, lose their worthwhileness.

To sum up and round off this part of my paper. Although it must be fully acknowledged that a religiously independent ethic cannot provide certain aids to the living of the moral life which are available to the serious believer, such an ethic is a real human possibility. Only because it is so can the teaching of Christianity itself be recognized as of high moral worth. Morality is a many-levelled structure, and there is no level on which a secular ethic is intrinsically unable to operate. The lowest level is the bargaining for benefits, such as personal security and dependable promises, in exchange for the restrictions of rule-obedience. On the way to the higher levels, there occurs that vital shift of perspective, from self-absorbed and self-centred to the distinctively moral viewpoint which has a genuine regard for the other person as a focus of respect, justice and love. If that shift does take place, there is no reason in principle why a person should not show (with no background of religious belief) the highest forms of self-sacrificing concern for others.

Morality and the moral viewpoint, whether religious or secular, are precarious human attainments. The religious is liable to lapse towards pre-moral authoritarianism and can swing between over-rigid legalism and an over-pliant "situation ethics". The non-religious has to maintain itself against the encroachment of sets of ideas, themselves valuable in their own special and restricted spheres, but which tend to redraw a human being as a socially or economically or psychologically determined being, and so diminish him. And paradoxically people in their freedom do often accept such freedom-denying views of their own nature.

Morality and Parenthood

Although I have been stressing that it is vital not to assimilate the moral with the psychological, it is quite as important not to sever the two. They clearly have common topics of interest, e.g. the development to maturity of the human person, the integration of his aims and desires, the management of conflict that dissipates his energies. To speak of "strengthening the individual" in stress may be partly a matter of finding ways of increasing his will-power, but it is notoriously difficult to achieve that directly or through sheer exhortation. Neither parent nor counsellor may be able to say categorically whether on a particular occasion of violence to a child it would have been possible for the parent to overcome a particular surge of anger. It seems there is a tension here in our understanding of human nature. On the one hand, we sometimes assume that "strictly speaking, no impulse is 'irresistible'", and that it is always true that "if the person had tried harder, he would have resisted it successfully" (Feinberg, 1970). Yet, on the other hand, we do think of a person as having finite reserves of energy with which to deal with crises and temptations. The morally strained person may never be quite like the shipwrecked man in the open sea, who swims till inevitably he is exhausted and drowns; nevertheless we allow that some temptations can be so strong that, given fatigue or depression, it becomes "unreasonable to expect [a person] to resist" (Feinberg, 1970; see also Funkenstein *et al.*, 1957). However we try to deal with this tension in our theorizing, practical tactics at any rate may concentrate on trying to reduce the incidence of crises of temptation: and to do so in several ways.

Although a parent may find it exceptionally hard or impossible to refrain from violence against a child once a crisis situation has built up, it may still be true that at some earlier point or points in the succession of events there will have been scope for free and reasonable action that would have averted the crisis. Since that might again be so in future recurrences, locating such points where the will can still be inserted could be an important co-operative task for parent and counsellor.

("...*that* is the point at which to phone the social worker/knock on the friendly neighbour's door...reluctant though you may be: far better that than let the crisis develop and control be lost.")

Instead of thinking how to strengthen will-power to oppose the hostile passions, it can be more profitable to find ways of changing the parents' whole complex of willing-and-feeling, by helping them to see if they have been misperceiving or misinterpreting their situation. A father, for instance, may have been seeing an infant simply as a *rival* for his wife's affections, rather than as an occasion for extending the scope of their affections. A baby's incessant crying may be misinterpreted as a malicious, deliberate wearing down of the parent's resources. Within such an approach, will and willpower, in a broad sense, do remain crucial; if anything is to be achieved, the parents will have to apply their minds to the corrected interpretation to which a counsellor may help them. They have to think against the grain of habit, holding themselves from lapsing to the primitive and distorted perception. Appropriating an insight can be a long and difficult task.

The case literature on child abuse makes it clear that very often such misperceptions do occur. For example, the violence "may really be aimed at the parent's own parent, who has failed, hurt or frustrated him..." (Gil, 1970). Or again a parent may have formed unrealistic expectations of an infant's ability to meet the parent's craving for affection; unrealistic, that is, in relation to the child's age and stage of development (Renvoize, 1974).

There are much broader practical implications in all this than has so far been suggested. Moral education in general, and particularly education for parenthood, needs to emphasize, far more than I suspect it does normally, this moral-psychological fact: that in some of our behaviour we act inappropriately or irrationally or badly, because we are not properly aware of the object of our actions as it is in itself. The importance of this is well presented by Peters (1973), in a study to which I am substantially indebted. To live the moral life is in part to learn to attend to the actual persons with whom we have to deal, as distinct from the fantasy-figures we so often set up in place of them. It is far easier to deal with fantasy-figures; they do not have an individuality to be mastered, so our manner of dealing with them practically can be crude and undiscriminating. The adolescent who is truculent towards a kindly teacher is not perceiving him as an individual human being, but in stereotyped terms as an authority-figure, largely a construction of his imagination. Discussion of such cases, in moral education, should certainly include also examples of parent–child misperceptions.

Once again, the point of view of morality is sharply contrasted with the egocentric or solipsistic point of view. I am still wedded to the latter if I see my children as primarily means to my own self-esteem, or as ministering to my desire for love. If that is my viewpoint, I am quite likely to turn nasty on them when they do not in fact beam back to me the response I want. The only reliable, self-sustaining remedy is for me fully to realize that my children are quite independent centres of experience, not existing in an adjectival sort of way *for me*. At one trivial level I do realize this: at another level I do not. I suspect there is a peculiar difficulty for some parents in acknowledging the other-existence of their children in infancy. Before a child is conceived, some of the self-concerned musings and questionings are perfectly in order: "Would children bring fulfilment, enhance our married life?" etc. But as soon as a child is born, the situation is altogether different. The nurture of the child lays obligations on the parents that are not at all conditional on the child's actually bringing the fulfilment they hoped for.

I have no delusion that a moral educator, however enlightened, can coax every pupil into taking up an inter-personal moral viewpoint. We can ask nevertheless that he should not delay or obstruct the taking up of such a viewpoint, for instance by suggesting that self-concern and duty to others can be counted on to coincide; though doubtless well-meaning, that is in the end a fraudulent assurance.

The effort to attend to and to understand the other person, import-ant as it is, does not *necessarily* lead to concern and love for the other (though, conversely, loving certainly demands attending to the indivi-duality of the person loved). It is possible to understand, and to be detached and cold. In particular, a couple may come to believe that they have blundered badly in having a family at all, and that it has added to, rather than alleviated, their life-problems. How could the individual be helped in this sort of case?

In some instances the most helpful thing might be the provision of enough support to the parents so as to reduce, for a spell, their fatigue, frustration and strain, and for a sufficiently warm and relaxed environ-ment to be temporarily provided in which their child can for the first time be enjoyed for its own sake, where it can be seen in a light in which it becomes lovable to the parents, and "distanced" just sufficiently for them to appreciate the child as an independent centre of experience. When stress returns, such episodes can be dwelt on as a focus for memory and imagination, and furnish some strength to bear the difficult periods with greater patience and control. Although a mother may well need occasional nights free altogether of a wakeful and demanding child, mere getting away is obviously not enough to meet her problem; the objective is not to escape from but to trans-form the parent–child relationship. Nor will the memory of a single idyllic interlude suffice; renewal and the expectation of renewal of such

interludes will matter the more, the more confined the parents' awareness is to present immediacies. The aim is not what I have just called
the "fraudulent" one of convincing the parent that the needs of the
child and her own individual gratification can be made at every point
to coincide, but to help her towards accepting the parental role as a
worthwhile one, for all its difficulty, one with which she can whole-
heartedly identify herself.

The unbelieving parent cannot be urged to pray and to meditate
prayerfully on the potentially loving relationships of the family group.
Imaginative dwelling upon the happier interludes could nevertheless
constitute a kind of non-dogmatic meditation, and given tactful and
gentle guidance serve as the nucleus for the growth of positive and
loving attitudes in place of the hostile and negative ones.

The sources of child-abuse are numerous. In some of the cases
documented, rather different things have gone wrong in the parent's
moral education. One source can be an over-rigid, over-demanding
and legalistic moral outlook, which is unrealistically and savagely
applied to young children. It may be that such a parent has not himself progressed from an inflexible superego *pre*-morality, the regulat-
ing of life by commands that are not to be tampered with, and which
(because their origin is inaccessible in the unconscious) do not grow
and cannot be appraised rationally. The commands can only be
reiterated with threats for disobedience. The vital component in moral
education, or re-education, here is the introducing of the contrast between the early, pre-critical conscience and the mature conscience, in
the forming of which critical reflection does play a large part and
questions about the point of morality and its rules are squarely faced.
Criticism need not, of course, involve a petulant, comprehensive
rejection of the parental morality. But a parent or potential parent
should be aware that the likelihood of his own children rejecting his
moral teaching is particularly high, if his severity and inflexibility
condition them strongly against it! The long-term strategy with regard
to morally over-demanding parents again lies in pre-parenthood
moral education. At the same time, it could be of great value in dealing
with a problem-parent of this kind, that counsellors should themselves keep clearly in sight the distinction between superego
"morality" and a reasoned self-critical moral view.

In the first part of this paper, I urged that secular moral education
and secular counselling should acknowledge, just as much as Christian, the pervasiveness of moral weakness and self-concern, and should
avoid Utopian and over-idealized accounts of human possibility. This
point has practical relevance to another aspect of our central problem;
the last I shall touch on in these unsystematic remarks. A parent who is
known in her neighbourhood to have harmed or neglected her child

may have the problem of coping not only with her intimate family responsibilities, but also with the righteous indignation or contempt of neighbours and acquaintances (Franklin, 1975). In this distinctively moral problem, the parent needs to be helped to avoid either of two extremes: (a) of being overwhelmed by intense feelings of guilt, from the sense that her actions have ostracized her from the human community, showing her to have some monstrous qualitative difference from the ordinary decent run of human beings; and (b) of dealing with her guilt by declining to accept a moral view of herself at all, seeing herself instead as a passive victim of circumstances and psychological storms. Response (a) depresses and paralyses and response (b) holds up the possible development of the personality towards moral autonomy. She would be helped if she came to realize that she is not in fact monstrously different from others. Others come close enough to similar violence and callousness to her own; many others again hurt each other in subtler, less dramatic, but not less damaging ways. This may make the guilt *tolerable*, but a movement to more responsible parenthood must not repudiate or disown the guilt. The measure of self-esteem that a person needs for the conducting of life may, in such cases, have to come from counsellors and (if possible) one or two understanding friends, until there occurs some diminishing of hostility from the neighbourhood.

Morality and the Counsellor

In helping to steer a person through these various hazards, moral and psychological, a counsellor has himself a difficult task in the management of his own attitudes. His constant problem is to acknowledge fully the universal nature of human moral frailty, without letting the acknowledgement in any way serve as a ground for *complicity* in the morally second-rate or squalid. Morally to condemn a person may indeed be destructive and inhumane, but it is ultimately no less destructive to *condone* moral indifference or callousness. Between the two lies difficult ground.

References

Bull, N. J. (1969). "Moral Education". Routledge and Kegan Paul, London; p 95f.

Feinberg, J. (1970). "Doing and Deserving". Princeton University Press; p 282.

Franklin, A. W. (1975). "Concerning Child Abuse". Churchill-Livingstone, Edinburgh; p 2.

Funkenstein, D. H. *et al.* (1957). "The Mastery of Stress". Harvard University Press, Cambridge, Mass.; pp 23, 26.

Gil, D. G. (1970). "Violence against Children". Harvard University Press, Cambridge, Mass.; pp 23, 26.

Nagel, T. (1970). "The Possibility of Altruism". Clarendon Press, Oxford.

Peters, R. S. (1973). "Reason and Compassion". Routledge and Kegan Paul, London.

Renvoize, J. (1975). "Children in Danger". Penguin, Harmondsworth; Chapter 2.

For Discussion see p 268.

19. Strengthening the Individual

Dom Benedict Webb

I make no claim to have any first-hand experience of dealing with adults who injure young children, and my role in this conference, as I see it, is to endeavour to put forward the Christian's approach to the individual who offends in this way. To be a Christian means to love, and to love is to serve, so that all of us who seek to find solutions to this form of violence must approach our work in a true spirit of service, service for the highest motives towards both the offender and towards every member of the team involved. I am simply a Roman Catholic priest, a Benedictine monk with a medical degree; for the past 20 years, I have been a housemaster in an independent boarding school, caring for other people's children between the ages of 13 and 18. I have a particular interest in medico-moral problems, in drug and alcohol abuse and above all, in educating young people to live the Christian life to the full.

History

This topic is certainly not modern. In principle and from a moral point of view it does overlap with the abortion issue which may be considered as a special example of child abuse which occurs to a baby before birth. Injury, murder and abandonment of children has been recorded in many times and cultures, and seem to form a central theme in Judaic development in both old and new testaments. Abraham obeyed the call of God to sacrifice his son Isaac and his obedience was rewarded by the life of his boy being spared. The Holy Innocents were killed in order that the life of the child Christ could be saved. The lives of young children were often offered in sacrifice in the false belief that some god's anger would be appeased.

In more recent times, the industrial revolution led to the subjection of quite young children to great cruelty when they were put to work in the factories and workshops of Victorian England and sent up chimneys by sweeps. Corporal punishment was the norm, often for trivial offences, of a rigid home discipline and for maintaining good order in schools. We live within the penumbra of the nineteenth century dictum: "spare the rod and spoil the child" (Proverbs 13.24), which I believe has an influence still on the choice of punishment by more parents than is commonly realised.

In 1833, the Factory Act was passed by Parliament and this limited child labour to some degree, but society was able to express its concern about the manner in which children were ill-treated only in 1884 when the National Society for the Prevention of Cruelty to Children was founded.

Child abuse covers a wide spectrum of mental as well as physical maltreatment of which death is the ultimate degree. Loneliness, rejection, lack of the normal signs of love, fear of the dark, unkind words and other forms of behaviour can be equally as wounding and damaging to children as physical violence; many of our problem parents of today were victims of mental trauma in their own childhood.

Aetiology

I have read a number of articles and chapters of books with the greatest interest and admiration, analysing the fruits of research into the causes of child abuse. I have been filled with admiration by the patience and dedication of the workers who have written them and I hope that their researches, which all seem to agree are only just beginning, will continue with ever increasing success. Their work suggests a continuity of influence from one generation to the next, for one reason or another, so that future generations of families will benefit from it.

Their work is largely concerned with immediate or proximate causes. If the offending parent is to be helped and strengthened, then the more remote causes must be considered. We live in a sick society. This is manifested by a general drift away from a belief in God, in His Commandments and in the acceptance of the fact that He loves each and every one of us. The spiritual dimension in man's life is no longer considered when solutions are sought for his tragedies. Instead of blaming pride, we follow the philosophy of Oscar Wilde who remarked that "lack of money is the root of all evils".

To abandon Christian principles in life is to release unfettered all the effects of hedonism which is one of the legacies of original sin. The faith that is implanted in us at baptism has to be nurtured if we are to grow up in the life of fellowship with God which we call Grace and it is on fellowship with God that love of our fellow men is founded. Lack of love leads to jealousy, jealousy leads to hatred and hatred leads to cruelty. So the individual citizen has to contend with an ever-increasing amount of vandalism and its attendant lack of respect for other people's property; with muggings and other forms of violence; with a crime rate, especially among juveniles, that is fast becoming alarming. Drug abuse and alcoholism release passions that should normally be under control. Successive Governments have passed a series of laws which permit practices regarded from time immemorial as sinful for the honest Christian; and so we have the Abortion Act which in practice means abortion on demand, homosexual acts are permitted between consenting adults, sterilization and contraceptive devices are encouraged with official backing and the divorce laws have been relaxed to the extent that marital stability is fast becoming a rarity.

A crumbling economy and a high level of unemployment in this country have led to insecurity in the family. A policy intended to remove this insecurity has been developed by introducing a complexity of welfare benefits, which the country can no longer afford but some of which are excellent and necessary; but this policy, far from solving the problem, has largely led to laziness and despair. In the resulting confusion, hope has been replaced by complacency, faith in God by material affluence, and so much compassion and sheer goodness have gone out of the window. No wonder that fear, frustration, anger, tension, resentment, all the emotions in fact that predispose to child abuse, have walked in through the front door.

The Ideal of the Christian Life

Love

C.S. Lewis points out in his book, "The Four Loves" that in French the verb "aimer" means both "to like" and "to love", two very different words in English! To "like" something is to take pleasure in or from it and the pleasure is enjoyed by the person who does the liking, it is directed to self; for example I say I like strawberries or going to the cinema. All too often the word "love" is substituted wrongly, e.g. I "love" strawberries. To "love" something, as St Thomas Aquinas says, is "nothing else than to will good to that thing" and is directed *away* from self. The soul of a human has two activities, knowing and loving. We know truth with our intellects and we love God with our wills, and so to love is to will good. We love God by loving our neighbour, who is anyone with whom we meet, family, friends, acquaintances, those involved in our work and, if we follow Christ's precept, our enemies, i.e.

those with whom we do not get on well. Ideally we also love God by prayer and obedience to his commands.

There are four common obstacles to friendliness, and these prevent us from breaking down the barriers of hostility. The first is laziness; we prefer the easy solution of opting out of a difficulty, we claim that we are too busy to worry about our friends, our children. The second is envy, expressed sometimes as jealousy or malice, by which we seek to establish our own importance, to flatter our own image, and we are too proud to climb down. The third, fear, is probably the most common because we disguise it as shyness or diffidence, or we become bullies, we stand aloof. Lastly there is anger, a variable quantity in every individual; it does not necessarily mean losing one's temper, but it is more common as sulking, that smouldering anger that leads to incontinence of speech and wounding remarks. St John says that "love drives out fear", and since fear leads to jealousy, hatred and cruelty, we conclude that they too are banished by love, for they are expressions of self-love, the greatest obstacle of all.

This seems to me to lie at the very root of all forms of child abuse, and unless everyone concerned with the treatment and protection of the injured child is motivated by love in this truest sense, we will get nowhere with the problem. Our love for one another, between husband and wife, between parent and child must have four positive qualities if it is to counter those obstacles. It must be generous, it must be based on respect, it must be courteous and it must be forgiving. When these qualities have been achieved, then a true, deep and lasting happiness has begun, and that is a happiness no one can take away.

The Value of Man himself

What is man? It is not easy to give a concise answer to this simple question. Certainly, from the moment of conception he is a person, created in the image and likeness of God Himself. There is in the world spirit, living matter and non-living matter; all bear the imprint of God's creative power. Spirits are made in His likeness, and the highest in the order of creation we call angels, spirits with no material element in them. Living beings have within themselves the principle by which they operate, whereas pure matter only operates in so far as it is acted upon. Man is a "bridge" between spirit and matter, unique in creation, because he is composed of both spirit and matter, soul and body. Rather as the water in a kettle placed on the fire is activated and heated by the energy of the flames, so is the body activated by the principle of the soul. Since the soul (or spirit) bears the likeness of God, so Man is created in God's image.

It follows that if every human is created in God's image, then He must pour his creative love into each and every one of us. He loves us with a love so intense that it is beyond our comprehension here on earth; we will only realise its magnitude when we finally join Him in eternal life. It is as though each person is a large shapeless lump of clay in the studio of the sculptor. Day after day He works on us, moulding, shaping us nearer and nearer to His image. The more we respond to His love, the more He responds to us and the quicker we grow into the finished article, the perfect image of Him. Sin unrepented is the great drawback, the condition which makes Him put away His tools and wait.

Forgiveness

I say "unrepented" sin. God is infinitely merciful, infinitely forgiving. Every single one of us is a sinner, and if we repent of our sins, if we say we are truly sorry, then He forgives us and continues His work all the harder. The situation is rather like that of the child in the nursery surrounded by all its toys. When bedtime comes, the one toy which that child will take to bed and cuddle is the oldest, the most worn, the teddy-bear with one eye missing, a limb off and sawdust leaking out of the scars. We are like that teddy bear, battered by sin but God loves us all the more for it, especially when we repent.

However wicked and depraved, however callous and cruel a person is, he or she is still loved by God. It is tremendously important for us to remember this, especially when we are in our moments of greatest depression, when we seem to have nothing but failures on our hands, when we are confronted with families exhibiting the worst cases of non-accidental injuries. To work with these families we need compassion and good judgement, as Miss Joan Court (1974) so rightly points out, but we need also that spirit of forgiveness, the acceptance that God loves the sinner, if we are really going to help them effectively.

Marriage

The concept of love underlies the Christian ideal of marriage, both as a sacrament and as a vocation. It was instituted by Christ as a loving dedication of life leading to the vocation of parenthood. To some it has become a vulgar joke, a drab façade of respectability, a pragmatic necessity. To others it is seen as a union of man and wife founded merely on mutual attraction; since the attraction is short-lived, so the partnership cannot survive for a lifetime. Real love is centred in another person, but what passes for love may indeed use another person but it is centred in self, it stretches no further than personal satisfaction or physical pleasure. "How often the young approach their union unable to take their eyes off each other; how often they part, because they are unable to take their eyes off themselves" (Barry, 1963). Love is never proved to be true love until self is overcome.

That is why it is so important to prepare for marriage. That is why the worst possible preparation is the pursuit of pleasure and sexual experience. The pursuit of pleasure is rooted in the love of self. The tragedy of the mad pursuit of sexual pleasure, which is so common, is that it makes those engaged in it increasingly inadequate for, or incapable of, the deep spiritual reality of married love. At its best it robs love of its nobility; at its worst it turns love of another into love of self, transforms love into hatred and denies even satisfaction to the craving addict. The further the pursuit of mere pleasure goes in these matters the more inevitable is its logical conclusion: apathy tempered by resentment, frustration which pleasure can no longer assuage (Barry, 1963).

What of the children from such a union? If the marriage continues, the position of a child is, to say the least, insecure since it is a constant reminder of a moment of weakness, perhaps even of infidelity from an adulterous union. All too frequently, it is conceived out of wedlock or even born illegitimately and in consequence it is unwanted, unloved and used as a means by one parent of taunting the other to express his or her resentment. If the marriage breaks down, as one in four now do, then the problems multiply as the father or more usually the mother, joins the ranks of the one-parent families. In every case of a broken marriage, it is the children who are the principal sufferers.

Strengthening Parents under Stress

Parental care is manifested by all mammals; the young are fed, protected and taught until they are able to fend for themselves, and this natural phenomenon normally reaches its climax in the human being. It is part of human nature. Any deviation from the normal is rare and means that there is a serious breakdown in the relationships within the family which normally ensure the safety of the children, especially during infancy. The demands made on all parents are considerable once a family has started and these lead to moments of crisis when hostile feelings towards children occur, even in normal people. But so deep rooted in our human nature is the protective instinct which prevents actual violence to the children, that it takes a considerable degree of intolerable stress to make a person lose control.

The Christian ideals are high and spiritual and do not appear to be easy to apply in such cases.

Ideals are romantic and noble at a distance and they shine through men like light through alabaster, but the mechanism of their practical accomplishment in the world is often sordid in the extreme. And therein lies the real test which will show whether those ideals are only illusions or whether they are founded on experience and understanding (Dormer, 1947).

It is my contention that only by the application of the Christian ideals of love, service, marriage, reverence for man and forgiveness that we will find a solution for child abuse. This again can only be accomplished by a team effort in which every member has these ideals at heart and in which the attitude of each individual is basically one of service and hence, of the closest co-operation; there can be no room for discord, jealousy or rivalry. They must steer a middle course between over-optimism and despair. Persistence and real, genuine kindness must prevail.

Clearly prevention must be the primary aim but since the diagnosis of these non-accidental injuries is usually the occasion for discovering one of these families the offending parents must first be diagnosed, both as a psychiatric and a social problem. Once an assessment has been made, then the strengthening process can begin. From the start, it is important to build on the shreds of any inner life they may have had earlier in life, to get them to see the real and urgent need for a spiritual life, and that their frustration with life is the product of an inner desert. This lack of marital stability cannot necessarily be attributed to one of the parents alone so that the sanctification in both their lives must be mutual, that is encouraged in the two parents together. Their failure to embrace their role of responsible parenthood must be related to a lack of reverence for God and for the role he defined in Genesis 1. "God created man in the image of Himself, in the image of God He created him, male and female he created them...God saw all He had made, and indeed it was very good".

The father's role is not only to be the breadwinner of the family but to be head of the family. He is the begetter of the child, the protector of the mother, the provider of the household and he possesses paternal authority in a special way. In spite of the Sex Discrimination Act, God has given him a basically dominant nature, his wife a basically submissive one; his wife wants him to rule and his children need his leadership. More than that, before his family, he is God's representative. If he develops a trust in God, he will assume those spiritual qualities which he will need to impart to his children to bring them to a well-adjusted adult life.

The mother's role is to be the heart of the family. It is she who must make the main emotional contribution to her children and show her love for them. The true spiritual love which I have earlier mentioned needs to be expressed through the normal emotions so that as the children grow up, they themselves learn to give their love. Furthermore, the mother must accept the child as it is; it may be very intelligent and possess all the qualities for which she hoped. It may be very ordinary with no special gifts or qualities. It may be born with physical or mental defects and therefore need more than usual loving care and attention. It is my experience that in those families with one child deformed in some way, there is a greater loving understanding from all the other members of that family, who are more united and able to express their love as a result. The mother's difficult task is to steer a middle course between over-protection and repression. The former leads to spoiling the child with the consequences of engendering in it selfishness and weaknesses of character. The latter leads to emotional immaturity and a sense of rejection, usually the consequence of a spartan up-bringing.

The Marital Relationship

Where the relationship between the parents is in jeopardy, where there is mutual antagonism and jealousy, their child becomes the scapegoat for their failures. There may be causes of insecurity and stress from outside, but fundamentally the cause lies within the lives of the parents themselves. It is essential to start the mending processes by re-establishing mutual understanding and respect, by eradicating the causes of selfishness that must be there, and by emphasizing the dignity which each must show towards self, and reverence which each must begin to show to the other. Guilt must be allayed by explaining that it is human to err, that fear, which is just another word for guilt, destroys love both for the partner and for the child, and that sin repented is sin remitted. Marriage must be seen as a nuclear state so that all the activities of those in the family revolve round an inner core of love.

The Children

What of the resultant relationship with the child? In the normal loving family, the child becomes the bond of unity between the two. It completes the trinity, using that word as an analogy to the Blessed Trinity in which there are three in one, three Persons in one God. Otherwise, it becomes a target, a target either of emotional over-indulgence or of aggression, whether mental or verbal or physical. Any emotional failure on the part of the parents leads to the child standing as a threat to one or the other, because of a failure in bonding between the two. This kind of emotional bonding can only be learnt over the years and if it does fail, a love-hate situation can soon develop with all the inevitable traumatic consequences.

Another situation can also be the cause of the abuse. In some of these families, the child is denied existence. Obviously physical neglect is the commonest manifestation such as malnutrition, or abandoning them to a locked room while the mother goes out to work and so on. But mental non-acceptance is also common when they are shut out of mind, ignored, not allowed to develop like other children (hence jealousy and hatred later on by the child itself). Here again the remedy must lie in eradicating the self-centredness of the parents; they are God's stewards of the children they have been given. Stewardship of its very nature implies responsibility, a lasting concern for the child, a degree of unselfishness which will extend to every moment of the child's life, and itself be a counter to the stress within the parent.

There is one form of abuse which is particularly intractable, namely that family in which one member is made the scapegoat and is denied its place within the family circle. It can extend to physical rejection by the whole group; the metaphorical "hunchback". Only a corporate conscience can remedy the harm, and in these cases the older children have to be "treated". The social worker dealing with this type of abuse requires the qualities of Mother Teresa herself.

The Team

At the risk of appearing to stick my neck out, I would like to comment on two areas of this work, both of which concern members of the team working for the good of these disturbed people. The first is the complex nature of service and the second the problem of confidentiality.

The degree of stress to which all professional people dealing with these unhappy families are subject is very considerable; unrelieved it can lead to anxieties and even despair. The decision, in each case, as to how to proceed should not be left to one individual to decide but should be made only after full discussion and by the "team" approach. Apart from G.Ps, and psychiatrists, professional members of the team fulfil an essential role often in very difficult circumstances. They require in their training a new approach to their career, to learn something over and above the skills of their work. Each of them enters into a personal relationship with his (or her) patients which imposes on him a real responsibility to that person, and this raises the whole position to a higher level. A personal relationship must be established on confidence and develop out of the integrity of the team member. This relationship can be inspired only if that member is motivated by a spirit of *service*. But in fact how difficult it is to serve truly, still more to teach others to serve. I think that there are three stages by which this is achieved. However generous he is, he will always start by asking himself "will I be a success?" or "shall I ever be able to give any real help?". So personal success becomes the primary consideration and it is unfortunately true that many get stuck at this stage for too long, and to their own cost.

The second stage in service moves to a higher ideal, that of serving the organization to which they belong which is a natural sequel for one in a dedicated profession. He can become a mere "admin." man, interested mainly in the smooth working of a system. This can prevent him from giving adequate time for a particular case; the individual can be crushed by the system because the sheer machinery of benevolence or government must think of the good of the majority; he is incapable, in the words of the Gospel, of leaving the ninety-nine in the desert to go and look for the one that was lost. To do so would be inefficient.

The third stage is care for these people as *persons,* as immortal personalities with a spiritual destiny and divine vocation. This can be done only by following the words of the Gospel where we read that Our Lord said: "I was sick and you visited me" (Mat. 25.36). "As often as you did it to one of these, my least brethren, you did it to me" (Mat. 25.40). This assertion of the infinite value of the individual person as representing Christ Himself gives us an entirely new dimension to the matter. It is only by making our motivation truly supernatural that we will really bring a lasting influence upon these families who are "sick".

"Should the Doctor Tell" — Police Involvement

The second area of this problem on which I dare to comment is the question of divulging information obtained in confidence by the doctor to a third party, such as the police. It has been recognized for a very long time (consider the Hippocratic oath) that any private information obtained from a patient is classed as a "committed secret" and may not be divulged unless permission is granted to the contrary. It is well recognized by some moralists, probably most, that there are occasions when, in special circumstances, there is an even greater obligation on the part of the doctor to divulge some of the information obtained from his patient, and these fall under the following four headings (Marshall, 1960).

1. When there is a serious threat to the common good (e.g. a threatened "coronary" in a bus driver).
2. When there is a possibility of serious harm to an innocent third party.
3. When the good of the individual who confides the secret requires it (e.g. threatened suicide).
4. When the doctor himself would suffer serious harm by maintaining the secret.

Clearly every attempt must be made to obtain the patient's consent to reveal the information in order not to undermine both the confidence of the patient and public confidence in the medical secret. It is equally clear that a child "at risk" for non-accidental injury is an innocent third party and therefore would come under the second category above. This would enable the general practitioner to enlist the help of the medical social worker, the health visitor and other team members.

When it comes to informing the police, the dilemma is raised to another level since the information could lead to prosecution. Each case must be determined on its merits by the doctor concerned in accordance with his conscience but he has to bear in mind that failure to invite police intervention could result in further serious injury or even the death of the child. On the other hand, if the parents are willing to help, there may be no need to inform the police. Others more learned than myself have given papers on this matter to amplify the implications of this grave decision so I will not develop the matter further. I think the practice of informing the police only after discussion and the approval of all concerned is a wise one.

Conclusion

In conclusion, the Christian approach is fundamental in dealing with parents who, under stress, deliberately injure their children. The approach must be that of "sharing and caring", caring for both the injured and the injurer.

References

Barry, P. O. S. B. (1963). Marriage as a vocation. *Ampleforth Journal,* 13.
Court, J. (1974). "Non-accidental Injury—A Symptom of Family Crisis and Stress". H.M.S.O., London.
Dormer, H. (1947). "Hugh Dormer's Diaries". Jonathan Cape, London.
Marshall, J. (1960). "The Ethics of Medical Practice". Darton, Longman and Todd, London.

For Discussion see p 268.

20. Means to Good Ends: A Theological View

Gordon R. Dunstan

It is to be remarked that, among the five participants invited to contribute to the final session of the symposium, three are drawn from disciplines other than the medical and social: one from moral philosophy, one from Benedictine spirituality, one from Anglican moral theology. This recognition by Dr White Franklin of the wider dimensions, not only of child abuse but of human personality and capacity, calls for a more than formal expression of appreciation. This I gladly voice.

The task laid upon me was, having to read the papers submitted and followed the discussion, to comment as someone committed to Christian theology and the study of its application to human concerns. The theme of the session is "Strengthening the Individual" and my commentary will be roughly consistent with that. Yet since there is an essential social interest to be served by philosophy and theology, my commentary will necessarily flow over on to social aspects also.

Most discussion in the earlier sessions concentrated on either the child abused or the abusing parents. Some (Shapland and Campbell; Richards; Tibbits) drew attention to the interaction between them. The element rather neglected, until the morning of the last day, was the professional workers themselves and their inter-action, not only with the parents and the abused children, but also with one another. To ignore the professionals and their own inter-action would be to ignore extensive case-work experience, studied and written upon particularly in the Institute of Marital Studies at the Tavistock Institute, to the staff of which I am indebted for my own limited understanding. It would also imply a fundamental difference between patients or clients and professionals, setting the latter apart as immune from processes common to humanity. To one who accepts an incarnational theology, belief that the Son or Word of God became man, not as one "that cannot be touched with the feeling of our infirmities, but one that hath been in all points tempted like as we are, yet without sin", such an implication looks unreal at the outset.

It may be well, therefore, to recall some of the characteristics of abusing parents, as described to us in the papers and in discussion. There is "a negligible relationship [of child abuse] to physical or psychiatric disorder" (Scott), though there was some discussion of what constituted "psychiatric disorder". There is emergence from childhood with low self-esteem (Scott; Pickett and Maton), an unsureness of a capacity to love or to be loved (Scott), ultra-sensitiveness to rejection (Scott), unrestrained anger (Scott), frustration of the demand for instant obedience (Storr, 1977); greed and envy (Hyatt Williams) and sheer frustration resulting in an impulsive outburst of force (general, in Discussion). It is no moralizing point, but a hard fact of observation and experience, that any of these conditions, and any combination of them, can show itself in the professionals as much as in the patients, though expressing itself rather differently. It is to be recalled, and remembered, that the highest peak of emotional tension in the three days of this symposium, with many voices heard at once, some in high tones, the chair momentarily ignored, occurred during the "case conference". We were angry, and more. It is also a fact of experience that professionals can collude, unwitting, with the parents or with either of them, being "appreciated" by one, "rejected" by the other. They can also act out between themselves, in the concerting of their efforts to help the patients and relieve their situation, the very pattern of interaction which, in the parents, has produced the family crisis. They can canalize their hostilities, collusions and the like through professional and bureaucratic channels: the case conference, the appeal to higher authority over the head of the irremovably obstinate colleague, and so on; and the ritualizing of the conflict may discharge some of its destructive force, but the common human elements are there. Again, recall instances cited in the symposium: the nurses in the day-centre "shooing the children out of the nursery and behaving like the mothers" (Carolyn Jones); the nurse who reduced a new mother to tears by removing, without a word, the nappy she had just put on for the first time to replace it folded in the "correct" manner (Richards); the child psychiatrist who felt "depressed" when he read of the "successes" claimed by American colleagues and surveyed his own work accordingly (Oliver).

An awareness of a common humanity is surely necessary for professionals if we are to help individuals at risk and if we are to be preserved from the fantasies of Olympian detachment, which, as every well-taught schoolboy knows, means a high-rise life of sophisticated squabbling among the gods, only absurdly obtrusive upon the life of man. The danger has been recognized in this group: Brandon pointed to the folly of assuming "the therapeutic omnipotence"; there has been frequent insistence that no professional should attempt this work without constant referral to colleagues, to check for bias or illusion. The realities of inter-action are not to be forgotten.

For a common humanity there is needed a common morality, one articulated, or expressing itself, in moral institutions apt to support and strengthen individuals and to facilitate a helping response from society to them in time of need. The common morality may have mixed origins, as ours has in western civilization, from Greek philosophy, Roman law and the Judaeo-Christian religion, to name only three ingredients of it. But common it must be, informing and penetrating social institutions and personal expectations and conduct (Dunstan, 1974, 1975). Moral institutions include conventions, common expectations of how we ought to behave to one another, professions and professional ethics, seen, not as domestic rules for self-protection and regulation, but as principles governing the use and application of knowledge and skills, and embodied not so much in written codes as in bodies of corporate, received, developed, kept sensitive, transmitted within the membership, and a system of law and legal institutions, capable first of distinguishing genuine moral fault or culpability from psychological or other incapacity, and second of dealing with the fault in ways which are above all just and, where possible, also remedial to the offender and protective of society.

Our symposium has rightly taken account of law and, accordingly, of punishment, retribution and rehabilitation. The concept of retribution calls for further exploration. It has been wrongly identified, in my view, with revenge and mere "gut reaction". On the contrary, when rightly understood and applied, it stands as a merciful and just restraint upon revenge. It asserts that there must be a just proportion of correspondence between the culpability of the offender and what is done to him in relation to his offence. It sets an upper limit, which must not be exceeded for any other reason, however useful or socially expedient. The *lex talionis* is restrictive: an eye for an eye (if you must). or a tooth for a tooth, but *no more*. Without this restraint, any of the other purposes which are now so popularly attributed to punishment, such as the reform or rehabilitation of the offender, the deterrence of others from the offence, the protection of society, could become a monstrous infliction of an unjust tyranny. It is odd that a generation which, in liberal western societies, rightly protests against the use of "psychiatric prisons" in the U.S.S.R., can shew itself to be so misunderstanding of the principle of retribution on which alone that protest logically rests.

We ask the wrong question, therefore, if we ask only whether punishment can ever do any good to the offender. Punishment, lawfully administered, is necessary in human society if only, human passions being so strong, to protect society from the inevitable alternative in vendetta, feud and organized or unorganized revenge. The present state of Northern Ireland is indicative. The first requirement of punishment is that it be just, that it matches not the crime but the culpability and the degree of fault, in the offender. After that and subject to it we are free to consider the best ways of punishing, having in view any good which may be done to the offender and any proper interests of society to be served. Punishment and restoration are not mutually exclusive alternatives. Hyatt Williams reported that therapy can begin with a prisoner convicted of grave violence or murder only when responsibility is admitted; acknowledgment of the justness of punishment is a step towards acceptance of responsibility. There must be, however, a common morality behind it all, behind the judicial and penal system and the common expectations of the public. The work of probation officers, the police, the courts and social workers, all tends towards frustration by contradiction when the common morality, itself normally dynamic and subject to organic change, is fractured or eroded by serious ideological intrusion from other moral systems (Lewis, 1976; Phillips, 1976).

The common morality has grown from diverse origins. The strands which compose it are inter-related and mutually dependent; they need not on that account lose their discrete identities, nor is it desirable that they should. The symposium has the benefit of Hepburn's paper, written with characteristic clarity, gentleness and power. There is nothing in it which he, from his religiously non-committed position, wishes to affirm that a Christian might wish or need to deny. The western Catholic moral tradition shaped by St Thomas Aquinas out of Aristotle, and transmitted by Richard Hooker to the Church of England, does not ground morality on religious revelation or commandment but on *recta ratio*, the capacity of the human mind, made in the image of God, to pass moral judgments and to commit itself to moral action (Dunstan, 1974). Christian theology builds on that foundation with a supportive commentary and with perceptible encouragements and sanctions apt for a further end, leading beyond mere morality to the re-creation of humanity in the image of God. This is not a ground for separation from the common human enterprise but for deeper commitment to it.

Christian theology, therefore, dictates commitment to a specific final end, and to proximate ends which it shares with men governed by other convictions or commitments. It sees as its end or goal the preparation of men for that eternal relationship with God for which they were created. Growth in relationship carries with it growth in likeness. So man is to be restored to the image or likeness of God seen in his

Son Jesus Christ bodily, in complete humanity. This end, and the means to it, are set before men ritually, liturgically, in prescribed ways and in the practice of prayer and other elements in the Christian life. Presupposed is the unassailable and precious identity of every single person; so, for instance, in liturgical language, the sacrament is given "for *thee*", "for *thee*", "for *thee*", not for a collectivity of persons. Yet the essential context of the action is a community of persons, the Church; and the end is not attainable for any man without implication in its attainment by the others as well; it can be no selfish or self-regarding pursuit. Hence the language of symbolism in which the first Christian experience was transmitted embodies this inter-reliance of the one and the many: the New Testament images are of a body, with head (Christ) and members; of a vine, with stock and branches; of a kingdom, a city, a household, a marriage. It is consistent also with this interpretation that the basis of the common morality is, on the personal level, respect for persons, and on the social or corporate level, trust. In the theological tradition, the first finds its basis in the incarnational theology of the New Testament, the second (which is presupposed as a foundation for the first) in the covenant theology of the Old Testament. But both have found eloquent expression from time to time by practitioners in the symposium, e.g. "commitment is the bedrock of security" (Rowe).

In pursuit of this final end, therefore, Christian theology commits us to intermediate or proximate ends, which may be taken together as the freeing of the human person from the many restraints, internal and external, physical, psychological, economic and social, which hinder him from attaining his final goal: delivery from crippling or inappropriate dependence or restraint. It can therefore suppose or suggest a common, unifying purpose for the many professional activities concerted in the service of men, of those gathered in this symposium. The Christian religion offers no substitute for professional knowledge and skill; rather it enhances their importance and sees for them a concerted, co-ordinating purpose.

The perceptive listener in the symposium will have noticed the by no means thoughtless use, by non-theological members, of language, apt to its context, with a theological ancestry and therefore with theological depths profitably to be explored. There was an exchange on the first day concerning some particularly damaged, damaging and intractable people, which evoked a cry, "are they *redeemable?*" Christian theology says, they are *redeemed*, they are of eternal value to God; the therapists are concerting their activities to enable them to feel their value, to be accorded their value in society, to live as what they are. Then there was an exchange about children's attitudes to parents, whether they do better to idealize them as what they are not or to hate them for what they are; it was the voice of a psychiatrist which cut the knot: "Forgive them", he said. Hyatt Williams's paper speaks of forgiveness and atonement in the therapeutic process. He spoke in terms of an analogy with what theologians call *grace*, a favourable, enabling relationship, given not earned, active in the acceptance of the other as he is in order to free him for change; inviting a response in good will and a commitment to it, but not withdrawn for lack of them. Technicalities in the full discussion of the word *grace* are considerable, and are complicated by diversities of ecclesiastical tradition. But if the delineation just given is acceptable as roughly descriptive of the theological understanding and of the therapeutic experience, then we have here another example of a point at which inter-disciplinary study would be to mutual profit.

There has been, inevitably, much discussion about the family itself, particularly the "biological family". Caution was expressed in an early session about the historical validity of some of the assumptions expressed, and reference was made to contemporary Cambridge studies (Laslett, 1965, 1972). Even so, signs of strain persisted. The biological family not only enjoys the favour of law; it is an entity to be respected to the extent of creating scarcely resolvable tension when decisions are made concerning children's welfare. On occasions when there is no clear, irrefutable case for taking the child away from its parents, should the child be returned to its "natural" home, either on the supposition that what is "natural" for it must be presumed to be for its benefit, or on the assumption that its presence may help to restore its parents and their relationship to a state compatible with growth all round, or on the assumption that their natural right to bring up their child is so entrenched that only for the most compelling reasons should it be violated? Nothing that is written here is intended to weaken that proper respect, nor to facilitate a casual attitude to family ties, particularly on the part of public authorities. Yet there are difficulties to be faced at the level of practice, particularly when scruples inhibit necessary decisions about placing children in "alternative families" (Rowe) and when social attitudes project stigma upon relationships regarded as "second best" or worse, and so damage the relationship themselves.

In an important sense this respect for the biological family has a firm foundation, in that man is a mammalian species with a highly developed and prolonged psycho-physical dependence of offspring upon parents. Yet, first, it must be observed that man's mammalian constitution, important physically and psychologically as it is, does not constitute his specific characteristic as *man*. Second, popular idealization of the biological family has been fortified in recent decades by religious idealization which in itself invites scrutiny. There are indeed *within* the family particular relationships which not only enjoy the clearest sanction of the Judaeo-Christian religion but are also used as models or symbols of divine relationship and divine activity, and so enjoy important theological significance as "signs" of God's working. Such are the network of moral claims and obligations within a kinship group which the bible speaks of being "bone of my bone and flesh of my flesh", or more simply, "one flesh", a phrase with primarily a moral reference and not a sexual one. Such are also the relationships of husband and wife, whose covenant is used as a sign of God's covenant with Israel and of Christ's with his Church; and of parent, particularly father, with child, used as a model for the Fatherhood of God. None of this is denied, but, rather, vigorously affirmed. What must be called in question, however, is the contemporary Christian idealization of the biological family as the unique embodiment of those relationships; it has, in fact, no firm place in the theological tradition.

In the Old Testament the unit denoted by the word "family" in the English translation was a tribe; and the tribal system was historically obsolete (though still theologically significant) by New Testament times. In the New Testament, the word "family" in our sense *does not occur*. The domestic unit which does occur is the *oikos*, in Greek, the *familia* in Latin; and this means strictly a *household*, a socio-economic group of persons of which some might well have been blood relations and others certainly were not; it would include slaves and servants and anyone else living in the group. Mary the mother of Jesus, and Joseph her husband, and his brothers and sisters are indeed mentioned in the Gospels; but they are nowhere designated a "family" as we now use the term; the "Holy Family" is a creation of a later pious imagination. The use of *familia*, then of "family", for *household* persisted throughout the middle ages and into the nineteenth century; even today we can speak with distinction of "the Royal Family" and "the Royal Household". Celibate bishops, like other magnates had their *familiae*: their household establishments of servants and officials through whom their jurisdiction was exercised. As late as 1851 in the official directions to the census enumerators, the word "family" was explicitly equated with "household" (Laslett, 1972), and "family prayers", where they persisted, would involve the gathering of servants and guests as well as biological kin. It was this *oikos*, this household "not of blood, nor of the will of the flesh", this non-biological unit, which was used as a model in the New Testament, alongside of the kingdom and the city, as a model for the Church; and for many centuries "households" of monks or of nuns were held to be the model community, apt to receive the fullest grace of God and to cultivate the fullest response, while the biological unit created by marriage and pro-creation was very much a second best.

The significance for the Church of the change in its self-under-standing from "the household of God" to "the family of God" is a matter for consideration elsewhere. The purpose of the present argu-ment is to emphasize that the social worker, for instance, agonized in conscience about the best placement for a child at risk, should be aware of his freedom to consider the pattern of relationships within a secure household as the primary consideration, and whether that security is embodied in a biological family unit or not as secondary. In fact, with the known increase in extra-marital conceptions, and of con-ceptions by artificial insemination from donor, both concealed in the registration of the child, the biological unit becomes increasingly wrapped in fiction, and the time is ripe for the whole question of blood-relationship, in its social and legal aspects, to be reconsidered. The concepts of legitimacy and illegitimacy of birth should themselves be brought under question. They had their place in feudal society; they may now be obsolete. Most of the civil and ecclesiastical disabilities attending illegitimacy have been removed; but the stigma remains, providing, among other things, motive for concealment. At a time when genetic counselling is coming more widely into medical practice, based, at its early stages at least, on the assumption that patients know and speak the truth about their genetic identity, false assumptions can be damaging. If a patient's parents are not those whom he believes them to be, and his birth certificate declares them to be, the information he gives, and the advice he receives, are equally useless if not worse. We may need, in short, for an age which has already accepted adoption and fostering, a new concept on which to ground the relationship of child to family, one guaranteeing commitment and security to the child once accepted into a parent–child relationship, irrespective of the circumstances in which the child was conceived. As a moral instrument the concept of illegitimacy is both useless and mis-directed; it attaches the moral judgment, not to the agents, but to the passive issue of their act. The case for enquiry, argued in the relevant literature, is weighty and should not for long be ignored (Ramsey and Porter, 1971; Wolstenholme and Fitzsimons, 1973; Jones and Bodmer, 1974).

It was suggested at the outset that a theologian would find difficulty in considering the strengthening of the individual in isolation from a wider social concern. If bad or obsolete social assumptions cripple individuals, or hinder work, professional and pastoral, for their well-being, then to challenge those assumptions may be a necessary strengthening task.

References

Dunstan, G. R. (1974). "The Artifice of Ethics". SCM Press, London.

Dunstan, G. R. (1975). (Ed.). "Duty and Discernment". SCM Press, London.

Jones, A. and Bodmer, W. (1974). "Our Future Inheritance: Chance or Choice?" Oxford University Press, London.

Laslett, P. (1965). "The World we have Lost". Methuen, London.

Laslett, P. (1972). "Family and Household in Past Time". Cambridge University Press, Cambridge.

Lewis, R. (1976). Academic gloss on delinquency. *The Times* 29 May 1976.

Phillips, Baroness (1976). Shoplifting. *The Times* 24 May 1976.

Ramsey, I. T. and Porter, R, (1971). "Personality and Science". The Ciba Foundation, London.

Storr, A. (1977). Sadism and paranoia. *J. Child Psychol. Psychiat.* (Book suppl. in press).

Wolstenholme, G. E. W. and Fitzsimons, D. (1973). "The Law and Ethics of A.I.D. and Embryo Transfer". The Ciba Foundation, London.

For Discussion see p 268.

21. Therapeutic Systems and Settings in the Treatment of Child Abuse

Arnon Bentovim

Working with families who have abused their children or who are at risk of doing so, uniquely extends and challenges the therapeutic skills of the professional worker who hopes to offer help. He needs a bewildering range of skills at a wide variety of levels. He must have a secure framework both theoretical and personal from which to view his intervention, and confidence that he can contain the family violence, inevitably communicated to him as a result of his therapeutic efforts.

Each family presents an individual challenge. Handled therapeutically, the result is the maximum benefit to the child and his family. Otherwise, a real danger exists of breakdown and family destruction. Some of the clinical situations to be faced, from the first moment that the professional realizes that he is dealing with a possible abuse situation, can be listed as follows:

1. the confrontation with the family, when a diagnosis of abuse has been made, to explain that history and clinical picture do not tally, or that the evidence points unequivocally to non-accidental injury;

2. relating to the family when the immediate safety of the child requires statutory procedures;

3. exploring the family relationships to understand how abuse could have come about, to assess the degree of danger to the child if he is returned to his family, or to determine the need for separation and treatment.

When a decision is made to separate a child, working with the family:

4. to ensure a continuing relationship between child, agency and worker;

5. to alter family relationships by carrying out the therapeutic work while maintaining a statutory role of authority;

6. to help the separated child or siblings to live with the violence of parents towards them, and yet not to fear or expect disaster from the world in general;

7. to work for reunion of parents and children despite separation and the anxieties of agencies and society.

Certain special difficulties arise over working with the family:

8. when the child has been severely damaged or has died;

9. when a child is at risk, there is resistance from the family, and there are agency anxieties but no statutory authority;

10. when a new-born infant has to be removed because of previous severe abuse;

11. when parents have experienced a penal borstal or prison sentence and wish to return to their family or re-make contact with a damaged child;

12. when the parents' psychotic condition makes it dangerous for them ever to take care of their children;

13. when re-abuse may have occurred, after return of the child.

Such a list, incomplete, yet full of tragedies, separation and confrontation, presents workers, medical, social, or police, with some of the most painful tasks of their careers, the counter-part of the pain which gives rise to the abuse in the first place. A number of recent developments in the theory and technique of psychotherapeutic work with individuals, families and institutions can help the worker in a task which is close to the one described by Main when he called psycho-analysis a "cross-bearing profession".

Therapeutic Settings for the Individual

The first area to consider is the setting in which the transaction be-tween worker and client, therapist and patient take place. Generally, consideration is given to the actual content of an interview, rather than where it takes place. The focus is usually on what and how the worker communicates, but increasingly attention is being paid to the space, time and setting offered, in which the client is given the room to communicate. The family where abuse has occurred may only be able to interact therapeutically within a very clearly demarcated area. This may have to be a residential family unit with a physical boundary as described by Lynch et al. (1975) or a special therapeutic nursery as described by the N.S.P.C.C. Battered Child Research Team (Baher et al., 1976). Another demarcated area is the family psychiatric day centre, described later. Separations, periods of care and hospital-ization can all be seen as creating boundaries and space in which the family has an opportunity to extricate its members from the spiralling system of negative feed-back and punitiveness described by Straus (1974).

The introduction of a therapeutic person, whether a mothering aid, "grandmother" substitute or skilled case-worker, also helps to create space in which the family can open up a closed self-destructive system. The idea of space in therapeutic encounter originates from the work of Winnicott (1971) while exploring the manifestations of the psycho-analytic situation between analyst and patient. The psycho-analytic contract has a very firm boundary in the sense of the time of meetings, the space, the room and its arrangement, the regularity of the meetings and the presence of the analyst. This apparently rigid arrangement, through its predictability and the care taken to create and maintain the setting, paradoxically gives the patient room to play, explore and confront himself, and the opportunity to dare to make a new beginning.

Play and Therapy

The concept of play and playing is an important one in therapeutic work. Winnicott describes the development of play from the use of "transitional" objects which enable the infant to re-create a sense of perfect care and so to deal with a moment of frustration, like having to get to sleep alone. He develops this theme to incorporate a broad variety of activities, imaginative play, fantasy and dreams which serve the same purpose, providing experience of the pains, stress and losses, inevitable to maturation and adaptation to our world (Mahler *et al.*, 1975). Winnicott also describes the process of relating to "the other one" through play. At first the infant has to have an illusion of total control and to be unaware of how much work "the other one" has to put in to enable him to play with freedom. Gradually he gains enough confidence to acknowledge the other and play with him. When the other is unavailable to hold the early omnipotent control of the world and then gradually to fail him, the infant becomes disillusioned and fails to adapt, with the development of pathological interaction. The recent Ciba Symposium on Parent–Infant Interaction (1975) gives many examples of the sensitivity of the infant and mother to impingement and interference, and of the resulting failures, which can lead to abuse.

Therapeutic work has to give the patient or client the opportunity to reverse the process by unlocking the frozen potential to "play" and develop. To achieve this, the therapist first has to be used by the patient (Winnicott, 1971) for whatever his needs are. The therapist has to allow sufficient play to go on between him and his patient for an illusion to be created that the patient has found what he has lost, or what he needed in the relationship with the therapist. Only later can he acknowledge the fact that the therapist is a separate person with a life of his own to be related to as another individual rather than as a magic part of himself. For instance, a patient of mine only acknowledged after a long period in treatment that I probably had as much of a struggle to get up in the morning for his early session as he did. Until then, he had maintained the illusion, necessary for him, that I awoke very early and worked for several hours before seeing him. Once he had acknowledged his own competence, he no longer needed to attribute omnipotence to me and could perceive my struggles. Similarly, parents whose own deprivation has left them with a need for parenting, need an illusion of being parented by the professional until they can discover their own competence. Then they can see the worker as he really is, rather than as their own needs dictate.

Within this therapeutic model with time and space for play, the patient can bring his object relationships, i.e. those with himself and significant others, and important experiences related to them. In particular he can bring the traumatic experiences for which at the time he was not mature enough to find a psychological place (Winnicott, 1974). Such unintegrated experiences are perpetually felt to be present or to be expected, and they may be re-created through action or feared continuously. A group of children whose sibling had been killed by a parent indicated in their play a constant preoccupation with the killing, either through stamping behaviour with toy wild animals, drawings of war and hatred, or through their attitudes to each other either a frozen response to being attacked or retaliating viciously. Only by experiencing the death in the therapeutic space could it be placed in memory rather than in the present where it shaped action and reaction.

A firm, well delineated therapeutic boundary is essential before there can be any reversal of the widespread severe medical and social pathology experienced by the abusing individual (Baldwin and Oliver, 1975) described as "cumulative trauma" by Khan (1974). Following re-experience in safety, a process of growth and integration through identification and trust can occur, and substitution for the negative of a positive feed-back spiral of development.

Therapeutic Settings for Families

The therapeutic system described for helping an individual may well help relationships in general. As one patient said: "You only change one bit of me and yet this relieves the pressure for me to be able to use the rest of myself." Altering the system in one area can have profound effects in other areas and can trigger off a new beginning. Unfortunately the homeostatic pressure against change within family systems when abuse and violence is present is particularly powerful (Straus, 1974). One marital partner is likely to choose another with interlocking problems. A partner, sympathetic and knowledgable about the other's deprivation or rejection as a child, may well have had a similar experience and be un-able to help cope with the crisis of childbirth and to meet the infant's needs, particularly if bonding has been unsatisfactory through early illness, prematurity or separation (Lynch, 1975).

Interest is growing in ways of helping the family as a group, rather than through treating each member as an individual. The boundary is not drawn around the individual and the therapist, but contains the whole family and the therapist. Such a setting meets all the family members' needs and uses their strengths as well as dealing with their deficiencies.

Ounsted *et al.* (1974) and Lynch *et al.* (1975) take the family into a hospital setting. Families are provided with an extremely solid, firm, containing setting and boundary so that they can begin the process of therapeutic reappraisal and change. Folkart (1967) has described the therapeutic admission of whole families to the Cassel Hospital.

Working in a paediatric hospital, in our management of child abuse, we have found a day parent pre-school child psychiatric centre an extremely valuable setting for many of the therapeutic tasks described in the introduction. After a period in a paediatric ward for initial diagnosis and management, attendances of parents and children can commence in the centre, observations of interactions and intervention become possible, and for those families where separation is not necessary, or where re-unions are being planned, the setting provides an enabling therapeutic milieu (Bentovim and Boston, 1973).

Families usually attend on one day a week and have an intensive therapeutic experience. Each day-centre social worker works with two families and about eight to ten families attend each day, working together as a group. Each family also has individualized help for the parent or child chosen from a wide variety of therapeutic modalities: conjoint family therapy, individual or marital case-work for the adults, individual dynamic or behavioural therapy for the child. In this setting, we mix families with abused or at risk children and those with behavioural or developmental problems, and we find that the mix can be therapeutic.

A visitor to the centre might see a fluid and apparently unstructured situation, with workers, parents and children interacting in a pattern of free play, interspersed with breaks for tea, coffee, meals and meetings. He might wonder how a parallel could be drawn with an individual therapeutic session with its boundary of time and place. In fact an examination of the process in the day centre does reveal some analogous functions. The setting is created by the families and the workers attending; people and activities occurring at regular times create the firm boundary which provides the necessary safety and security for change to take place. This can be recognized by the anxious reaction to absences, lateness of families or workers, or by the problems created if families starting in the centre or those who have to accept them into the group are inadequately prepared. Without attention to the boundaries there is no "play" within the centre and no possibility of trying new roles and new ways of relating.

The importance of the boundary's function is shown by the effect on the therapeutic milieu of resistance to entry or exit. If the difficulties are too great, if newcomers are excluded and old patients are not allowed to leave, the structure of the centre becomes rigid, dysfunctional and unhelpful. With entry or leaving too easy, the danger to the therapeutic milieu is that the culture and the group's therapeutic potential are lost. Without new workers or families there is insufficient energy and charge brought to the situation; with too much movement in and out, energy is dissipated. The systems model (Emery, 1969), used here to describe a therapeutic institution and those within its boundary, can also be seen to apply to an individual and his therapist, and their mutual play and interplay, which also needs to be free of unnecessary impingement.

It is possible to be more precise about the therapeutic transactions within the centre. Sub-groups form; workers interact with their families and attempt to modify parent–child vicious circle by direct intervention, or by giving alternative models of action. Individual or family casework gives an opportunity to talk about problems experienced and to find alternative solutions. Parents meet together and help to change each other's view of parenting and parenting roles, children play and modify each other's behaviour. The workers themselves form a supportive sub-group and they in turn need parenting by senior staff and help in formulating aims and monitoring effectiveness. The combination of therapeutic processes creates an extended family network and provides more resources than are available to any one family. New learning development and maturation may become possible.

The day centre setting also provides an opportunity to work with families conjointly. Family therapy with pre-school children and their families was felt in the past not to be feasible. This was partly because their language development was thought to be insufficient to create a group which could communicate in such a way that a therapist could relate equally to all the family members and partly because of the difficulty of satisfactorily controlling young children's activity. In fact when parents respond and echo their young children's regressive behaviour, the therapist soon finds the common themes, so useful to take up when family members are together with him. Special consideration has to be given to techniques (Bentovim *et al.*, 1976). For example play material and seating must be suitable so that young children have the opportunity to speak, to play and to be heard. Two therapists can be helpful by attending to both verbal and non-verbal language and beginning to integrate them. Feelings expressed and behaviour observed between family members need to be noted and fed back to the family by the therapists. Their interventions however do need to reinforce the parents' ability to parent their children, rather than make children of the parents with the therapeutist's assuming the parental role. Limit settings for the children, and who should put rules into action have to be worked out between parents and therapists. If therapists have to control children, they need to hand their power over to the parents so as not to undermine them.

Communications from young children are often powerful and naked in meanings, and the meanings should not be conveyed to the parent until the therapist is sure that the parent shares the child's understanding.

Treating the family as a group can be powerful and effective, since the "treatment" goes on working between sessions, By opening up the family system, a change for the good can be reinforced and internalized by the family's togetherness, just as the "closed" nature of the pathological family system can ensure the reverberation of misery, distress and anger.

Clinical Example

To illustrate some of the theoretical points, practical work with a family over an extended period is described. The family was referred by a perceptive general practitioner to whom the mother was complaining that she was finding her three-month daughter, Polly, extremely irritating. She found herself slapping her, stuffing things in her mouth, throwing her down in her cot when she was crying. She was aware that at these times Polly was just asking for social interaction and attention. Her husband often had to step in and take over her care and she was clearly at risk for major abuse. The mother was aware of her tendency to hit out at Polly, and realized that she was getting a good deal of pleasure from her cruelty. There were none of the early characteristics of separation or illness at the time of pregnancy, but what was striking was the story given about the events of the birth. The mother described a nightmare occurring in the first days of Polly's life when she vividly dreamt of her husband being seduced by an unknown girl. She told the midwife in hospital, who immediately gave her the correct interpretation, jokingly, saying that it was probably her daughter growing up, taking over from her and seducing her father. This had a profound effect on this mother and immediately set off intense feelings of depression, which at first she could not understand.

It later emerged that this dream and the midwife's conversation had reawakened painful feelings, which she had been able to set aside for some years, about her relationship to her own father. With the barely disguised dreams, provoked by the birth of a daughter, and the intense emotionality of the period after the birth, these feelings had flooded back to invade her attitudes to both her husband and her daughter. Until her puberty she had had an over-close and sexualized relationship with her father, which had been over-stimulating and had resulted in a distorted relationship to her family of origin. Her father later attempted to over-control her relationships with boy-friends and she was distant from and rather rejected by her mother, a rejection accompanied by frequent slaps. Her brother had a similar over-close relationship with the mother and a distant relationship with father. This family pattern of relationships was clearly dysfunctional and can be seen to constitute a form of psychological abuse for the mother in this case and for her brother. It distorted her ability to find a feminine identification for herself free of parents' involvement and she was not allowed to feel in possession of her own body.

The intrusion of these feelings disturbed the normal birth process that brings together both parents and earlier experiences crystalized in one. Instead of pleasure and joy at the birth and a bringing together of what was good in previous and current relationships, there was the experience of a re-birth of all that could be harmful and dangerous. These emotions are connected with fear and guilt about having a child at all, with the return of unresolved and unresolvable conflicts for the child who had nowhere to put events, which had no place for her in her understanding at the time. She was put once more in touch with them and with the intense resentment that she must have expected from her own mother because of her own activities. The situation was then felt as being repeated by her own daughter, in fantasy at least, and she then felt a similar anger and rage towards her as she expected from her mother for the same crime. There must have been many factors at work early in her family's life which led her parents to make such gross over-stimulating contact with the children of the opposite sex. Such powerful reactions within families can take over and shape each individual's behaviour subsequently and deny them their own individuality.

The first concern in this case was the child's safety. For a time this seemed to be ensured by a network of helping agencies at home: the health visitor and G.P., who acted with the father as surrogate parents. But during an unfortunate absence of the G.P. and health visitor a crisis occurred and the mother came to us in a panic. She felt that her daughter was rejecting her, and was turning away, perhaps in the same way as she was experiencing abandonment by her community helpers. In the absence of the parent figures who were providing a good supportive experience for the mother, she was left with her own internal feeling of having rejecting parents, her confusion being projected onto the child and resulting in a feeling that the baby was turning away. It was felt that this was a danger point and that anger and abuse could be released.

The immediate response was to take both mother and baby into hospital. This was a similar move to the admission of families described by Lynch *et al.* (1975), and in this situation the boundary could be provided that could re-assert the separateness of mother and child and keep mother in touch with her good parenting feelings rather than leave her to her angry rejecting ones. The opportunity was taken to help Polly's mother with her earlier feelings in an attempt to begin to resolve her life situation and an individual therapeutic relationship with a social-worker was set up as described earlier. It emerged that she had never talked to her family about her feelings concerning the relationship with her father, and indeed complete lack of communication had contributed to the considerable distance between her mother and herself. Like any woman caring for a baby, she needed to feel support from her own mother so that the infant in her could feel cared for and looked after. She expected punishment, and we felt after a good deal of individual work that there was a need to move to a family therapy modality in order to help the family themselves to resolve some of these difficulties.

A meeting was arranged at which the mother was encouraged to talk to her own parents about the earlier events in the family, so as to allow for a new beginning in their relationship which had been frozen for so long. This was an emotional and distressing confrontation which needed much therapeutic facilitation and holding. However, it relieved a log-jam for the mother, although at first, it had repercussions on the grandparents' own relationship. This was strong enough to bear the strain and even improved with some help from their own daughter. Family secrets have a powerful effect in preventing family members from getting close and making relationships which facilitate maturation.

The next step after discharge was to initiate regular attendance at our parent–child day centre which both parents were able to attend fairly regularly due to the father's shift work. In this situation there was the possibility of observing and helping the parent–child relationship and encouraging their relationships with other parents and families. My social worker colleague and myself continued working with the parents in a family therapy modality. The earlier work had taken the form of individual work with mother, and the next stage was to extend the work to the family system itself, after the original problems between the mother and her own mother had begun to be resolved. In particular work was focused on the parents' own marital relationship and their ability to work together to meet their children's needs.

As an example, on one occasion we were discussing the way in which both parents felt infantilized especially by the father's parents when they visited them. On one weekend they had followed the grandparent's plans and not their own. They were not able to confront them with the fact that their very little children did need to have periods of rest and not over-stimulation, but this they felt quite unable to tell the grandparents. This shed some light on the father's own position with his parents and their choice of each other as marital partners. Whilst the parents were telling us this, it was clear that they had stopped being concerned about Polly now 2 years old and a new baby who was born in the family subsequently. We observed that, instead of almost sub-consciously noticing when the baby was bumping and falling over, they were so completely focused on their own anger and irritation with feeling in the child position with the grandparents that they could not act as parents to their own children and save them from hurting themselves. We pointed out to them how much conflict there was between their rage at not being allowed to be grown up, and yet their wish still to be little and dependent, and without responsibilities. Because of this conflict they were quite unable to meet the needs of their own children, who were left for us to care for.

On another occasion the issue presented itself of helping the parents to control their lives rather than be controlled by events. The fact was discussed that the family always arrived late for their sessions. They arrived in a chaotic way, burst into the room with babies, prams and general clutter. Polly immediately forced the therapist to stop her climbing on his desk and throwing his papers around, although toys were available for her. Meanwhile, the parents were describing the chaotic chain of events which had led them to their lateness, each getting into the other's way and nothing being achieved. Through their chaotic manner of communicating to the therapists they could be shown just how little in the way of boundaries they had for each other, they all demanded immediate attention in an infantile way from each other and from the therapists and there was nobody to be the grown-up and who could set controls for them, again a demand being made on the therapists. They were in a system whose elements were in constant turmoil with no-one providing control.

Over a long period, by making demands of them to come for sessions regularly with a particular constraint of time and place, this family was given the experience of firm and concerned parenting without excessive over-exciting demands and consequent failure to respond. By example and by helping them to understand, it was hoped that they would be able to carry out the basic family functions. These include providing for each other's needs as adults, meeting their children's needs for nurturance in appropriate doses, with failure when necessary to help the children use their own resources, for appropriate socialization and sex models, and maintaining the generation boundary they did not experience themselves. In this case the family was discharged with no further evidence of risk of abuse to date.

References

Baher, E., Hyman, C., Jones, C., Jones, R., Kerr, A. and Mitchell, R. (1976). "At Risk", N.S.P.C.C. Battered Child Research Team. Routledge and Kegan Paul, London.

Baldwin, J. A. and Oliver, J. E. (1975). Epidemiology and family characteristics of severely abused children. *Brit. J. Prev. Soc. Med.* **29**, 205–221.

Bentovim, A. and Boston, M. (1973). A day centre for disturbed children and their families. *J. Child Psychother.* **3**, 46–60.

Bentovim, A., Boston, M. and Elton, A. (1976). Family therapy with very young children and their families. (To be submitted.)

Ciba Symposium, (1975). "Parent–Infant Interaction". Elsevier, Holland; Vol. 33.

Emery, F. E. (1969). (Ed.). "Systems Thinking". Penguin, Harmondsworth.

Folkart, L. (1967). Some problems of treating children in the in-patient setting. *J. Child Psychother.* **2**, 46–55.

Khan, M. M. R. (1974). "The Concept of Cumulative Trauma (The Privacy of the Self)". Hogarth, London.

Lynch, M. A. (1975). Ill-health and child abuse. *Lancet* **2**, 317–319.

Lynch, M., Steinberg, D. and Ounsted, C. (1975). Family unit in a children's psychiatric unit. *Brit. Med. J.* **2**, 127–129.

Mahler, M. S., Pine, F. and Bergman, A. (1975). "The Psychological Birth of the Human Infant". Hutchinson, London.

Ounsted, C., Oppenheimer, R. and Lindsay, J. (1974). Aspects of bonding failure: the psychopathology and psychotherapeutic treatment of families of battered children. *Develop. Med. Child Neurol.* **16**, 447–456.

Straus, M. A. (1974). A general systems theory approach to a theory of violence between family members. *Social Science Information* **12**(3), 105–125.

Winnicott, D. W. (1971). "Playing and Reality". Tavistock, London.

Winnicott, D. W. (1974). Fear of breakdown. *Int. Rev. Psychoanal.* **1**, 103–108.

For Discussion see p 268.

22. Strengthening the Individual?

Jan Carter

There may be an important paradox in the task of strengthening the individual that our present professional values and services overlook. The paradox that I should like to suggest is that the individual is only strengthened in relation to others, that is to say in community, and that our failure to grasp this may reinforce constraints which have prevented the constructive direction of professional help.

An illustration may help. I started to think about the nature of community and the nature of professional values as a result of a discussion about possible ways to organize this session. I had hoped to invite a parent or parents who had received help in dealing with their problems of child abuse to join us, so that we could discuss together the approaches and methods that they had found helpful in their contact with professionals, and the approaches that they had found confusing and perhaps destructive. This idea was unacceptable to some members of the conference and I wondered why this should be so.

This made me think about the validity of many of the assumptions behind professional thinking in child abuse. For instance there is in our thinking a distinct boundary drawn between the helper and the helped. There is a hierarchy of professional values which places the helper at the top and the helped at the bottom. There is the helper's demands that the helped fit into his routines. There is the way the depersonalization of the helped is achieved by the abstractions of research and clinical reports.

The Helper and the Helped

I should like to suggest that in the field of child abuse we have developed two quite separate cultures: the helper culture (the professional) and the helped culture (the child abusers). Normally, contact between the two groups is minimal and is restricted to official occasions in the office or clinic, or at a home visit. One culture is regarded as dominant, morally superior and persuasive. The helped are expected to fit into the helper's social and moral expectations and one way of enforcing this is to draw a picture of certain stereotypes about the helped (to be described later), which emphasize his degree of social distance from the norms considered appropriate for him by the helper.

In our society there is little doubt that professionalism implies the idea of the social and intellectual dominance of an élite. For this reason it is clearly difficult for professionals to participate or to share in a community, the boundaries of which encompass those whom they are trained to help. Many of the premises of professionalism seem to have been based on the philosophy of individualism, to which ideas of inter-dependence and community are in opposition. The philosophy of individualism (i.e. the social theory of the free and independent action of the individual) has had profound effects on the development of modern professionalism. Howard Jones has described the development of professional social work as the gradual scientization and humanization of the basic ideology of capitalism. Similar analysis could be made about medicine and the law, but his basic argument is that social work arose at a time in the nineteenth century when the dominant mode of social production (capitalism) needed an individualistic creed (Jones, 1975). Individualism, in the sense of taking personal responsibility for their own actions is a very important part of professional thinking. It is seen most clearly in the doctrine of professional autonomy. However, the idea that a professional's action is right if he considers it to be right and if he acts in good faith is a doctrine which has come under fire recently, particularly in inquiries such as those into the death of Maria Colwell and Stephen Meurs.

In fact it is becoming more and more difficult to substantiate the doctrine of professional individualism. To explore fully the positive and negative aspects of this doctrine would require a detailed philosophical, political and social analysis beyond the scope of this paper. But it could be more useful to conceive of twentieth century professionalism as one side of a dualism rather than as the unbridled exercise of indivdual autonomy. For professionals cannot exist in a vacuum. Social workers, paediatricians, lawyers and child psychiatrists actually need the "helped culture" to confirm their own. The variation in degrees of dependence between the professional and his patient/client depend on many factors, including for example, the way the professional group is organized: whether it is largely mediated by the state (as for doctors in the N.H.S. and social workers in local authority social services departments) or mediated through a "market-place" referral system (as for barristers and solicitors). As the social and economic variations in professional organization proceed, it is important to recognize that professionals are as dependent on the culture of child abuse as the reverse. In fact, such social and economic structures encourage a psychological dependency (but not inter-dependence) between the two groups. It is difficult to admit that we need the families of abused children as much as they need us. Except at the level of professional jokes, such dependence is rarely expressed and then only one side, the dependence of the parents, is analysed.

The problem is to ask whether mutual dependence could be acknowledged as inter-dependence. So far I have argued that many professional assumptions are antithetical to the idea of inter-dependence and community because professional culture and family culture are discrete and rarely meet. Further, the distance between the professional and the client is given considerable justification by the philosophy of individualism. Because dependence is two way, a more mature inter-dependence could possibly develop. This would concentrate less on the symbiotic dependence that I have been describing and more on the inter-dependence and community shared by the helper and the helped. This position has a great deal in common with Professor Dunstan's argument that professionals and parents have a common humanity. Such inter-dependence results less from the effects of socially induced dependence than from the notion of community based on the acknowledgement of a common human interest.

In one other area both professional individualism and socially induced dependence between professional and patient may have contributed to unhelpful thinking about the abusing families. This lack of inter-dependence or of common or shared experiences between the two groups would appear to have reinforced the idea that the failings or defects of abusive parents are located solely inside them. Nineteenth century individualistic thinking held the individual responsible for his own problems, his unemployment, his physical or mental handicap and his mental illness, and above all, for his social and moral inferiority. This thinking was of course embodied in the Poor Law (Jordan, 1974).

"Blaming the Victim"

In the twentieth century, confining our professional gaze to the individual and family defects of the child abuser has become an explanation in itself for the problems of child abuse and neglect. Take the family with child abuse as an example:

Several interesting psychiatric features emerged. Abnormal personality was a significant finding among parents.... Mothers were generally emotionally immature and dependent. Nearly half were of subnormal intelligence... Battering may at best be an ineffectual method of controlling the child's behaviour .... One third of the fathers had a gross personality defect and half the mothers were neurotic. ... Nearly a third of the fathers had a criminal record.

Mothers reported that their husband was rejecting the child and failed to help in bringing it up. ... Although almost one third were unmarried, three-quarters ... had conceived premaritally (Smith and Noble, 1973).

Such statements about parents of child abusers are common.

As Martin Rein has pointed out (Rein, 1969) progress itself has contributed to the institutional rejection and thus the dependence of many of the people we discuss. More automation means less manufacturing jobs and has left more people out of jobs and as dependents on social service department caseloads. More medical care has provided environments in which young premature and handicapped children live longer, extending their dependence on the "chronic" sector of the N.H.S. More "rehabilitation" programmes in housing have torn down cohesive communities and replaced them by the non-communicating crowds in tower blocks where young mothers pass their days in depression (Richman, 1974).

To explain the failings of child abusers simply as the function of innate defects is simplistic. Complex social and economic forces are closely associated in processes which we do not fully understand in the problem of child abuse (Carter, 1974). Abnormal personality, emotional immaturity, dependency, borderline intelligence, child abuse and neglect, gross personality defects, neuroticism and crime are not necessarily the sole results of individual or familial pathology and defects. Commenting on the similar components of the so-called deprivation cycle, Rein (1969) says:

a valid alternative analysis would focus not on personal defects but on institutional rejection and the indifference, which leads to development of protective sub-cultures which wall people off from the threatened destruction of their personalities.

William Ryan (1971) has called this process "blaming the victim". As he explains:

the stigma, the defect, the fatal difference... is located within the victim, inside his skin. With such an elegant formulation, the humanitarian can have it both ways. He can, at the same time, concentrate his charitable interest on the defects of the victim, condemn the vague social and environmental stresses that produced the defect (some time ago) and ignore the continuing effect of victimizing social forces (right now). It is a brilliant ideology for justifying a perverse form of social action to change, not society, as one might expect, but rather society's victim (p 7).

Within child abuse the possibility that the problems of individuals could be seriously related to the social fabric has never been taken seriously by policy makers and rarely by researchers, with the exception of David Gil (1970) and Giovannoni (1971). Researchers get answers only to the questions they pose and the question of the way broad social processes interact with the individual or family have not been considered or measured. Perhaps a partial answer to this represents a hidden vested interest of professionals in maintaining a new population of child abuse dependents.

The Community and Communities

Having suggested that we need to move from an outdated philosophy, which locates social and personal inadequacy entirely within the individual, I can now return to the concept of inter-dependence. Not only in child abuse are there important stirrings to assess the value of inter-dependence and community.

Theologians, for instance, have also been attempting to free themselves from the constraints of Victorian individualism and, in grappling with the meaning of inter-dependence, have suggested that individuation is only achieved in the community. Martin Buber, the Jewish existentialist, started from the single "I–thou" relationship, which was to be distinguished from the "I–it" relationship. "I–thou" relationships are relationships between persons, and "I–it" relationships denote treating the person as a thing. He enlarged the single "I–thou" relationship to the idea of the community (Gemeinshaft), the living unity of a group with a common spiritual basis and a genuine "I–thou" relationship between its members (Buber, 1947). John Baillie, the Protestant Scottish theologian, has said:

Christianity can only be understood as a community affair. This does not mean it is not a personal affair, on the contrary (it is) because it is a community affair that it is personal — for only in community can personality be developed (Baillie, 1942).

Social and political scientists have emphasized the importance of the dialectical relationship which exists between an individual and the community. Marx insisted that the individual could only develop in a human society where men were freed from the dehumanizing arrangements of production in a capitalist society. In recent decades, social-science research findings have emphasized that it is only in certain *kinds* of community that individual human development is possible. Recent research in institutions has shown that some kinds of communities can actually have negative and harmful effects on the individual. As it happens such institutions or communities have many of the characteristics of the "two cultures", detailed earlier in the paper as illustrations of the split between the professional and parent culture in child abuse.

For instance, in the social sciences, the writing of Goffman (1971) marked an important beginning. He drew attention to the ways in which self-contained communities such as mental hospitals, prisons, concentration camps and monastries had many features in common. These "total" institutions were fundamentally split in two, with a wide gulf between the larger group, the inmates and the smaller group, the staff. There was relatively little interaction between these groups and often some hostility associated with social distance.

Next, the organization of such communities was authoritarian, in that the programme was imposed centrally by officials who belonged to a strict hierarchy. The inmates who spent all day in each other's company were given very little choice in their activities. They proceeded to meals, toilets and baths and under strict routines. The implicit purpose of these procedures was to induce the inmate to lose his personal identity and to accept the community's definition of reality.

Following Goffman, research workers from many backgrounds have detailed the negative effects of the institutional community, drawing attention to the excessive power and authority of officials, the relative impotence of the inmates, the heavy dependence on rituals and routines. In Britain, the deficiencies of such communities have been detailed in studies about the elderly (Townsend, 1962), the mentally handicapped (Morris, 1969), mentally ill (Wing and Brown, 1970) and the physically disabled (Miller and Gwynne, 1972).

To illustrate this kind of research may be useful. King *et al.* (1971) discriminated between two sets of practices in children's institutions. The research workers examined the quality of care received by the children in everyday living and found wide differences between different institutions. By means of a child management scale, the rigidity of the routine, the amount of mass rather than individual treatment, the degree of de-personalization and of social distance between staff and children was assessed. Considerable differences in practices led the authors to suggest that one major set of practices, the institutionally orientated ones were harmful, while the child orientated practices were not. Wing and Brown (1970) looked at related issues of institutionalism in the management of schizophrenics in the mental hospital. They were interested to know how far the social environment actually affected patients' symptoms and whether it actually caused improvements or deterioration. They showed that there was an important association between an impoverished social environment and negative symptoms, such as withdrawal and regression. The most important factor in improving patients was a reduction in the amout of time spent doing nothing. Also, a restrictive ward routine seemed to play a part in the continuance of negative symptoms. In other words, the more patients were free to choose their daily living practices such as when they went to the shop or left the hospital grounds the less likely they were to be withdrawn or regressed.

These examples of communities are chosen to demonstrate the fact that the communal environment exerts a powerful effect on an individual. Although these arguments apply to residential communities at present, there is a national study of day centres and day hospitals where a view of the results of a pilot study demonstrates that many of the same negative patterns may operate (Carter and Edwards, 1975).

At the same time, the studies which have detailed the negative effects of communties have provided us with implicit clues about their possible positive effects. At an empirical level the status of the evidence about the positive rather than the negative effects of communities is rather more tentative, perhaps because research is done more often in "bad" environments. The fundamental issue is the degree to which the individual can seek individuation and this seems to depend on such matters as:

his degree of involvement in setting the aims and deciding the programme;

his degree of personal responsibility in running the place;

the amount of choice he has over his activities;

his participation with the wider community, i.e. those communities which interlock with his own.

All these issues revolve around the way the issue of professional dominance and the separatist professional culture is dealt with. For example in day centres and day hospitals, inspection of everyday living practices indicate silent messages about the superiority of the professional culture. Separate quiet rooms for staff to rest, separate lunch arrangements for staff, separate (and usually better) toilets for staff, the non-reciprocal use of Christian names of patients and clients by the staff, all are messages about superior and inferior cultures. All the vital decisions about admission, length of stay and discharge are taken by the staff. Staff in day communities are often critical of the members' refusal to take responsibility, whilst continuing to deny them access to the process of jointly making their own decisions; perhaps this is the nub of the paradox. Until professionals contribute to settings where all individuals (whether patients/clients or workers) are recognized as inter-dependent, it is unlikely that individuation will flourish. At present professionals contribute to environments by emphasizing their own individualism. By denying their inter-dependence with their clients or patients they reject in turn *their* individualism. Yet it is only through healthy community and inter-dependence that individuation and taking of personal responsibility can develop.

Conclusion

How can inter-dependence and community be helpful in managing child abuse cases? Several contributors to this meeting have suggested in detail the potential impact of varying community approaches to child abuse cases (see Chapters 7, 17 and 21 by Richards, Mann and Bentovim). These ideas need not be repeated here. Most of the suggestions aim at divesting the professional of his control and involve substantial devolvement of responsibility for child abuse by placing it back on the community. So far as the management of child abuse is concerned the community is largely an untapped force. The similarity shared by the professional working with child abuse and his colleagues in the better documented children's homes, psychiatric hospitals and prisons is the absence of a clearcut and distinctive technology for intervention. Perhaps this also justifies a new look at his role. Professional dominance is easier to justify in the operating theatre than in the child abuse clinic or outpatient department, the mothers group or the community centre, the residential unit or the play group. In those situations, where the technology is unclear or uncertain, perhaps the views of the professionals should have the status of just another set of opinions, neither superior nor inferior. This after all may do no more than reflect the inter-dependence of the community itself.

Until we try such ideas and step outside the limitations of our professional rigidities, our pessimism about dealing with the problem of child abuse is understandable. While such pessimism may be justifiable, as applied to ourselves, about the parents and the families it is less defensible. It may be that we have stayed in our own culture trapped within our own isolated dominance. It may be that which now fails us.

References

Baillie, J. (1942). "Invitation to Pilgrimage". Pelican edition 1960.

Buber, M. (1947). "Between Man and Man". Fontana edition 1973.

Carter, J. (1974). "Child Abuse and Society in The Maltreated Child". Priory Press, London.

Carter, J. and Edwards, C. (1975). Institutional care and community care. Paper presented at D.H.S.S. sponsored C.C.E.T.S.W. workshop on training for day care, Southport, 1975.

Gil, D. G. (1970). "Violence Against Children". Harvard University Press, Cambridge, Mass.

Goffman, E. (1971). "Asylums: Essays on the Social Situations of Mental Patients and Other Inmates". Penguin, Harmondsworth.

Giovannoni, J. M. (1971). Parental mistreatment: perpetrators and victims. *J. Marriage Fam.* November, 649–657.

Jones, H. (1975) (Ed.). "Towards a New Social Work". Routledge and Kegan Paul, London.

Jordan, B. (1974). "Poor Parents". Routledge and Kegan Paul, London.

King, R., Raynes, N. and Tizard, J. (1971). "Patterns of Residential Care". Routledge and Kegan Paul, London.

Miller, E. and Gwynne, G. (1972). "A Life Apart". Tavistock, London.

Morris, P. (1969). "Put Away". Routledge and Kegan Paul, London.

Rein, M. (1969). The Strange Case of Public Dependency. *Transaction* March/April, 16–23.

Richman, N. (1974). The effects of housing on pre-school children and their mothers. *Develop. Med. Child Neurol.* **16**, 53–58.

Ryan, W. (1971). "Blaming the Victim". Orbach and Chambers, London.

Smith, S. and Noble, S.(1973). Battered children and their parents. *New Society* 15th November.

Townsend, P. (1962). "The Last Refuge". Routledge and Kegan Paul, London.

Wing, J. and Brown, G. (1970). "Institutionalism and Schizophrenia". Oxford University Press, London.

Discussion

(*Chapters 18–22*)

The plan for the last session had been to discuss with the theologians and the philosophers who had studied the documents and had been present throughout the meeting, what views they now took of the subject. Particularly they had been asked to address themselves to the question "how can the individual be strengthened?". As a contrast to theological, philosophical and moral speculations (Chapters 18, 19 and 20), a psychiatrist and a social worker were invited to speak on what they themselves actually did. In the event the group was unable to accept that this was a question that should be asked or could be answered. Individuals do want personal help of course, but in child abuse the problem had ceased to be an individual's problem at both ends of time. If it be true that usually it is the parenting of the parent or caretaker that is at fault, two or three individuals are already involved, and, since the child is abused in the family setting, again a number of people are involved. To this number are added all those who investigate or "treat". The idea that the psychopathic abuser is not responsible for his actions appears to have been accepted without discussion. Such a person is not to be trusted with the care of a baby at all and the necessary treatment is not aimed at rehabilitating the family but, in the first instance, at protecting the child.

In any case, whether it was the individual or whether it was always the total family that needed help, the first requirement was that a helper should be available. That helper could be effective whether professionally trained or not, but with lay helpers a professional adviser was essential in the background. To use the analogy of the medical cure as of a sickness was misleading. The nature of the help was something entirely different. First aid to ensure the safety of the child was of paramount importance. After that the task was to promote the development of a family for the child, a family whether biological or substitute that takes its place in the community.

Other families, themselves involved in abuse, could play their part. The psychiatrist sees the abusing person as someone left with unresolved problems which block his development and will continue so to do unless and until they are resolved. Without resolution repetition remains an ever present danger.

From the point of view of society a crime has been committed and the discussion moved to consider whether punishment could help let alone strengthen anyone. To the question whether punishment does any good, the answers varied. It was not meant to do good; it was necessary to society; it was to be used only as a last resort and then only if it was of advantage to the punished. Whatever its purpose, it must be just and absolutely related to the offender's culpability. One of its functions was to get the criminal to face and to accept responsibility for his crime. This would seem to rule it out if the argument be accepted that the responsibility rests not with the abuser but rather with the failure of his parenting by his own parents.* Perhaps punishment is reformative, certainly it is a protection for society. Everyone agreed that the concept, despite attempts to simplify it, remained complex. Sometimes the wrong person was punished. Children must see removal from their families as a form of punishment. The severely brain-damaged child suffered an even worse "punishment", although this is a misuse of the word, by being ejected from society into an institution where he lingered unvisited and unloved. If the individual could be strengthened, the time for strengthening was before and not after the abuse.

To the theologians and the philosopher the idea of community commended itself. Although each person is unique, he needs to be liberated from the stresses and constraints imposed by the community as well as from within himself so as to become truly and freely a part of the community. The basis for a code of morality and whether one could exist effectively without a "religion" (see Professor Hepburn's essay in Chapter 18) was not discussed.

One psychiatrist said "it is not unknown for a psychiatrist to think, even if he doesn't say it, the patient needs a parish priest more than he needs me!", but no suggestion was made as to how the priest could be made available and acceptable to the abusing family. The psychiatrists

---

* To be accepted in moral philosophy and in law, a complete absence of responsibility requires the presence of very severe psychopathic disorder. Only where there is no real freedom can there be no real culpability.

had techniques to tempt families into interaction between members, then with other families and finally with the community. If it be true that God is in everyone, the ultimate aim of the Christian theologian is to enable man to realize his relationship with God and to change, with Jesus as his model of what man can make of man. The two approaches, conversion (seen as a process) or the resolution of developmental blocks, could achieve such a fundamental alteration. Both aimed at getting man into relationship with the community. Perhaps both share more than is at first apparent.

23. Child Abuse as a Challenge

Alfred White Franklin

Child abuse in its modern guise has now established itself as a fact of life in society in every part of the western world and is met everywhere with horror and dismay. Two hundred years ago the same shock and a similar outcry greeted the high infant mortality in foundling hospitals and this was repeated during the nineteenth century with the scandals of "Burial Clubs" and of "baby-farming". By no means all of these disposable babies are unwanted. For some the mother's pregnancy may have been a tragedy, for others only an inconvenience, but for many a pregnancy is needed to fit a pattern in the mother's mind. The baby is loved with selfish love for the part that it is expected to play and abused when it fails to play it. This failure is likely to lead the mother to try again. The techniques of disposal have changed and the outward appearances. Central to them all is the same theme that some babies and some young children have no natural place where they belong, where they can rely on love, security and the satisfaction of their biological needs.

No one disputes that every child who survives birth has a right to live and to the satisfaction of these needs. If the parents fail, whose is the responsibility to provide a substitute family? Wives no longer *belong* to their husbands, but the concept of a child as a chattel lingers on. Society has now arranged that a wife can look after herself on her own. Biology has not so far made this arrangement for the child. What he needs from his family for his normal development is spelt out on p 2. Without the satisfaction of these needs he is deprived and disadvantaged, possibly for life.

A child is also in some sense the property of the "state". He is part, not always an easily recognized part, of the "state's" capital assets. He is the future soldier, worker, voter, taxpayer and parent of the next generation. He therefore merits and receives the "state's" protection. His entitlement to education has been legally recognized in England for over a century. His entitlement to proper care by his family cannot be assured by even the most caring laws.

What the state can do is limited to passing child protection laws, to legal action when these laws are transgressed and to the provision of either a rehabilitation service or an alternative family. What it ought to be able to do is to ensure that children are given priority in our society and that the external environmental stresses on families with children are reduced to a minimum. But this task, difficult as it is, and perhaps impossible to fulfil, is not enough. The reports of the cases offered in Chapter 2 by Dr Cooper and the observations of Dr Oliver in Chapter 3 reveal once again complex kinships of individuals whose reaction to almost any difficulty is violent. They appear to reject not only their children but also all the restraints and codes of behaviour on which society as a cohesive institution depends for its life. They are first material for research, for theses, for understanding, then as understanding grows, so does sympathy and in the end identification so that we too risk feeling resentment against the state and its arrangements and lodge blame there. This involves us in the fantasy that were there no poverty there would be no abuse.

The Scapegoat

Members of the general public, whose voluntary exercises in compassion have been gradually replaced by state action, are still able in conscience to pass by on the other side. But when the statutory compassionate service fails, the public demand for a scapegoat is understandably violent, for, without a positive resistance, violence breeds violence. The violence has to be projected on a person, and, whatever the findings of public inquiries, this can never be just nor justified. These inquiries have been useful in drawing attention to the existence of the problem. Now many believe them to be counter-productive, since they sap the confidence and weaken the resolve of the workers. But when something has gone wrong and a baby has died or suffered permanent damage under the very eyes of the protecting and rehabilitating service, to whom or to what does blame attach?

What may seem to some a decision even more dangerous than to blame one person is to make the state the target. The organization of society is always imperfect but remains tolerable to the majority as long as and only just as long as it contains within itself the means for making improvements. Blueprints for Utopias are not hard to fashion or to find; not one carries any guarantee of betterment for a single individual. This, then, is one challenge, with which the study and the experience of abusing families faces us. And the challenge is readily recognized in Chapters 17 and 22. If the eradication of child abuse needs a really radical alteration of society, this possibly is too high a price to pay. Nor is success guaranteed.

Society's multifarious activities are seen in different lights according to the viewer's position in society. The solving of one problem is likely to produce another and, as society can never be all things to all men, systems of priorities and of checks and balances have to be devised and, having been devised, be generally agreed. At present society is greatly exercised about child abuse. There is less general tolerance of violence in all its forms, particularly intrafamilial violence, while paradoxically individuals succumb as readily as ever, if not more readily, to the temptation to perform violent acts and to achieve group aims through collective disruptive acts, mindful but not caring that what they do may destroy society. The end is held everywhere to justify the means.

Family Health

The recent past has seen an astonishing improvement in health and especially in child health. "Unnecessary" largely environmental disease and death are now diminished, and as the tide of infection and malnutrition has receded, ugly residues remain on the shore, death and disability from child abuse among them. Lord Taylor in his opening remarks reminded us of the heavy toll in earlier times of "overlaying" seemingly commoner during parental intoxication, but accepted as accidental. Now it looks as if in every single form of infant death and damage from accident the question has to be asked: "Was this in fact non-accidental?"

Along with improved child health has come the smaller family, of which both the cause and the effect are worth examining as parts of the social scene in front of which the drama of child abuse is enacted. Population control and contraception as part of family planning are acclaimed as good. That they encourage laxity in sexual behaviour seems probable, although a general erosion of authoritarian, imposed moral systems, must share the responsibility. Inevitably, the methods are used by 12 and 13 year-old children, encouraging them to enjoy the pleasure of coitus with impunity and without pregnancy and a baby. Should the methods fail, recourse may easily be had to termination of pregnancy, what was once called procurement of abortion and is seen still by some as fetal murder. To whatever moral or ethical arguments these practices give rise, termination on medical prescription following diagnosis of fetal disease or deformity or of a high risk of abnormality meets little opposition. And so society, which castigates child abuse at the hands of parents, compelled to these acts by their own internal or external circumstances, is to be found approving of this destruction of prenatal life, though not yet of euthanasia.

Some of the circumstances which seem to predispose to child abuse are described in Chapters 2, 3 and 4, and included are early sexual activity, changes of partner and too many babies too close together and too soon. The challenge here is to our laxity over sexual behaviour. Can such behaviour in the background of abuse be condemned when the majority demand sexual freedom for themselves? Is child abuse part of the price that society has to pay for these liberties and for our present approval of permissive legislation?

Cultures and Subcultures

A whole vista of challenges was opened to our gaze when we began to contemplate society and especially that part of society in which child abuse predominantly flourishes. Much was heard about sub-cultures, presumably always minority groups to earn the title "sub". That we should try to understand minority groups is certain, but how far do we promote the interests of sub-cultures at the expense of the major culture? Before such a question can be answered, the nature of society itself must be examined, and consideration be given to such further problems as what person or persons can speak for society or for a sub-culture, what beliefs or aims or habits of life are shared between members of a society and what authority should a society exert over its members if they wish to remain members and if that society is to survive. The alternative society, a name for opting out now so readily on the lips, combines acceptance of what organized society not only offers but gives, with a refusal to recognize that there is a responsibility towards that society and a duty to accept its authority in return. Although this may not seem relevant to a discussion of child abuse, both opting out and the balancing need for some acceptance of authority are indeed absolutely relevant.

First of all at the level of the family and its members comes the tendency to isolation, the opting out of the family, and second the therapeutic need for restriction within boundaries. One of the characteristics of the abusing family is its wish for isolation from neighbours. Loneliness, and friendlessness and refusal of help, are ways of opting out of community and sharing, so that the family is "a law unto itself" with violent reactions to authority and especially to any person who may be regarded as a representative of authority. In his discussion on psychotherapy, Arnon Bentovim (Chapter 21) referred to the need to work within a boundary. Those who are concerned with the upbringing of children are made aware of the child's normal need for a boundary. He has to discover how far he can go in his behaviour and he encroaches further and further on his parents' patience and love until he finds the limits. The immature adult or adolescent shares this compulsion. Child and adult reveal behaviour increasingly disturbing to those in contact with them, until they find the boundary. Without a boundary they become lost.

Tradition and age-old wisdom have defined boundaries through rules and traditions of behaviour admittedly not all of which are good, but when parents no longer wish to exercise the authority of these rules and traditions, and children and immature adults are no longer willing to accept this authority, confusion and chaos result. Morality is regulated by a show of hands, the democratic way of life is satisfied, but the maintenance of law and order becomes increasingly difficult, and so does self-control.

A further relevance to the family problems of child deprivation and abuse is given by the effect of these ideas in changing the philosophy of social workers. The modern social workers and their clients repeat the pattern of parents and their children. Help in problem solving replaces the traditional authoritarian approach. Identification with the client brings the social worker to the level of the client, one hesitates to say down to his level, because this is a value judgement about the difference which not all the clients or the social workers accept. That this attempted identification is exploited by the client is a common experience, but more serious than this is the frequency with which it fails to bridge the communication gap between professional and client. This failure provided a recurring theme throughout the symposium and is considered in more detail in the discussion of the case conference (p 279).

Some Questions of Law

Is legal practice undergoing any similar change? Several serious legal questions arose during the meeting. The underlying challenge was provoked by the question of the value to society as well as to the whole *dramatis personae*, clients, children and professional workers, of treating child abuse under the criminal law, prosecutions being brought before courts where the adversary system prevails and where basic information is not necessarily available. Underlying this is the question of the nature of justice and what is the aim of the sentence to be pronounced upon the guilty party.

Retribution, punishment and rehabilitation are dove-tailed to the application of three different principles of justice, those respectively of rights, deserts and needs, and, since to combine all three is impossible, the emphasis must be laid upon one. Certainly the social worker and the doctor in their professional capacities would seek to make the last, the needs of child and family, pre-eminent. But since even the professionals are human beings who think and feel like the rest of the society to which they belong, they must also acknowledge the necessity for both retribution and punishment. Indeed Canon Dunstan reminded us that the right understanding of retribution shows that "it stands as a merciful and just restraint upon revenge" (p 242). Miss Tibbits (Chapter 14) raised many questions about punishment and in the discussions concern was expressed that the sense of being punished served to isolate abusing families even further and to stress their own already low self-value. Pressure to secure the implementation of the Finer Report recommendations was unanimously supported. The whole question would then arise of transferring as much as possible of the legal management of child deprivation and abuse to family courts, where they would be followed by problems of parental rights and of access by biological parents.

Apart from the paramountcy of social justice and of securing the best solution for the child, which would be expected to be guiding principles in a family court, the innocency of the judiciary and at times the naïvety of its ideas about family behaviour remain of deep concern to professional workers. The traditional concepts of the child as a chattel, of the blood tie, of a mystical ability of a child to "recognize" its mother even when they have not met since the labour ward, months or years before, of the ability of the court to "recognize" brutal abusing parents by their appearance or by their demeanour during the hearings and pronouncements such as "no parent would purposely plunge a child into boiling water" have all been found in recent reports. All are false and everyone of them is calculated to mislead the court.

General disquiet was expressed and concern about how our present increased knowledge of child development could be communicated to the legal profession. The differing needs of children at different ages require especial emphasis and must sooner or later find acceptance in legislation about children. One practical measure could be the promotion of arrangements for some "feed-back" to the court about the short and long-term effects which had flowed from their decisions. In this context the proposal was made that the local authority to whom parental rights had been transferred should be in law as much accountable for the subsequent welfare of the child as biological parents.

Parental rights were not deeply considered except in two particular contexts, first in relation to the proportion of parents with whom their own offspring are recognizably unsafe. By what technique would it be proper and safe to deprive such parents of their rights? Who should be entitled to make the decisions and on what grounds? How could parents exercise a right of appeal? The baby born to such parents can be removed under a place of safety order or a care order, but the baby is left in limbo and is deprived of the chance to make those early relationships with substitute parents on which so much of its future emotional well-being is believed to depend. The baby is saved from physical abuse or death, but condemned to emotional deprivation. As long as a chance remains of restoration later of such a baby to its biological parents, some access must be allowed and, so often this, as in Dr Cooper's Mary (Case 1, p 7), is harmfully disturbing both to baby and substitute parents. While the solution of these problems would tax the judicial wisdom of a Solomon, a general doubt was shared about the extent to which the courts understood what was involved and about their tendency to favour the biological parents at the expense of the baby.

The second context was the right of a parent to refuse to admit a health visitor or a social worker to her home or to prevent an inspection of a baby or a child. Such a worker may apply to a magistrate and seek the company of a police officer to compel admission (see footnote on p 177). This hardly improves the worker's relationship with the client. To some, hearing these arguments, it seems that the existing relationship cannot be good when access is refused and the dangers to the child have been so great in past cases, that a stronger resolve to secure admission is both justified and necessary. The supervision order was also criticized for its weakness. If the object is to give parents the feeling that they are trusted, the very existence of the order must indicate to them that that trust is limited. The further limitation imposed by making the acceptance of visiting at the discretion of the worker an obligatory part of the order should not offend parents, especially if it was shown to be necessary to provide the information for the court on the basis of which the order could eventually be revoked.

Some details of legal procedure continue to worry the professionals and the need for them to develop the feeling of "being at home" in court was recognized. Some uncertainty persists about the admissibility of evidence concerning earlier abuse of siblings when the care of the next baby is under scrutiny. The proposals in Section 64 of the Children Act 1975 should help to ensure that a total picture of the family is presented to the court and the Department of Health and Social Security is urged to move quickly over the assembly and constitution of the panels of guardians *ad litem.**

Prediction, Prevention and Confidentiality

Although prediction and prevention loom large in current thinking about child abuse, they were not included in the programme of the

---

* The present position is described in D.H.S.S. Local Authority Circular, LAC(76)20.

symposium. Nevertheless they arose. Prevention before injury was stressed by Dr Oliver (Chapter 3) with his tragic experience of mentally handicapped children for whom only prevention would have been of use, and illuminated by Dr Richards (Chapter 7) in his studies on mother–child relationships. The social worker, the health visitor and the midwife are all directly concerned in this exercise. Ray Helfer's interpretation of the three stages of prevention was commended. Most workers are still involved in tertiary prevention, that is to say the prevention of further abuse following the diagnosis of the abusing family. Secondary prevention depended on the identification or prediction of vulnerable families, to whom moral support and explanation could be given. True primary prevention meant concern with the grandparents and their parenting ability, assuming that their failure here was the key to the vulnerability of the "at risk" family.

The social services often held much information about several generations of such families. Hospitals, too, had disconnected records of incidents which, taken singly, lacked significance. If and when all this social and medical information was drawn together, the resulting picture, like a completed jigsaw puzzle, could be both unexpected and frightening. Details about the father and any or all of the consorts and their families could also be enlightening and form an essential part of the family survey. It follows that about foster parents, too, no assumptions should be left untested. Such collation occupied much time, and considerable detective skill was needed to identify members with changed names and a multiplicity of addresses. The whole enterprise of identification was made possible by this kind of study, but whose was the duty and the responsibility to carry it out? The meeting agreed that this was a question that needed urgent thought.

Some concern was expressed about the switch from midwife to health visitor during the baby's first year and whether this interruption in the continuity of care and of observation is wise. A concentration of attention on vulnerable families at the expense of those who were obviously succeeding, although a change that would offend the principle of equal shares, would be one way of reducing the present excessive case load of workers.

One serious worry centred on confidentiality. Suppose a family were registered as "at risk" (the general topics of registers and reporting were not on the programme), should that family be informed? There are those who think that they should be, that all documents and reports should be available to them and that they should hear what transpired at any case conference. To the doctor, accustomed to moving out of earshot of the patient while his case is being discussed, the attendance of the client at the actual conference would be unthinkable and considered to be against his best interests, but the doctor immediately after the consultation communicates to the patient the result or as much as is thought wise under his particular circumstances. A medical attitude would favour a reasonably frank discussion after the conference. What is against such sharing is the fear that relationships would be damaged and future work jeopardized. For these reasons the outcome may not be communicated to the parents who are, in this way, treated like children who are not old enough to know the truth. The worker carries certain ideas and decisions in her mind of which the family is ignorant and a false relationship based on fear results. In many medical instances, the first step in the management of a serious condition is for the patient to accept its reality, and this may well be true of child abuse. Either through fear of offending or of spoiling a relationship, or through tenderheartedness, the worker is in collusion with the client in a denial of the truth. Here is another challenge to accepted practice.

What parents should not know as a general rule is the name of the first person to draw the attention of the professional workers to the supposed plight of the child or children in the family. An exception would be when the informant was found to be acting maliciously. A recent decision, not unanimous, in the Appeal Court which ordered the professional body concerned to disclose the informant's name, appears from the child abuse angle to be against the public interest. The members of the symposium were given the reassurance that despite this decision the question of disclosure remains at the discretion of the judge.

The Case Conference

Many of these points were raised by the case conference which preceded the final session and which rehearsed the discussions about a family whose records are printed in the appendix. The presentation was excellently well done and its profound and disturbing effect on the audience called for comment from Canon Dunstan (p 241). The functions of the various members were well illustrated. The police, whose role was not obtrusive in the symposium, substantiated the claim to provide a background which social workers lacked time to discover. They may like the clients, as social workers do, but they do not necessarily believe them and they avoid being conned more readily because of their wide experience of villains and their access to other members of the family. They are more prepared to talk to older children while social workers, fearing to do this, prefer to watch play and the handling of dolls and toys. The forensic doctor, whether surgeon or physician, is an expert on injuries and can recognize the method by which they were produced, although not identifying the assailant. This kind of doctor, experienced in court cases and not in any therapeutic relationship with the client, has great advantages in presenting the medical aspects of the case in court and the court in his area comes to know what may be expected from him. The paediatrician, the general practitioner and the social workers, provided the usual medical and social information and it was observed that there was no report from the school.

The conclusions of the case conference are omitted from this account. They were severely criticized at each stage, and with unavoidable hindsight many critics heatedly proposed alternative solutions. When the temperature of the meeting fell to normal once more, many of these criticisms were seen to be without real foundation and the protagonists to be acting out of their own insecurity and the unease intimately connected with the making of decisions in these complex family situations.

Certain other points, not included so far in the general discussion in this Chapter, deserve mention and can be considered as further challenges. First of all comes the idea of the case conference as it might strike the client. Here is a body of well trained people, all from caring professions, who have been working as a group for 10 years, a well-established team on christian-name terms, bringing into a professional arena a family as an object of study to be described in technical terms. Should not this strike terror in the client's heart? And must not this technique separate the abusing family from common humanity? Can human beings in such a team make decisions of the greatest importance to other human beings, the clients, without adopting a pose of superiority, without using previous experience of other abusing families and so denying the unique character of the clients? Can the client listen to and accept with any understanding at all pronouncements based on the team's discussions? Is true communication possible?

These considerations raised the question of labelling. An abusing parent, a batterer, to be "known to the police"; how do these labels strike the person labelled? How self-fulfilling are labels? By founding fresh categories of people, do we encourage the growth in size of the categories, as it were inviting those to join them who do not rightfully belong but who exploit the label? For example, "if I am not rehoused, I'll batter my baby", or "if you don't agree to abortion, I'll just kill the baby when he is born".

Some Other Questions

Reference was made to selective mating, spouses needing each other to be unsatisfactory. The part played by grandparents has already been referred to. Should the grandmother be able to overrule her daughter's wish to have her baby adopted and would grandparents act with greater wisdom when they will not approve of a daughter's boyfriend or consort and instead of forbidding the union accept cohabiting or even marriage (note the order), provided there are no babies?

Perhaps the most serious anxiety is about the difficulties in communication between professionals and clients. Andrew Mann in Chapter 17, discussing the Maria Colwell Inquiry, concluded that the main lesson was that the professionals, by reason of their professionalism, could not communicate. His plea was for the greater use of lay volunteers who spoke the same language as the clients but who would need the backing of the expertise of the professionals. This suggestion was not discussed in depth but it did not raise any noticeable adverse emotional or intellectual response from the professionals present. Indeed these had already given a partial assent by their self-criticism and their general feeling of failure to achieve the desired success in prevention and control. Perhaps the workers are too optimistic about what can be achieved. Certainly the questions were asked whether the "treatment" of parents was sufficient and whether what was done to help them could be relied on to help the children. The paper of Joanna Shapland and Anne Campbell in Chapter 10 gave the child's point of view and Carolyn Jones in Chapter 9 stressed the importance of following up what happened to the children. It is, after all, their protection and the advancement of their interests that remain the purpose of the whole exercise.

Because the symposium was intended to examine the background and to discuss underlying problems, many of the usual subjects discussed at meetings on child abuse were omitted or only touched on lightly, for example, the medical contribution to diagnosis. In considering the long-term effects of deprivation, Dermod MacCarthy's work (Chapter 8) on linking small stature to emotional deprivation was supplemented by reference to studies on the physical effects of undernutrition on brain growth in early life. Doctors were in increasing difficulties over finding time to deal adequately with the work produced as the result of child abuse and over gaining access to the wide range of information essential to the proper management of disorders of family life. More research, too, was needed, and particularly some general agreement about methods to be used in assessing the progress of child and family. Without some standardization of methods and tests, opportunity and information would be wasted.

The main medical contribution came from the psychiatrists. Everyone agreed about the importance of recognizing those parents with psychiatric illness in whose hands a baby was not and would never be safe. But the bulk of abusing parents were not "psychiatric cases", nor could they be regarded as sick persons. Usually as part of an inability to cope with life, they were unable to cope with children, but as far as a psychiatric report to the court went, they were psychiatrically normal. The danger here is that their ability to care for a baby or a child could only be tested by observing their responses when charged with this responsibility. The question then follows of the feasibility of trying to treat parents while the offspring is not in their care. More attention should be paid to the treatment of the deprived child himself.

Many of the children are born out of wedlock and if this fact is not it-self to be a disadvantage to them, the wider question of illegitimacy in-trudes itself into the discussion. The time may be ripe for an enquiry by a multi-disciplined committee into the continued usefulness of the concept of legitimacy of birth.

Conclusions

The members at the end of three days of hard thinking and serious dis-cussion felt that it would not be possible to construct and agree any specific resolutions or recommendations. They did wish to place on record certain anxieties which were generally shared.

The first concerns education. At some stage in life children should be made aware of the functions of families and what the proper care of babies and young children involved. What needs to be recognized is that in many existing families today these lessons are not learned and there-fore some other learning opportunity must be created.

In the teaching of professionals, a proper balance is not necessarily maintained between technical education and the caring element. Expertise and ability to communicate can be in some sense contra-dictory influences. Nevertheless foster parents and volunteer lay helpers often lack the required technical knowledge and this may contribute to failure which might be avoided by the greater use of professionals to advise and assist.

The difficulty in supplying information to the members of the legal profession is another grave anxiety, since it is the administration of the law that in the final result dominates the lives of parents and children when family life fails. Courts prefer short, succinct reports, but many members felt that such reports should be regarded as summaries and should be accompanied by much fuller accounts of all the particulars likely to be relevant. The assembling of panels of guardians *ad litem* under Section 64, Children Act 1975, should help over this and is regarded as a matter of urgency (see p 277). The anonymity of inform-ants should be protected. The weakness of supervision orders and the problem of access to families under suspicion or under supervision are also serious worries.

The court does not have enough opportunity to hear what happens as the result of its decisions, so that to learn by experience must be difficult. When the care of a child has been handed over to the local authority the matter is not really concluded and some measure of accountability such as is exercised in wardship cases by the official solicitor might be beneficial to the child. Access by biological parents to foster homes and nurseries presents another difficulty. Such visits, necessary if rehabilitation is likely or possible, do create serious emotional problems. The removal of parental rights is clearly a most serious step. On the other hand, from the baby's viewpoint, until this "divorce" is made absolute, a new life with fresh and good emotional relationships cannot begin. This problem needs careful study.

Concern is felt about the right of biological parents to know what is being reported about them and when and whether they are under suspicion as abusing parents.

Finally, do we have to accept that in the course of nature and in any society, families will fail to achieve the purposes listed by Spence and spelled out in the Introduction. Sometimes, when they fail, it will be because of psychiatric illness or because their personal responsibility for their actions is diminished. Sometimes they are caught in a social and environmental trap for which society as a whole must take some of the responsibility. But in the end what counts most must be the character and the quality of the individual.

In the study of child abuse, its origins and results and of our treatment efforts, we can discern another challenge. This most serious challenge, to be accepted by all, philosopher, theologian, priest, social worker, lawyer, judge, policeman, teacher, psychiatrist, paediatrician, is to the present way of life and to the partial breakdown of human relationships. The sense of community, which flows from shared beliefs and a shared culture, is under attack on all sides. We have concentrated on the science of communication and are losing the art of communicating. We can flash an instant message from one end of the world to the other by satellite, but somehow we do not know what to say to help our neighbour. When we do try to speak, he, in his isolation, somehow cannot hear.

Appendix Case Conference on Family R

Participants:
Dr L. J. H. Arthur, *paediatrician*
Det. Sup. P. Baylis, *police*
Mrs J. Heath, *senior hospital social worker*
Dr W. Milburn, *police surgeon*
Miss S. Mountain, *social worker student*
Dr R. E. Smith, *general practitioner*

The participants re-enacted this case conference during the meeting. No account of the decision is included, but the reference is made to the discussion after the case conference, which was a lively one and served to raise many of the matters about which anxieties are felt by professional workers in their relationships both to clients and to each other.

The reader may like to examine the following reports, by the social worker and the consultant psychiatrist.

Social Worker's Report on Family R for case conference on 8 March 1974

Re: Dorothy (28.9.72) Place of safety order taken 26.2.74.

Family

Mother: Sarah R. (2.5.49) housewife (divorcee)
Father: Henry, present consort
Patrick (4.11.66)
Marjorie (15.10.68)
Fred (13.5.70)
Dorothy (28.9.72)

Home Circumstances

The family lives in a council house. The house is reasonably well furnished and usually quite clean, although often very untidy. The children are well fed and generally well clothed.

General Background

Sarah has been known to the Department since 1961. On 20th January 1961, her mother, Mrs H. had been admitted to hospital after an attempted suicide bid (overdose of cold cure tablets). Mrs H. had made a previous suicide bid the year before when she tried to gas herself and her children. Mrs H. was formerly married to Mr R. who is the father of Sarah and her younger sister, Jenny. Mrs H. had four younger children by her second marriage, but she and Mr H. later adopted Sarah and Jenny to make them full members of the H. family. Between 1961 and 1965 Mr and Mrs H. experienced considerable difficulties in caring for Jenny and were receiving regular visits from the staff of this department. In December 1965, Mrs H. approached the children's department again expressing concern about Sarah's association with Derek R., but Sarah refused to end her friendship with Derek and subsequently left home.

She had already left grammar school without taking G.C.E. examinations and married Derek, against her parents advice. In September 1967, Derek approached us for advice on the marital difficulties which were then being experienced by Sarah and himself. Sarah was 17 years old at the time and she evidently felt the strain of running a home and caring for a young baby.

Over the next months, the condition of the home deteriorated as a result of Sarah's apathy and depression. The situation was aggravated by Derek's lack of help and support for his wife and also by his association with another girl of which he made no secret. He was seldom in employment for longer than a week or two, and financial problems arose with arrears of rent, gas and electricity. The conditions of the home caused such infections as impetigo and nappy rash in the children and Marjorie was particularly affected when she was a baby.

In 1969 the social worker, making a home visit, discovered the children left unattended. Mrs R.'s attitude when tackled about this was casual and her tendency to leave the children alone continued. On these occasions neighbours anonymously reported Mrs R. to the police or children's department. It was felt at the time that her leaving the children was a symptom of Sarah's pessimism as to the future of her relationship with Derek.

In May 1969, Sarah left Derek and moved in to her stepfather's home with Patrick and Marjorie. She made application for separation from her husband and managed adequately by herself during this period. However, the couple were reconciled in October of the same year and Mrs R. became pregnant. After Fred was born (13.5.70) marital relations became progessively more and more strained, mainly because of Derek's lack of incentive and real effort in finding and holding down a job. Both partners raked up all their past reasons for argument to add fuel to their present quarrels.

During this period Sarah was the dominant partner in the relationship, probably as a reaction to Derek's childishness. Whereas he responded to advice in a petulant manner, Sarah intelligently accepted social-work help. Derek persistently broke in to the electricity meter and the supply was disconnected several times as a result. Eventually, in November 1970, Derek began a short prison sentence for non-payment of a fine.

In March 1972, after months of increasing tension, Derek attacked Sarah, thereby giving her grounds for divorce which she had long been seeking. At this time, she was in the early stages of her fourth pregnancy. The divorce became effective in April 1973. Since that time there has been a marked improvement in the home conditions. The house is kept clean, although it is often untidy, and the children appear well cared for and happy. The effect of the divorce has been to relieve Mrs R. of the burden of worry over her husband's conduct and her outlook is now much more optimistic than previously.

Henry, whom Mrs R. has known for several years, moved in with the family in January 1974. Mrs R. feels that the arrangement is working well, and the children refer to Henry as "our new daddy". The whole family enjoys weekend outings in the car with Henry and he evidently has gained popularity with the children for the toys he has bought them and the time he spends with them.

There have been some difficulties in the establishment of a relationship between Henry and Dorothy, mainly because Dorothy is unused to contact with male adults, and as a result does not respond to Henry's demonstrations of affection for her. This leads to frustration, particularly as Mrs R. has a warm physical relationship with all her children, and Henry's impatience results in flashes of anger. The incident under review happened in such a situation.

25.2.74 10.00 a.m. Telephone call from a neighbour who wished to remain anonymous, claiming that Fred and Dorothy were being ill-treated. It was alleged that Fred had two black eyes and that Dorothy had cigarette burns on her body.

11.45 a.m. Visited. Saw Mrs R. and all the children. Fred had two black eyes, but Mrs R. says these occurred as a result of a fall. Baby Dorothy had bruises on the side of her face and around her left eye. Mrs R. tearfully admitted that "Henry hit her last night". She said that he had done it before but that he has a quick temper and does not intend to hurt the children as he loves them. Marjorie had traces of a black eye, and her mother said this was caused accidentally, as Marjorie moved away when Henry went to slap her arm.

Later. Dorothy admitted to children's hospital.

26.2.74. Place of safety order taken out on Dorothy. I saw Mrs R. at the hospital on the day after Dorothy's admission. She was very distressed by the place of safety order and its implications. Henry's attitude to the present situation is one of great concern. I feel that he was deeply shocked by the consequences of his actions, and he appeared to be genuinely worried in case he had caused Sarah any pain as a result of his blow. I take Sarah and Henry's prompt attendance at the hospital on the following day to be a favourable sign, indicating their real concern for Dorothy. Sarah is deeply distressed by the incident, but says that she was thankful for my intervention, as she could not have brought herself to report this fundamentally worrying situation.

Report of Consultant Psychiatrist, April 9, 1974

Re: Dorothy (28.9.72)

I have interviewed the mother of this injured baby and also with her consent, Henry. They were aware of the purpose of my seeing them and had no objection.

I first saw Henry, aged 28 years, on 18 March. He informed me that Mrs R. could not come on that date as she had an appointment at an orthopaedic clinic following their recent road accident when Henry was driving. The only information I have about him is what he himself told me and in some respects he seemed quite frank but at times was vague and claimed difficulty in remembering.

He appeared to be of normal intelligence but a rather immature and inadequate personality who was not yet sure of his role in life. He is the second of six children, his three brothers are married and his two younger sisters are at home and he appears to have been the odd one out and to have had a rather roving life. He gave a history of some court appearances: for taking cigarettes from a machine as a juvenile; some driving offences, he thought about three, and probation a few years ago for "doing a job" when he got into bad company. He said he was not harshly treated as a child; his father only once really laid into him and then hit him very hard with his fist, he could still remember it but did not know why. He left home at 21 and went round Europe looking for work and living on his savings. On his return to England he met a man with a borstal background and got into trouble. He then worked in various cities doing a variety of jobs mainly in the building trade. For the past 18 months he had been working as a machine attendant.

He said he had known Mrs R. for several years and had lived with her since just after last Christmas. He was fond of her but did not intend marrying her unless she improved. He said she was intelligent but very untidy, spent a long time in front of the fire reading and watching TV and did not bother very much. He described how he painted, decorated and carpeted the house; according to Mrs R. he began decorating last summer before he cohabited and from the reports it would seem that there has been a marked improvement in the material conditions of the home.

Henry said he was very fond of the children and agreed with my suggestion that he might be seeking affection through them. With regard to Dorothy's injury, he said he was feeding her like he always did, with a spoon, she got very stubborn and he smacked her across the face. He angrily said he did not strike her with anything else and the doctor who said he did must be a quack. This was the only time he showed any signs of anger, or any other positive emotion, and I could not say whether his reaction was due to righteous indignation or to guilty over-protestation.

He was vague and somewhat inconsistent about his future plans except that he did not intend marrying at present. If Dorothy was committed to care, he thought he would leave so that Mrs R. could have her back. He would like them all to be together again so that they could start afresh. But he also said that in a way he was sorry he got into this situation; he had no worry before, just lived his own life. He had always felt you are on your own in this world and had to make your own way and he loved to explore and see different faces and places. When asked whether he would lose his temper with Dorothy again, he at first said he was very doubtful whether it would happen again, then said he was sure it would not. He gave no history of nervous disorder but said that in the past he had suffered from migraine and the present worry had caused a recurrence of headaches.

I interviewed Mrs R., aged 24 years, on 26 March. Her family had been known to the social services since 1961, her mother had a history of two attempts at suicide and Mrs R. gave a history of a very disturbed and unhappy childhood due to parental quarrelling, between her mother and stepfather, who had both been divorced, and also between her mother and her own father prior to their separation when she was ?4½ years of age. She said her stepfather had once been bound over for beating up her mother. Her own father also beat her mother and she thought he was more sadistic because she remembered him hitting her mother with a belt. She could not remember much about him but remembered him hitting her for not eating eggs at breakfast. She stayed with him for a fortnight in 1966 and he treated her as though she was beneath him and not on his level.

Mrs R. seemed to be of normal or possibly good intelligence but to have little pride in herself and was rather unkempt when she came for interview. She said that as a child she was shy, had few friends and always did as she was told. Her stepfather was rather strict and at 16 she had to be in for 9 p.m. Her only contact with the police was once when she stayed out late and her stepfather had telephoned them. She passed the 13+ and went to grammar school and was top of the class in physics and chemistry. She took "O" levels in art, English language, Spanish, and physics with chemistry, passed in art and Spanish oral, but failed the rest. Her mother could not afford to keep her longer at school so she left at 16. She married a few months after leaving school, her parents having given her the choice of giving up her boy friend or leaving home. She knew that her husband had been in an approved school. He stopped working when she was 5 or 6 months pregnant, kept her short of money and later physically ill-treated her.

Mrs R. said she was fond of Henry but had no intention of rushing into marriage after the disaster of her first marriage. She was a poor housekeeper, untidy and did not mind the children messing the place up; she thought this was better than the way she had been treated. Henry was strict and treated them as though they were older, expecting them to take their shoes off because of the carpets and keep their bedroom tidy. With regard to Dorothy, she felt rather pushed out because he wanted to do everything for her even to changing her nappy and she felt he was taking her role. She was present when Dorothy was injured, he had finished feeding her and she was screaming; Mrs R. thought Dorothy resented him. He hit her twice with his fingers, not with anything else, and then he cuddled her. The bruising did not come out until the next day. Mrs R. had not previously seen him lose his temper except once after a row with his mother when he became very moody and uncommunicative but was not violent. She was fairly sure that it would not happen again but thought there would be some difficulties with Dorothy due to her being away and she wondered how he would react if Dorothy were really difficult.

Both the mother and Henry seem to be rather damaged and inadequate personalities who, as often happens, have come together. Henry seems to have an immature and possessive attitude towards Dorothy and there are differences concerning the children's upbringing. On the other hand he appears to have caused a substantial improvement in the general standards of the home and in this respect to have compensated for the mother's deficiencies. But for the forensic medical report, I would have thought that supervision would be appropriate in this case.

The forensic doctor believes that part of Dorothy's injury could only have been caused by hitting with a hard object, such as a stick, belt or knife handle. Both partners, and especially the mother, seem not free from doubts about the possibility of a further incident but such concern is not necessarily a bad sign. There is also doubt as to how long Henry will remain in the household.

In the circumstances, I consider a care order is necessary to safeguard Dorothy. It is, however, a very serious matter to deprive a child of its natural home and this home is by no means wholly bad; in some respects it is good. I think it would be reasonable to try to return Dorothy to her home, initially for short periods, as soon as possible.

Index